The
DEVIL & the
DEEP BLUE SEA

Dear Shaun —

with much gratitude —

Lili Panno~~~ —

Nov 6/13

The
DEVIL & the
DEEP BLUE SEA

An Investigation into the
Scapegoating of Canada's Grey Seal

LINDA PANNOZZO

Fernwood Publishing
Halifax & Winnipeg

Editing: Eileen Young
Text design: Brenda Conroy
Cover photo: male grey seal on Sable Island beach,
    titled *Old Man and the Sea*, by Damian Lidgard
Cover design: John van der Woude
Printed and bound in Canada by Hignell Book Printing

Published in Canada by Fernwood Publishing
32 Oceanvista Lane, Black Point, Nova Scotia, B0J 1B0
and 748 Broadway Avenue, Winnipeg, Manitoba, R3G 0X3
www.fernwoodpublishing.ca

Fernwood Publishing Company Limited gratefully acknowledges the financial support of the Government of Canada through the Canada Book Fund and the Canada Council for the Arts, the Nova Scotia Department of Communities, Culture and Heritage, the Manitoba Department of Culture, Heritage and Tourism under the Manitoba Publishers Marketing Assistance Program and the Province of Manitoba, through the Book Publishing Tax Credit, for our publishing program.

Library and Archives Canada Cataloguing in Publication

Pannozzo, Linda, author
The devil and the deep blue sea: an investigation into scapegoating of Canada's grey seal / Linda Pannozzo.

Includes bibliographical references and index.
ISBN 978-1-55266-586-2 (pbk.)

1. Seals (Animals)—Control—Atlantic Coast (Canada). 2. Sealing—Canada—Management. 3. Atlantic cod fisheries—Atlantic Coast (Canada). 4. Atlantic cod fisheries—Closures—Atlantic Coast (Canada). 5. Fishery management—Canada. I. Title.

SH362.P35 2013   333.95'9790971   C2013-905875-3

Contents

For Jasmine

I envy the beasts two things —
their ignorance of evil to come and
their ignorance of what's said about them.

— Voltaire

Author's Note

In 2009 I was working as a researcher for the non-profit research and education organization Genuine Progress Index Atlantic (GPI Atlantic), which was developing indicators to measure environmental quality, sustainability, well-being and quality of life for Nova Scotia. One of the areas we felt the province had made steady progress over the years was in its protection of wilderness. However, at the time, Hay Island, one of the province's wilderness areas — and the subject of the first chapter of this book — had to our dismay been opened up to commercial sealing. Not only that, but the newly elected NDP government had proposed to change the *Wilderness Areas Protection Act* to accommodate it. They argued that the grey seal population, which had been growing, was harming biodiversity by eating too many fish, namely cod, and stunting the recovery of the species — a species that had been brought to its knees from overfishing nearly two decades earlier.

At the time, public hearings were held by the government's Law Amendments Committee to make sure it was making the right decision over changing the legal protection of Nova Scotia wilderness; along with a number of others, I presented a submission on behalf of GPI Atlantic arguing that wilderness areas are intended to provide sanctuary to all native biodiversity, not just those species particularly favoured by some humans. I also argued that allowing commercial activity of this nature went against the spirit of the Act. However, I was most impressed during the hearings by the number of scientists from Dalhousie University in Halifax who presented submissions arguing there was no science to support the view that the seals were holding back the recovery of cod. One prominent scientist told the Committee that the seals could even be helping the cod. This led me to wonder, "If there was no scientific basis for the argument then what was really behind the push to kill the seals?"

Finding answers to this question led me to a number of places, some quite unexpected. I began to imagine the research process as one that resembled a journey, which began with me parked for some time in the complex and often confounding world of food webs and grey seal diet studies. When the trip resumed I was happily plummeted into the expansive fields of population dynamics and the study of historical ecology. But then I was led to the rather disquieting exploration of our relationship with the grey seal and other marine mammals, and with nature in general. It really wasn't until I was faced with the murky, uncomfortable and sometimes questionable, world where science and politics overlap, that I realized the process of writing this book was going to have to involve looking at something else.

Over the years as a freelance journalist and researcher I've been drawn to "resource-based" controversies; when I look back at a number of them, I see that they all have a number of things in common. For one, they are usually highly polarized. Think of the charged protests over the cutting of old growth forests or closer to home, the clashes over the harp seal hunt — one story that has gripped and divided the east coast for five decades. In these and countless other stories around the globe, the issues tend to get distilled in the mainstream media as a battle between two opposing forces: between the environmentalist and the logger, or in this case the animal welfare activist and the sealer. In a way, it's this conflict that has defined these stories, usually characterized by easily digestible sound-bites and stereotypes on all sides — with usually only two presented.

But the truth is, the issues don't break down over neatly defined lines like these. In all of these controversies the simple dichotomies don't even begin to address the complexity of the issues at hand. The pressures facing people who depend on a steady supply of "resources" for their livelihood are real, and sometimes tragically so. It is this broader analysis of the economic system in which the fishery takes place — one that demands limitless growth on a finite planet and one that often pits big business and profits against small communities — that is noticeably absent from the discussion. This is where I had to ultimately go: to explore the real battle that most of the time is being waged off our radar screens.

When I looked back in the CBC radio archives, I found an interview given in 1977 by Richard Cashin, the head of the Newfoundland Fishermen, Food, and Allied Workers Union at the time, who was passionately representing the sealers during the protests against the harp seal hunt and trying to sway public opinion in their favour. He said: "The seal to us, to me anyway, is a symbol. If today you take the seal away from me, tomorrow you'll take the cod, the next day the lobster, the next day my right to live in a small village … It's a fight for survival." His words proved uncannily prescient and in many ways they are as true today as they were back then. The seal is really a symbol and the issues are about survival: the seal is a symbol of how our relationship with nature has gone completely askew, and the story shows how this estrangement — from the natural world and each other — not only threatens the viability of small coastal communities but our survival on this planet. That's what this book is really about, and the story about the grey seals and the cod illustrates it.

This book is not a "he said, she said," piece of reporting. You will hear from various sides on the issues — but I also try to go much further than that. It is an overview and critical analysis of the science and the debate within the context of our political and economic system, presented in an attempt to get to the bottom of what's really going on with the seals-cod issue. I am under no illusion that this book will convince seal cull proponents to change their minds or that it will pursuade the mainstream environmental movement to address root causes of our degradation of the natural world. But I do hope that it brings to the discussion some of the layers of complexity, historical context and economic analysis that have been sorely lacking.

Acknowledgements

I am indebted to my good friend Bruce Wark, a veteran journalist and influential former professor at the University of King's College School of Journalism, who provided me with invaluable editing advice on an early draft of the manuscript. Special thanks to Zoe Lucas and Damian Lidgard, for all the beautifully composed photos of Sable Island grey seals. Their dedication to sharing the magnificence of the island, particularly with those of us who have never been there, is an inspiration. Thanks to Rebecca Aldworth of the Humane Society International for kindly providing photos of the Hay Island seal hunt and to David Lavigne of the International Fund for Animal Welfare for the food web graphic. Thank you to Simon Copas, who created the map that appears at the beginning of the book. I also want to thank everyone at Fernwood Publishing: Eileen Young for copy-editing, Debbie Mathers for making the manuscript changes, Brenda Conroy for proofreading and text design, John van der Woude for the cover design, Beverley Rach for managing the book's production and especially my stalwart editor Errol Sharpe, for his insights, kindness and sharp eye. I also want to thank my family and friends, especially Laura Landon, Suzie LeBlanc, Cait Redmond, Steve Myrden, DeNel Rehberg Sedo and Peter Walker for their ongoing encouragement. I owe a very special debt of gratitude to my mother for her support and abiding affection and to my husband, Michael, and our daughter, Jasmine, whose love and commitment to making this a planet that's fit to live on makes me believe all things are actually possible.

I want to sincerely thank all those who generously contributed their time, knowledge and expertise to this book. Some went well beyond the call of duty. They know who they are. The affiliations of all those I interviewed, listed alphabetically below, appear in the book:

Rebecca Aldworth, Marc Allain, Gary Andrea, Shannon Arnold, Danny Arsenault, Dean Bavington, Don Bowen, Ian Boyd, Alida Bundy, Tony Charles, Jae Choi, Robert Courtney, Bridget Curran, Howard Epstein, Sheryl Fink, Ken Frank, Susanna Fuller, Mike Hammill, Sidney Holt, Jeffrey Hutchings, Sara Iverson, David Johnston, Peter Koeller, David Lavigne, Damian Lidgard, Heike Lotze, Kenton Lysak, Zoe Lucas, Debbie MacKenzie, Judith Maxwell, Robert Mohn, Denny Morrow, Robert O'Boyle, Daniel Pauly, Isabelle Perrault, Raymond Plourde, Sara Quigley, Robert Rangeley, Greg Roach, Neil Rooney, George Rose, Michael Sinclair, Douglas Swain, Harry Thurston, Julie Tompa, Liette Vasseur, Carl Walters, Diana Whalen, Hal Whitehead, Ronnie Wolkins and Boris Worm.

Any material in this book that has not been cited is a result of personal communication or correspondence with those I've interviewed.

Acronyms

ATIP	Access to Information and Privacy
ATV	All-Terrain Vehicle
BIO	Bedford Institute of Oceanography
CBC	Canadian Broadcasting Corporation
CEAA	*Canadian Environmental Assessment Act*
CERN	European Organization for Nuclear Research
CIESM	Mediterranean Science Commission
COSEWIC	Committee on the Status of Endangered Wildlife in Canada
DDT	Dichlorodiphenyltrichloroethane
DNA	Deoxyribonuclec Acid
DFO	Department of Fisheries and Oceans
EA	Environmental Assessment
EAC	Ecology Action Centre
FAO	Food and Agriculture Organization
FRCC	Fisheries Resource Conservation Council
GDP	Gross Domestic Product
GPI	Genuine Progress Index
HSI	Humane Society International
ICES	International Council for the Exploration of the Sea
IFAW	International Fund for Animal Welfare
ITQ	Individual Transferable Quotas
IUCN	International Union for Conservation of Nature
IUU	Illegal, Unreported, or Undocumented Catches
LHC	Large Hadron Collider
LSLE	Lower St. Lawrence Estuary
MSC	Maritime Stewardship Council
MSY	Maximum Sustainable Yield
NAFO	Northwest Atlantic Fisheries Organization
NAMMCO	North Atlantic Marine Mammal Commission
NDP	New Democratic Party
NOAA	National Oceanic and Atmospheric Administration
OHV	Off Highway Vehicle
OTN	Ocean Tracking Network
PBDE	Polybrominated Diphenyl Ethers
PCB	Polychlorinated Biphenyl
POPs	Persistent Organic Pollutants
SARA	*Species at Risk Act*
SSB	Spawning Stock Biomass
TAC	Total Allowable Catch
TAGS	The Atlantic Groundfish Strategy
WWF	World Wildlife Fund
ZAP	Zonal Assessment Process

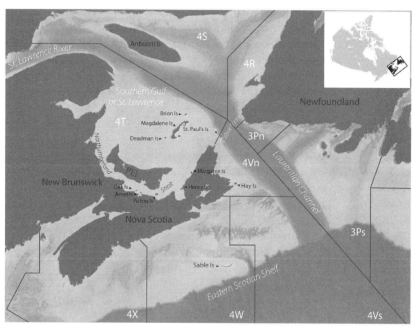

Northwest Atlantic Fisheries Organization (NAFO) fishery management areas and main grey seal pupping colonies in Atlantic Canada.

Chapter 1

Sanctuary Lost

And silence fell: the rushing sun
Stood still in paths of heat,
Gazing in waves of horror on
The dead about my feet.

— Walter de la Mare, from *The Massacre*, 1970

These grey seals, Mr. Speaker, don't need the ice to have their babies on, they just slide on the beach anywhere and have a baby; they can slide up on the street to have a baby. They will be before long — they'll be out here on the street. They're out here in the harbour right now and they'll be up on the streets of Halifax if they keep accumulating — and I don't know how these fish stocks are standing it inshore, I really don't. I'm being told they're not standing it ... They've got to go and find the food, so watch out, they're coming up these streets.

— Harold Theriault, Member of the Legislative Assembly of Nova Scotia, Digby-Annapolis, *Hansard Reporting Services*, March 29, 2007

It's mid-February 2008 and Rebecca Aldworth's first time on Hay Island, a "tiny wind-swept grass-covered rock," as she describes it, located about an hour's boat ride southeast of Sydney, Nova Scotia, and nestled to the south of Scatarie Island, one of the province's largest offshore islands. No one lives on these islands today, but archaeological evidence of fishing villages, long abandoned now, dates back to the 1700s. Before that, Nova Scotia's indigenous people, the Mi'kmaq, would have frequented these wild spaces, especially in the less frigid months of the year. For decades, Scatarie Island and the much smaller Hay Island were given provincial wildlife management area status, which meant it was permitted to hunt waterfowl and deer, but the hunting or trapping of fur-bearing mammals was prohibited. Today the islands are part of the Scatarie Island Wilderness Area — a designation that provides the highest level of protection in the province.

But it isn't an interest in the island's past that brings Aldworth here. It's her interest in the wildlife. Exposed to the raw and relentless winds of the north Atlantic, and often shrouded in a veil of fog, Hay Island is the domain of thousands of grey seals that congregate each year to whelp, or give birth. The law governing Nova Scotia's protected spaces was also supposed to protect Hay Island's grey seals, and for years it did. But this was no longer the case. On this particular day in February, Aldworth makes her way onto the island's beach to document the seal hunt as part of her job as the head of the Humane Society International.

Originally from Woody Point, in the heart of Gros Morne National Park on the western coast of Newfoundland, Aldworth says that like most Newfoundlanders she'd never actually seen a seal when she was growing up, but she had eaten seal meat.

> Most of the seals in Newfoundland are far offshore. But at a very early age I saw a television documentary about the seal hunt and I remember watching a [harp] whitecoat being killed in front of its mother and calling to my mother in tears asking "What is that?" and I remember she said, "It's the seal hunt and we're against it." And that really stuck with me for life.

Today, ice floes are Aldworth's "second home," and she's spent the last thirteen years observing the harp seal hunts on the ice in the Gulf of St. Lawrence. But it's her first time seeing a grey seal. "Grey seal pups are really different than harp seal pups," she says. "Harp seals are really docile and trusting, but grey seals are feisty, they're full of attitude, and they can be funny and charismatic, interactive, and curious." Aldworth says the time she spends on the island with the live seals makes what comes next even worse. "When the hunters arrive, it's absolutely devastating to watch."

Aldworth describes what happened on Hay Island that day in 2008.

> As we were walking up to the area where the killing was happening, there was this little whitecoat grey seal and it was just crying, making the loudest distressed noise, and there was nobody around this seal, so I couldn't figure out what was happening. As I got closer I saw there was a pail next to the seal with wooden bats covered in blood.

Aldworth speculates that the seal pup had just witnessed what she was about to see:

> As we came up over the ridge we saw about seventeen sealers and maybe between thirty and fifty seals that they had herded together. They were just clubbing them as fast as they could, and the sight and the violence of it, it was the worst thing I've ever seen in all the years I've witnessed commercial seal hunting. Animals just four weeks old being beaten to death inches away from each other and inches from newborns. The newborns were crawling through blood

and the mothers were trying desperately to protect their newborns. Seals make a very human cry — it's a very haunting cry and it echoes throughout the island. And, when you see what this island can be and what it should be — one of the greatest wildlife spectacles that could be seen — and then watch it turned into an open-air slaughterhouse. It's a very hard thing to watch.

The grey seals that congregate on Hay Island every year to breed are part of what's called the Eastern Shore herd of grey seals, the smallest of three herds in the northwest Atlantic identified by Fisheries and Oceans Canada (DFO). In 2010 this herd was estimated to be between 20,000 and 22,000 seals; Hay Island is where the majority of the roughly 3,000 pups were born. The largest herd congregates every winter to whelp on Sable Island, which sits about 300 kilometres southeast of Halifax on the eastern Scotian Shelf. The size of this seal colony — the world's largest — is estimated between 260,000 and 320,000 animals. The Gulf of St. Lawrence herd whelps on ice and on islands in the Gulf and its population is estimated between 55,000 and 71,000 seals.[1]

Typically, grey seals, which have a natural lifespan of between thirty and forty years, are found on both sides of the north Atlantic. While they are not considered a migratory species, the three herds do migrate extensively along the Atlantic coast, foraging for fish. In the summer months, for instance, seals from Sable Island and the Eastern Shore can be found foraging in the Gulf of St. Lawrence, and some seals from the Gulf can be found on the Scotian Shelf.

In late December the females haul out onto ice, undisturbed islands, or exposed reefs along the coast, where the pupping begins. The majority of the pups on Hay Island are born by mid-January. For about fifteen to eighteen days they're called "whitecoats" because of the colour of the thick layer of insulating fur. While they're nursing they are inseparable from their mothers. According to scientists, the short and intense nursing period — about two weeks for grey seals — is possible because the grey seal mother's milk fat content is decadently high — about 60 percent — when compared to the only 4 percent in cow's milk. The hooded seal has the highest milk fat content (68 percent) of all mammals: as mothers only nurse for four days, it holds the record when it comes to lactation brevity. While they nurse, grey seals gain about three kilograms a day and double in weight to about fifty kilograms when they're fully weaned.

By about a month of age the pup's white coat is replaced by a thick, water-repelling, black-mottled silvery one, suited to a life at sea. At this stage, when they're called "beaters," because of the way they beat the water with their front flippers as they learn to swim, they can be legally killed. In

1987, Canada banned the killing of newborn harp and grey seal pups at the whitecoat stage and hooded seals at the blueback stage.* But once they've shed their birth-coats they're fair game. Once fully weaned, the pups stay put for about two more weeks, fasting before they make their way into the ocean for the first time as swimmers.

The process allowing the Hay Island seal slaughter all started in the spring of 2007, when the Liberals brought forward a resolution to control the growing seal population.[2] Liberal Harold Theriault was especially indignant. He said that the seals in general were eating too many fish and that if they weren't controlled, like the mice in his cupboards, they'd "eat us out of house and home." Then it was Sterling Belliveau's turn. The former commercial fisherman-cum-politician represents Shelburne for the New Democratic Party. He talked about how as a young man he used to kill grey seals as part of the federally subsidized bounty program. From 1978 to 1990, a bounty was paid to licensed fishermen who provided the lower jawbone of a grey seal as proof of a kill. Belliveau lamented that fishers today don't garner the same kind of respect that they once did: "The bible is a good indication about fishermen and having respect for fishermen," he said. "The disciples, the majority of them, were fishermen." In no uncertain terms, Belliveau was on side with the fishermen, who he said had enough "evidence" to support a "seal harvest."[3]

The resolution also garnered vociferous support from the Tory Minister of Fisheries and Aquaculture, Ronald Chisholm, who talked about how the province was already on board with developing a commercial sealing industry by providing financial support to develop marketable products from grey seals. He told the Legislature that there was also no doubt in his mind they posed a huge threat to the fishing industry: "Grey seals are implicated in the downturn of our groundfish stocks and the fishing industry is unanimous in calling for a reduction in the seal numbers." Calling it a "downturn" was a bit of an understatement.

By the early 1990s, an event of unprecedented proportions in Atlantic Canada set the stage for our present-day relationship with the much-maligned grey seal. They had always been easily blamed for anything that went wrong in the fishery and this time things had gone horribly wrong. On July 2, 1992, then federal fisheries minister John Crosbie announced that the epic Newfoundland and Labrador cod had collapsed. The so-called "northern stock," which supported the largest cod fishery in the world, was nearly wiped out, and the spawning stock — or the population of adults old enough to reproduce — had been reduced by 99 percent. The cod had become com-

---

*   Hooded seals shed their first coat in utero and at birth have a short, coarse-haired coat, slate blue-grey in colour. They moult this coat once they're fifteen to twenty-seven months old.

mercially extinct. Dalhousie biology professor and cod expert Jeff Hutchings calls the decline of Canadian cod "the greatest numerical loss of a vertebrate in Canada's history." He provides this astonishing comparison: by weight, he says, the loss of mature cod alone was equivalent to that of twenty-seven million humans.

The collapse was an event that clearly registered our ravages of life in the seas but it also threw 40,000 people out of work, unraveling the very fabric of rural life throughout Atlantic Canada. Small coastal communities that had for centuries been rooted in the comings and goings of fish were devastated. It was nothing short of an ecological, social and cultural catastrophe. The arrival of modern trawler fleets in the 1950s — equipped with fish-finders and sophisticated gear — marked the beginning of the end. Whole schools of cod could now be found, caught, processed and frozen 24-7. These factory-freezer trawlers were so effective that 200 of them were able to catch eight million tonnes of northern cod in just fifteen years. By comparison, it took roughly 250 years to catch that many fish after John Cabot's arrival in 1497.

In 1990, Leslie Harris, President of Memorial University, chaired an independent review of the state of the northern cod stocks. He described the offshore factory trawler as "the most destructive fishing machine yet de-vised by human ingenuity."[4] Members of the traditional, small-scale, inshore fishery, who operated from small boats closer to shore, had warned since the mid-1980s that the cod were disappearing, but the government had failed to respond. While senior bureaucrats within the DFO did, remarkably, attempt early on to blame the collapse on seals and the environment, today there's little disagreement that overfishing combined with short-term economic thinking, faulty assumptions and government mismanagement caused the cod collapse, turning one of the most fertile fishing grounds in the world into a wasteland.

Fast-forward two decades, and the cod, for the most part, still show no signs of recovery. Estimates vary depending on the stock, but scientists say that only a tiny fraction of the original cod biomass is left in Atlantic Canada. Furthermore, while the early 1990s marked the commercial extinction of the cod stocks, today some are now very close to being biologically extinct. Small-scale inshore fishers, pushed to the brink of financial collapse, blame the seals for the fish not coming back. Unlike the cod, the grey seal population has rebounded in the last five decades — in 2010 the three herds combined were estimated to total between 330,000 to 410,000 animals. Fishermen say that, since they aren't benefiting from the presence of grey seals — seals wreck their gear, eat the fish, and spread a parasite that infects cod and other groundfish — the only way to fix the imbalance is to kill the seals. But many scientists and conservationists believe pointing a finger at seals is a misguided and even dangerous oversimplification; they speculate that culling seals could result in a number of unintended consequences. They also argue that focusing on the grey seal diverts attention away from other possible causes of the cod's demise, including the government's mismanagement of the fisheries, and that efforts to improve fishing productivity should first address fishing practices. They argue that within this context, the push to kill grey seals as a way to protect the fish is nothing short of Orwellian.

Back at Hay Island the stage was being set. Over the course of a few months in 2007, with support from all parties, the grey seals on the island would become the target of a hunt. But the problem was that Hay Island was part of a protected wilderness area. At the time, according to the law governing wilderness areas, commercial activity was prohibited unless the activity protected indigenous biodiversity. In other words, the Minister of Environment — Mark Parent, at the time — had the discretion to authorize a seal hunt on Hay Island if he could argue that the commercial activity protected the area's biodiversity. The Tories alleged the seals were eating too many of the fish swimming in the ocean around the island, threatening marine biodiversity. However, the wilderness area designation did not apply to the waters around Scatarie or Hay Islands: it only applied to the land above the mean high water mark. In order to apply this section of the *Fisheries Act*, it had to be shown that the presence of seals was detrimental to the island's ecology. As it turned out, an internal biological review of the matter concluded the seals did not pose any threat to the island's biodiversity. In fact, the study found they may even be supporting the island's biodiversity.

That finding didn't seem to matter much though. Momentum was building. In February 2008, the year Aldworth first set foot on the island, commercial sealers were given a limited period of access to the island. Fisheries Minister Ronald Chisholm, who requested the access, said in a media release that his department was "working to protect fish species in the Hay Island area." That year, the DFO set a Total Allowable Catch (TAC) of 2,200 Hay Island seals. Sealers killed about 1,000.

It wasn't until the summer of that year that Minister Chisholm's department prepared a follow-up to the Hay Island seal hunt and gave it to Minister Parent. It looked at the effects of the seals on the marine biodiversity. Not surprisingly, it found that the hunt provided no noticeable benefits to the marine or fish biodiversity but that more hunts were needed for further study: "Evidence that this reduction has assisted in this goal is difficult or impossible to state without a complex, scientific, multi-year approach."[5]

The next winter, the Tories authorized another hunt — this time 200 Hay Island grey seals were killed. The week before the hunt was set to start, the Newfoundland pelt buyer unexpectedly backed out, leaving the sealers scrambling to find another buyer. They did locate one, but the number of pelts requested was much lower. The reality was that by 2009 a seal pelt just wasn't worth much anymore — $15, compared to seven times more just four years earlier. As well, the market for seal meat had become virtually non-existent, except as feed for fox and mink being raised on fur farms. Despite all the rhetoric about the market for seal products, in reality it had been drying up for years. The U.S. had banned the import and sale of seal products in 1972, as part of its *Marine Mammal Protection Act*, and in 2009 the European Union followed suit — banning the importation of seal hunt products. Russia was next, in 2011, banning the import of seal products; in 2009 it had banned its own hunt of harp seal pups in the White Sea because of fears the population was reaching dangerously low levels.

By 2009 questions were also being raised about the legality of authorizing a hunt in a protected area and whether the government itself could be fined for breaking its own law. Penalties for breaking this law were also very tough. Individuals in contravention of the Act could be fined up to $500,000 per day or put in prison for up to six months; corporations could be on the hook for $1 million a day. In a letter written on February 17, 2008, to Mark Parent, Debbie MacKenzie, head of the Grey Seal Conservation Society (a non-profit organization based in Halifax that advocates for a healthy ocean ecosystem and argues that the grey seal is intrinsic to that) wrote: "A year ago, the provincial Crown was reported to be prosecuting individuals for offences under the Wilderness Areas Protection Act that arose from illegal seal hunting on Hay Island." Though it didn't state any specifics in the letter, MacKenzie was referring to a group of sealers led by Robert Courtney, a haddock fisher from Cape Breton and president of the North of Smokey Fishermen's Association. They had already been sealing illegally on Hay Island, apparently with the approval of DFO. They may have been doing so to test the province to see what might be possible in other protected places like Sable Island — a subject we'll return to in the next chapter. Once the province discovered what was going on it ordered the illegal sealing stopped and served several of the sealers with warnings. The sealers ignored these and were eventually charged. MacKenzie poses the question: "Might the Crown next have to defend itself against a prosecution under the same law? Could the matter go to court as a civil case, say, if some well-heeled seal hunt protester decided to finance a lawsuit?"

By the time the NDP took power in the summer of 2009, civil servants within the departments were getting cold feet, worried that maybe the Minister of Environment didn't have legal authority to allow the hunt after all. Howard Epstein, a lawyer and long-time environmentalist, who has represented a Halifax riding for the NDP since 1998, comments:

> I began to pay attention to this once we became the government. The way it was presented to us at caucus was that, even though

under the Tories the government had authorized a hunt, there was concern within the departments about whether the Minister actually had legal authority to do that and so they wanted to clarify the legislation to make sure there wasn't any doubt about it.

Sterling Belliveau, who had voiced his support for the two previous grey seal hunts under the Tories, was given two portfolios in the new NDP government: Fisheries and Environment — a combination many at the time felt was a conflict of interest. In his weekly editorial in the *Coast*, journalist and former journalism professor Bruce Wark didn't mince words: "Being an NDP environment minister, you'd think Belliveau would have fought tooth and nail to preserve the sanctity of every square inch of protected wilderness," he wrote, but instead "there was Belliveau giving himself the power to allow a slaughter of grey seals in the protected wilderness of Hay Island." Wark pointed to Belliveau's other role as Minister of Fisheries, "a department that desperately wants us to blame the seals for the continued decline of the cod stocks wiped out by decades of overfishing."[6]

In our interview, Epstein was more cautious: "I tend to see at least two government departments as having a strong regulatory mandate that includes regulatory oversight of other departments. One is the Department of Justice and the other is Environment." Epstein wouldn't go so far as to say Belliveau's appointment represented a conflict of interest but he did say it was "very undesirable to have either the Minister of Justice or the Minister of Environment carrying a second portfolio."

In the fall of 2009, Belliveau proposed changing the *Wilderness Areas Protection Act* to, he said, "strike a balance between economic and environmental interests," and allow a hunt on Hay Island without having to consider the hunt's effects on the area's biodiversity.In other words, the amended Act, if passed, would allow the hunt without needing to resort to any dubious arguments about the island's biodiversity or about the seals eating too many fish: more importantly, it would remove any legal ambiguity.

"This is where I think it got very difficult," says Epstein, who was also a member of the Law Amendments Committee at the time. He commented:

> The bill proceeded through the legislature and it got to the stage in the process in which the public is allowed to come and make comments on bills and there was a lot of information that came to the Law Amendments Committee that gave government members of the Committee serious reason to question the wisdom of the changes to the legislation.

Over a period of two days in November 2009, Bill 50 was scrutinized. The committee, made up of five members from the ruling NDP, two Liberals and two Tories, received submissions and listened to testimony from nearly two dozen people representing a wide range of interests. On the one hand, the Bill was an environmentalist's nightmare, but on the other it was a dream come true. Along with the changes allowing a commercial hunt on Hay Island, the Bill also included changes affecting off-highway vehicle (OHV) use in protected areas. So while the Minister was gaining power to authorize a hunt, he was losing it when it came to OHVs.

Raymond Plourde is the Wilderness Coordinator of the Ecology Action Centre (EAC), an environmental organization based in Halifax that's been in existence for more than four decades; its marine conservation program started in the wake of the groundfish collapse. Plourde says, "at the time there was a significant push on from ATV and snowmobile groups to open up some or all of the existing Wilderness Areas to recreational use. We had been pushing to get that clause out of the Act for years and that's where our attention was," he says. "I certainly agree that the argument used to allow a seal hunt on Hay Island was weak and the amendment was against the spirit of the Act but we just didn't have time to get into that issue too." Plourde ultimately felt the EAC was strategically better placed to focus on OHV use in protected areas and that, when it came to the seals, he would leave it to the "other well-qualified voices" scheduled to appear.

Epstein remembers the marine biologists from Dalhousie University in Halifax who came to give evidence: "They did not believe the seals were in fact a problem with the cod stocks and that therefore, there wasn't any compelling ecosystem reason to allow a hunt — that it would have no effect on the recovery of cod stocks."

Boris Worm, for instance, a professor of Marine Conservation Biology at Dalhousie University who has written extensively about the recovery of fish stocks told the Committee in November 2009: "I felt compelled to come here because I realized that the seal hunt issue is intertwined with the motivation to recover fish stocks in Nova Scotia." Worm argued that the motivation for a potential cull, or for allowing a hunt on Hay Island or elsewhere was not supported by the current science. "Both grey and harp seals cannot be implicated as a major factor, either in the collapse or the non-recovery of the groundfish stocks in Eastern Canada." Worm told the committee that not only were the seals not harming groundfish stocks, they may have been helping them recover. The latest science was showing that overall cod is not the preferred prey of grey seals, that they feed on fatty forage fish for the most part, and that these fish, particularly herring and sandlance, if not eaten by seals, would be having an even greater effect on cod because they feed extensively on cod larvae. He said seals were integral to marine ecosystems and that their role was a positive one. Worm added finally, "I don't think commercial interests should be allowed in wilderness areas."[7]

Hal Whitehead, a Dalhousie professor who has studied marine mammals for more than thirty years and is a world-renowned researcher on whales, also voiced his dissent about allowing a seal hunt in a protected area. At one point the following, rather telling, exchange took place:

> Harold Theriault: Mr. Whitehead, in Australia right now they're going to do a cull on the kangaroo for a few reasons — the population has doubled there so they figure they should cull the animals out. They're disturbing their golfing, they can't seem to golf without hitting one of them, they can't drive up the road without hitting one. Do you believe that should be done, that the herd should be brought down to a manageable level, in Australia?
>
> Hal Whitehead: I don't know enough about the situation there, I'm afraid.
>
> Theriault: You don't?
>
> Whitehead: No, I'm sorry, I can't comment on that.
>
> Theriault: If there were eight million seals here, on our land in Nova Scotia to Labrador, eight million, and they were disturbing our golfing and driving up and down the roads, do you believe that we would have a cull of the seal herd?
>
> Whitehead: I think to kill seals to make golfing a little less difficult, to me that doesn't seem like a good plan. I think the chances of seals interfering with traffic on Nova Scotia highways is small and probably something we don't need to consider at the moment.
>
> Theriault: Because we keep those animals culled down.
>
> Whitehead: No, I don't think that's the reason.[8]

Representatives from a number of anti-sealing groups made presentations at the hearings on Bill 50 as did Liz White from the Animal Alliance, Bridget Curran of the Atlantic Anti-Sealing Coalition, Debbie MacKenzie and Rebecca Aldworth. Aldworth showed the committee slides of the Hay Island hunt — a move that would later prove that a picture may indeed be worth a thousand words.

Several others argued that wilderness areas are intended to provide sanctuary to all native biodiversity, including grey seals; they felt that allowing commercial activity of this nature went against the spirit of the Act. In all, about ten people made presentations opposed to the changes allowing a seal hunt on Hay Island. "Very compelling" was how Epstein described the evidence provided by the Dalhousie scientists. "The other thing that happened at Law Amendments is we were shown slides of how the hunt took place, and a number of these were pretty vivid and dramatic as well, so I think pretty well everyone who was on law amendments from the government caucus came away from this feeling that this bill was ill-conceived and that there was no good reason to go ahead with it."

At this point politics got in the way. Epstein comments

> Two things happened at the caucus meeting that were fairly emphatic. One was that Sterling Belliveau, the Minister of Fisheries, said that from his perspective the issue was one that had to do with credibility of the government in the fishing community. There was a group of fishers who supplemented their income from fishing by hunting seals on Hay Island and that although there weren't a lot of individuals involved — maybe five boats, maybe twenty people — what Sterling was saying was that if we said "no" to these people by not allowing the legal framework to be put in place, that not only would it offend them, but this would be read as a very negative signal about the new government and this would be fatal to our chances of re-election. It was put in terms of votes.

Epstein explained that Belliveau wasn't alone in opposing the recommendation against amending the law. "The house leader and deputy premier, Frank Corbett, said that, because this bill was presented as a government bill, there was no backing down from it." Epstein recounts: "He said that it was not a free vote, that people weren't going to vote their consciences, that this was a government bill and everyone had to vote for it."

The next day Bill 50 was brought back to the House. It passed, with the NDP voting for it en masse — except for Epstein. Since he was not allowed to vote his conscience, he wasn't present for the vote in the house. "Either you have to vote for it, vote against it, or you're not there," he explains. A vote of abstention was not an option.

Hopes Pinned on Chinese Market

The following February, with the ink barely dry on the new law, the sealers were ready to go, with a buyer secured — it was supposed to be a lucrative year. But instead, just a few days before it was set to begin, the hunt was called off. In an interview, Courtney, the spokesperson for the Hay Island sealers, told me that in 2010 the federal and provincial governments had promised them some money but the province never came through. Because the rest of the world had begun shutting its doors to seal products, the Canadian government had been wooing the Chinese to expand its market. In 2006, it announced a five-year management plan, along with increased quotas and trade missions, working hand-in-hand with the Canadian seal industry to promote seal products in China. The province was going to help with funds,

Live grey seal pups on Hay Island, 2011.
Rebecca Aldworth/For HIS.

says Courtney, to make the hunt financially viable and to develop the samples of seal meat as a marketable product.

Senior bureaucrat with the provincial Department of Fisheries and Aquaculture, Greg Roach says,

We didn't get our ducks lined up in time for the 2010 harvest on Hay. That was a clear irritant with the harvesters. It was very shortly after that when we did have a program in place to help develop the products. We got that rolling later in 2010 for meat products and it was also used for 2011, again for a very modest harvest to produce products and samples, largely for the Chinese market.

Roach says that, although the sealers asked for $50,000, the province only came through with $35,000. "We wanted to make sure they were paid for the products that were used for the product development."

Courtney says that, in 2011, with the money they did eventually get, they killed about one hundred Hay Island seals as well as another hundred from Henry Island, on the western side of Cape Breton Island and a few from the tiny Amet Island in the southern Gulf of St. Lawrence. The animals were skinned and the meat was cut up, packaged and frozen but, without a market, according to Courtney, it all still sits in a freezer somewhere in Newfoundland.[*]

Having no market has meant that, since the winter of 2011, the slaughter on the island has been suspended — a setback Courtney sees as temporary. He says the Chinese have expressed interest in another product, one better tailored to the Chinese marketplace: "The Chinese want the whole animal, the intestines taken out, and the body, head and all, blast frozen." Courtney says they aren't really interested in juvenile seals, they want the adults, males in particular. "They'd have to be transferred to blast freezers and we're looking

---

[*] In 2012, with the loss of the European Union (E.U.) and Russia as markets for harp seal pelts threatening the viability of the hunt, the government of Newfoundland and Labrador offered the sealing industry financial support to stockpile seal products from that year's hunt in hopes that the market would open up again in the future.

Dead seals with whitecoat pup in foreground, 2008. Rebecca Aldworth/For HIS.

Seal hunt on Hay Island, 2011. Rebecca Aldworth/For HIS.

at doing a project on [Prince Edward Island] to see if that would work," he says. "We were working towards this but we're just waiting for the Chinese border to open up."

If the Chinese border were to open up, sealing industry representatives say they're not sure how to even go about "harvesting" the adult male grey seals — the ones they say the Chinese want. In 2006, Denny Morrow was secretary and treasurer of the now defunct Grey Seal Research and Development Society, a group promoting the development of a grey seal market. He was also the executive director of the Nova Scotia Fish Packers Association. At the time he told a provincial legislative committee on resources that ensuring the meat is "pristine" and free of gravel, sand, or grass in order to meet the regulations of the Canadian Food Inspection Agency would be challenging, especially given that the current method of killing is by shooting when the seals are on land. In response, Nova Scotia MLA Ernest Fage suggested that an alternative to shooting them might be drowning them in underwater traps. He wondered if Morrow's society could get the permission to do so. Morrow replied: "We've already thought of the net idea and we're thinking about what time of year we can get the concentrations of adults on the islands, maybe before they start their reproductive cycle."[9]

Courtney also says the Chinese don't want the carcasses processed by Canadians. They plan to do that work themselves, in China. "They want the skin, meat, heart, liver, the whole thing just as it is. Some of the markets [in China] want just the penis, I guess some others want just the fur, some just the meat."

Seal penises — when powdered and mixed with wine — are used as aphrodisiacs in Chinese traditional medicine: they can fetch upwards of $500 in medicine shops in Toronto. In 1997, a team of Canadian scientists analyzed the DNA from supposed seal penises sold in shops in Canada, the U.S. and Asia: they found that some were bona fide seal organs, but some were actually parts from domestic cattle and dogs. The paper published in *Conservation Biology* noted that the presence of unidentifiable species, possibly including the protected Australian fur seal, suggested the legal trade in seal products was being used as a cover for illegal trade.

According to the International Fund for Animal Welfare (IFAW), in the mid-1990s the Chinese company Shanghai Fisheries bought 50,000 seals from Newfoundland's Terra Nova Fishery. Stories about the clandestine sales of seal penises abound but are no better described than in the 1998 book by former Newfoundland sealer and fisherman Michael Dwyer. In *Over the Side, Mickey,* Dwyer paints a relentless and at times horrifyingly honest account of the Newfoundland harp seal hunt in the spring of 1997. Dwyer spent twenty days aboard the long-liner *C. Michelle* with seven other crew members. He describes in sickening detail not only the horrors visited upon the crew, having to endure near torturous conditions and squalor, but also upon the seals. In one scene, Dwyer describes the value of male or "old dog" seal penises:

> An old dog organ, as every sealer knows, brings in the best kind of money. Last year, on our first trip, we had brought in 550, almost a large fish containerful. Very discreetly, they were loaded onto a pickup that disappeared in the night. We received more money from that tub of organs than we did from the tractor-trailer loaded with pelts, meat and fat. Asians loved them. Nothing less than six inches

was acceptable. They averaged seventy dollars each and we only had to handle them twice.[10]

In spite of the fact that seal penises are so valuable, the Canadian government says it is promoting the meat in China. Announcements have now been made by two of Canada's federal fisheries ministers that China was going to the be the sealing industry's salvation: however, as Courtney says, the border still remains closed and seal meat sales to China are on hold.

"If the Chinese border opens up, where will you get all the seals to meet the demand?" I ask Courtney. "Sable Island is the heart of the grey seal population," he says. "Unless you do something there to clean up the seals, bring the population under control, it isn't going to make any difference for the fish."

As pressure was successfully being applied by a small group of sealers on Hay Island, momentum for a massive seal cull was building at higher political levels. By the end of 2009, the federal government would have in its possession a macabre plan of how to kill more than half of the grey seal population on Sable Island. By the end of 2012 there would be two high-level recommendations to the federal fisheries minister for a cull starting in, but not limited to, the southern Gulf of St. Lawrence. The magnitude of a cull, should one be authorized, would involve nothing short of tens of thousands of seals.

Chapter 2

Graveyard of the Atlantic

> In mid-ocean, the grass has begun to build a world, a thin white world in the shape of the new moon. The grasses raise up their green spires like swords to defend this new religion of land — Sable Island.
>
> — Harry Thurston, *Marram*, 2001

When maps were first being drawn of the world more than five centuries ago, there was the "known world" and there was everything else. Usually drawn near the margins of these maps, where the great expanse of the untravelled deep waters lay, were the sea monsters — scaly and green, with horns and daunting tusks — rearing their fearsome heads from the dark depths. In one such map of Scandinavia dating back to the 1530s, from Martin Sandler's 2008 book, *Atlantic Ocean: The Illustrated History of the Ocean that Changed the World,* one sea monster, striped orange and brown with webbed feet, a shark's fin and face of a bird, is being attacked by another sea monster, grey with the snout of a fish, bearing ferocious fangs. Elsewhere on the map another monster with a red gaping mouth is so mammoth that it towers over a sailing ship and spews water like a fountain from its blow-hole; yet another is flaming red, snakelike, and wrapped around a schooner, its open mouth on deck, no doubt devouring the crew.

That was where our knowledge ended, back then. Yesterday's sea monsters are the marine mammals we know today — whales, dolphins, walruses, seals. In a short time these mythical and demonized creatures moved from the edges of the maps to become "inexhaustible resources," and targets of merciless and enormously lucrative killing sprees.

Heike Lotze, a Dalhousie University biology professor who specializes in human impacts on marine ecosystems, says that by 1900 most marine mammals and birds had already been hunted to very low levels. In 2004, she and a colleague reported that of the sixteen marine mammal species recorded in the Atlantic region of Canada, three were hunted to extinction before 1900, seven were severely reduced in the nineteenth and early twentieth centuries and another four were targeted in the twentieth century. The three extinct species include the globally extinct sea mink, the extirpated Atlantic walrus and the Atlantic grey whale, an easily targeted coastal species that was wiped out before large-scale industrial whaling began.

Although whaling in the northwest Atlantic, which started in the 1500s, first targeted northern right whales, once they were depleted, hunters turned to humpback whales, which became the most important targets in the eighteenth and nineteenth centuries. Hunting was then extended to fin and blue whales in the late nineteenth century and then shifted to sei, minke, pilot and killer whales in the twentieth century.

The other group of marine mammals that underwent unprecedented levels of exploitation were the pinnipeds: fin-footed semi-aquatic mammals, including the Atlantic walrus as well as the family known scientifically as *phocidae* — or "true seals" — including the harp, hooded, grey and harbour seals. These seals lack an external ear, distinguishing them from another family of pinniped, the eared seals or *otariidae*, which includes the sea lions and fur seals.

In the 1600s, the population of the Atlantic walrus on Canada's east coast was estimated to be in the hundreds of thousands, but, because they were extremely vulnerable on land and slow to reproduce, they were unable to withstand the onslaught of sustained killing for their ivory tusks and blubber. As a result, they disappeared from Canada's east coast and are now only found in the Arctic, where they continue to be hunted. In 2012, in the most recent international assessment of Canada's pinnipeds, the status of the Arctic walrus was unknown, but some populations were thought to be declining because some aboriginal harvests were considered unsustainable.[11] In 2006 the Committee on the Status of Endangered Wildlife in Canada (COSEWIC) designated the species "special concern."

Today, eighteen species of phocids or "true seals" exist on the planet and nearly half of these are either critically endangered, threatened or their status is unknown. The recent 2012 assessment lists harp, harbour and grey seal populations as being of "least concern." Harp populations are believed to be stable or increasing and grey seal populations increasing, while harbour seal populations are showing recent and rapid declines on Sable Island, possibly as a result of shark predation. The hooded seal, which is still commercially hunted, is listed as "vulnerable," with numbers in decline.

Once the floating ice nurseries of the harp and much less numerous hooded seals were discovered in the Gulf of St. Lawrence and on what's called "the Front" off the northeastern coast of Newfoundland by European sealers in the mid-1600s, it wasn't long before they were exploited as mercilessly as the whales and walruses. By the 1800s, sealing had reached full throttle: by the middle of that century nearly 400 vessels and 14,000 sealers headed out to the pack ice nurseries. The peak year was 1832, when sealers returned with more than 740,000 sculps — the word for the seal hides with the fat attached. Between 1830 and 1860, some thirteen million harp seals were landed, and some say that perhaps even double that number were killed, since the official figures do not include the unborn pups of females killed and to the extent that firearms were used, it excludes those that were shot in open water and never recovered.[12]

Historically, the teeming seas could have easily sustained eleven million and maybe even as high as fourteen million harp seals at any one time; indeed, a seal hunt of the magnitude that was sustained over many decades would not have been possible without a harp seal population of enormous abundance. However, by the early 1970s the unregulated hunt reduced their population to less than two million, forcing Canada to introduce a quota system of management. By 2012, the population had recovered to between seven and eight million.

The annual harp seal hunt, one of the most polarizing issues on the east coast of Canada, has perhaps best defined our relationship with the seal. At one time it was the white-coated seal pups that were killed for their fur, but public outcry over the hunt's cruelty — rooted in the 1964 CBC series on hunting and fishing produced by Montreal-based Artek Films, which included footage of the seal hunt on the Magdalen Islands and in particular a controversial clip of the skinning of live seals — eventually resulted in the European Economic Community ban on importing whitecoats in 1983 and an eventual prohibition of this practice altogether just four years later. Today, seal pups must have begun to shed the thick white fur and be in what's called the *ragged-jacket* stage before they can be killed. This rule extends their life for at least a couple of weeks.

For many vehemently opposed to the slaughter of seals, this was a minor victory, and anti-sealing groups, particularly the International Fund for Animal Welfare (IFAW), the Sea Shepherd Conservation Society, and Greenpeace redoubled their efforts to end the hunt altogether, charging that the hunt was cruel and inhumane as well as being unnecessary because seal fur was a luxury item. By 2009, nearly five decades after the seal hunt protests began, lobbying of decision-makers in Europe — the largest market for seal fur — coupled with palpable and sustained public pressure was about to finally pay off.

In anticipation of a decision by the European Union regarding the import of seal products, in the spring of 2009 the Canadian government amended the *Marine Mammal Regulations* to try to address the thorny issue of cruelty. According to the DFO the changes were meant to clarify the steps that should be followed to ensure the seals were killed both "quickly and humanely" before being skinned.[13] The regulations were to outline what's called the "three-step process" of killing a seal, starting with the first step, referred to as "striking." According to the amendments, a firearm, not a hakapik or club, should be the primary weapon for killing seals older than a year of age because by then their skulls are thicker and cannot be crushed very easily. In step two, sealers are supposed to "check" that the seal is actually dead by palpating the cranium after striking it to see if the skull is crushed. Prior to the amendment, a "blinking reflex test" was required to determine if a seal was dead: a glassy eye that did not blink was thought to be a good indicator of death but veterinarians found it wasn't a reliable indicator and that a non-blinking seal — thought to be dead — could regain consciousness during the skinning process. In the third step, sealers are to "bleed" the seals by severing the two axillary arteries of the seal, located beneath its front flippers. Bleeding ensures that the seal is dead and sealers must wait a minimum of one minute after bleeding the seal before skinning it.

However, according to animal welfare groups, the changes made to the regulations do nothing to ensure a quick and humane slaughter. For the killing to be humane they say animal welfare experts are clear: the three-steps of the process need to be carried out in rapid succession, but the amended regulations do not require it. Instead, they allow a sealer to check that the skull is crushed "as soon as possible" after it's shot, which critics say leaves a lot of room for suffering to take place.

David Lavigne has been the science advisor for the International Fund for Animal Welfare (IFAW) since 1999. Before that he was a zoology professor at the University of Guelph; he's been studying seals since 1969. He explains: "The regulations in fact allow a sealer to shoot an animal on ice or in the water, then hook it, drag it along the ice, then hoist it on deck," and all these steps are performed prior to making sure it's actually dead. In other words, the absence of any time requirements between the three steps means that a sealer could potentially bleed the seal — the last step to ensure that the animal is dead before skinning — hours after shooting it.

In the summer of 2009, the European Union — and its twenty-seven-member countries voted in favour of banning the import of seal products and goods derived from seals including fur, meat, oil, blubber, and omega-3 pills made from seal oil. The ban exempted products from traditional hunts carried out by Inuit. The loss of the E.U. market had a profound impact on the Newfoundland and Labrador seal hunt. According to one commentator, in 2011, after the E.U. ban, the hunt brought in about as much money as a busy department store in Corner Brook would in a month, about $1.5 million.[14] Later that year, Russia, Belarus and Kazakhstan also banned the import of harp seal pelts.

Despite these dismal market realities, in 2011 the DFO set a TAC (Total Allowable Catch), or upper limit on how many harp seals that could be killed commercially, at 400,000, the highest harp seal quota ever set since quota management was introduced in 1971. With a record TAC set, another record was about to be set. When all the pelts were counted, less than 10 percent of the TAC or 37,600 seals were landed by commercial sealers — the lowest number in at least 250 years. The lack of sea ice and of markets seemed to be conspiring, and few sealers made the journey in search of the nurseries. The DFO TAC of 400,000 was carried over to 2012, when roughly 70,000 harp seals were killed in the hunt.

Harp and hooded seals have historically been the backbone of the commercial sealing industry in Canada, largely because of their numbers. But other lesser-known seals were also hunted. By the time the images of the harp seal hunt were being flashed on television screens everywhere, grey and harbour seals had already borne the brunt of human assault.

By 1949 the grey seal — also commonly called a horsehead because of its head's elongated shape — had been unreported for so long that some biologists believed it to be extirpated in the northwest Atlantic. Around the time of the early French arrivals, these seals remained year-round along the northeast coasts of Canada and the U.S. with whelping rookeries that they often shared with their gigantic relative, the walrus, though at different times of year. Some have speculated that what ultimately saved the grey and the much smaller harbour seals on the northeastern seaboard from the fate of the walrus was that they had been replaced by the much more abundant harp seal as a prime source of oil.

In 1927, the federal government placed a bounty on the "muzzles" of harbour seals because at that time they were said to be eating too many salmon. But because it was difficult to tell whether the nose, which was to be presented by the fisherman to collect the bounty, was from a grey seal or a harbour seal, both were being killed. Within a decade the grey seals had become very rare but some did remain, finding sanctuary in more remote locations. The Second World War provided them (as well as commercial fish species) with some respite, so that during the war both the grey and harbour seals managed to secure small footholds. After the war the bounty on harbour seals continued but this time, in order to prove the seal killed was in fact a harbour seal, the fisherman had to provide the lower jaw bone — which would be much smaller than that of a grey seal. The grey seals were left alone for some time until in 1967, the federal government decided that the grey seal population also needed to be "managed" and an annual cull took place at their traditional rookery sites for nearly two decades: on the pack ice in the Gulf of St. Lawrence, on Amet, Camp, and Hut Islands along the coasts of Nova Scotia, and on Sable Island. Between 1978 and 1990, the government added a bounty program where fishers were paid for presenting the lower jaw of a dead grey seal. But once the culling and bounty efforts ceased, the grey seal population rebounded. It will be recalled that the vast majority — possibly as high as 330,000 — can be found on Sable Island, making it the world's largest grey seal colony. It also makes it a place where it would be possible to kill a large number of the animals in just a few days.

Last Grey Seal Refuge Under Threat

Like the tip of an iceberg, Sable Island is the emergent part of a much larger sand deposit on Sable Island Bank, an area totalling about 28,000 square kilometres on the Scotian Shelf, flanked on its eastern edge by The Gully, a legally protected submarine canyon of corals and a unique population of non-migratory bottlenose whales. The crescent-moon shaped island itself is about 42 kilometres long and 1.4 kilometres wide at low tide and is sculpted constantly by restless seas and incessant winds. Its backbone of undulating dunes is held together by the long roots of the marram grass, which feeds the island's famous wild horses.

The two ends of Sable Island extend below the ocean surface creating underwater sand bars — and giving the island an actual length double what we see. It's these hidden, but deadly, sandbars that are partly responsible for giving Sable Island its other name: "graveyard of the Atlantic," because of the ships that wrecked there — more than 350 of them recorded. Buried beneath the continuously moving sands, some of these wrecks, occasionally and unexpectedly, reappear like apparitions.

The other thing making the mid-ocean location of the island treacherous is the fog — thick as milk for 125 days a year — created by the collision of the frigid Labrador Current originating in the Arctic and the warm Gulf Stream originating at the tip of Florida. These two ocean currents officially meet at the Grand Banks, off Newfoundland, and their combination also created what was once the richest fishing ground in the world.

The island is a unique and fragile mid-ocean sanctuary. Apart from the

North beach, late December, Sable Island. Photo courtesy Zoe Lucas.

Adults hauled out along the south beach on the east spit, mid February when pupping season is mostly over, Sable Island. Photo courtesy Zoe Lucas.

Whitecoat pup and a moulted pup, north beach dune in late January, Sable Island. Photo courtesy Zoe Lucas.

Female and her pup and an interested male, early January, Sable Island. Photo courtesy Zoe Lucas.

world-famous horses — descendants of animals brought to Sable during the late 1700s — Sable also has the largest dunes in eastern North America, and several species at risk including the roseate tern and the Ipswich sparrow. It's also home to the largest colony of grey seals in the world.

In 2009, under growing pressure from the fishing industry the DFO commissioned a study to examine the costs and logistics of "managing" the Sable Island grey seal population. It hired CBCL Ltd., a Halifax-based engineering firm, to consider two options: first, to figure out what it would take to slaughter 220,000 seals over a five-year period; and second, to consider how to conduct a contraceptive vaccine program targeting 16,000 females each year for five years.*

According to the study, obtained through an Access to Information request, either of these two options would have to take place between December and early February when the beaches and dunes of Sable Island are covered

---

* DFO scientists say sterilization is not the favoured approach for reducing grey seal numbers because the possible benefits to cod would not materialize in the short term. Sterilizing mature females with the vaccine would have an immediate impact on the grey seal population (i.e., fewer pups born in the future) but the number of seals currently eating cod wouldn't change. Logistically, they say, it would also be difficult to capture the females for the injection. Injecting the weaned pups would be much easier because they are already on the beach before they're able to swim, but DFO has never completed the study to find out if injecting the weaned pups renders the animal permanently or partially sterile. In any case, the impact of this would still not be immediate enough to save the cod from extirpation, they say.

Grey seal pup, late December, Sable Island. Photo courtesy Zoe Lucas.

Female grey seal on the alert, mid September, Sable Island. Photo courtesy Zoe Lucas.

Grey seal pup resting in the marram grass, early January. Photo courtesy Zoe Lucas.

with nursing mothers and their babies. The logistics of killing and moving tens of thousands of seal carcasses over a twenty-five-day period would be gruesome, at best: mobile crematoriums and modified tree-harvesting equipment would be needed and the operation would cost upwards of $35 million — a figure which compares to roughly half the value of commercial landings of all groundfish species in Nova Scotia in 2010. Adult seals would be killed with rifles and the pups with either rifle or by clubbing. To achieve the goal of 100,000 dead seals in twenty-five days, the engineering firm estimated that ten seals would have to be killed every minute, filling a tandem dump truck with seals approximately every ten minutes, seven hours a day.

Thirty modified tree forwarders would load the carcasses to one of the twenty or so mobile crematoriums where they would be incinerated.* If the carcasses were not incinerated then the onset of rot and disease would be fast,

---

* Units called "Air Curtain Burners," designed to burn wood waste with special mechanisms to control smoke, could be used for incineration. These have reportedly been used in animal disease outbreaks. However, the manufacturer's website notes that sand, likely to be present on a dead seal carcass from Sable, could smother the fire. In this case, combustion of the cadavers would require wood in a one-to-one ratio — that's 15,000 tonnes of wood, which would also have to be brought to the island. This detail was overlooked in the study.

Female and her pup, late December, Sable Island. Photo courtesy Zoe Lucas.

resulting in biological hazards and health and safety issues for the workers. If they weren't incinerated, they would have to be transported daily off the island — slung from shore by helicopter to a supply vessel — and brought to a place on shore. According to the study, this scenario was fraught with difficulties, including the fact that 100,000 intact carcasses would weigh roughly 15,000 tonnes and would require 500 trips by tractor-trailer from an onshore marine terminal to a disposal facility. Since this would be taking place in the winter months, the carcasses would likely freeze inside the containers making disposal difficult. It's also currently not legal to dump 15,000 tonnes of dead seals into a Nova Scotia landfill.

"To any reasonable person, this is a holocaust situation and I don't use that word lightly," says Bridget Curran, director of the Atlantic Canadian Anti-Sealing Coalition. "There's no science to support claims that seals are responsible for groundfish stock depletion or are responsible for the failure of groundfish stocks to rebound," she says. "It's a ridiculous scheme, it's unnecessary, it's inhumane and has no basis in science."

Denny Morrow strongly favours a cull of grey seals on Sable Island, and in 2004 led the call to cull half the population. He says that seals are the main culprits for the non-recovery of the cod, especially as their numbers rise. "These are very large predators, adults can weigh 600 to 1,000 pounds," he says. "They're eating a lot of fish."[15]

Morrow is also concerned about parasite worms that seals can pass on to cod, possibly affecting the health of the fish while making them less commercially attractive. "We've found that fish that we've gotten in that moratorium area off eastern Nova Scotia has been so infested by these parasites that even if the fishery were open, we wouldn't be able to do anything with the fish. You can't economically pick [the worms] out." For Morrow, the main issue here is that, if there were fewer seals, there'd be less cod infestation, which is making business difficult for fish packers. He says it is affecting the survival of Nova Scotia fishing towns. "Our young people, who would like to stay and fish, increasingly have to move," he says.

In fact, many fishermen and fish processors have complained that the worm affects other groundfish too — haddock and cusk — forcing some groundfish processors to stop processing haddock and other groundfish from the Scotian Shelf. Manually removing the worms is no doubt time consuming and expensive, and wormy fish are hard to market. In addition to making the fish less commercially attractive, they argue the seal worm affects the health of the cod. But on this, the science suggests otherwise.

Parasites are part of the normal stomach flora of all marine mammals. In the case of the grey seal, the seal worms don't make the seal sick, but they do produce millions of eggs. Debbie MacKenzie says the worm eggs, which are released into the ocean ecosystem when the seal defecates, are essentially food — a form of zooplankton. She says small crustaceans eat the eggs and then the small crustaceans get eaten by fish. Once inside the fish, the egg develops into its larval stage, comes out of the fish's gut and lodges into its flesh. "It just sits there in a little coil and it waits until a warm blooded animal eats the fish, and completes the cycle," explains MacKenzie. The worm doesn't damage the flesh of the cod but it does distress fishers, she says. "The fishermen hypothesized that the worm load was killing the fish and they forced the DFO to look into it and there was a surprising outcome," she says.

In 2009, the DFO reported the findings of a study of cod in the southern Gulf of St. Lawrence, which showed that fish with more worms were actually in better physical condition than those with less worms. This suggested that cod that were better at foraging — finding food — were in better condition and also more likely to ingest seal worm. The study found no evidence that the seal worm was harming cod, let alone killing them.[16]

According to the DFO, the CBCL study that looked at the logistics of a Sable Island grey seal cull was only a fact-finding exercise, which was meant to assess, technically, what would be required if a cull were to take place. Any decision to implement the study's recommendations would be made by the federal Minister of Fisheries and Oceans, who, at the time, was Gail Shea.

In January of 2010, about two months after the CBCL study was submitted to DFO, Shea announced a TAC of 39,000 grey seals on Sable Island. Then, almost as if the left hand didn't know what the right hand was doing, in 2011 Environment Canada announced that Sable Island would become a national park reserve.* Many environmentalists, including naturalist Zoe Lucas, who heads the Sable Island Green Horse Society, Mark Butler of the EAC and Chris Miller of the Canadian Parks and Wilderness Society, welcomed the decision because they argued it raised the level of protection for the island's unique biodiversity and extremely fragile sand-dune ecosystems.

But some were not so sure about the new park status. Prior to becoming a park, Sable was protected under the *Canada Shipping Act* and experienced very restricted access — anyone wishing to visit the island required both permission from the Canadian Coast Guard and enough gumption or money to land a boat or plane there. Under this scenario the island received 200–250 visitors a year. Parker Donham, a well-known columnist and commentator in the province, started a "Hands Off Sable Island" Facebook group, which had more than 2,000 members. The main sentiment of the group was that dangerous levels of tourism would damage the island's ecological integrity.

But according to Lucas, a resident of Sable Island since 1982 and arguably its most impassioned and knowledgeable advocate, national park status "is the best possible thing that could happen to Sable." The alternative was that it gets taken over by the Canadian Wildlife Service, an organization which she says has been a handicap for Sable for some time. "Their idea was to shut down the Canadian Meteorological Service, remove all the human presence on the island and put up 'keep off' signs." Lucas says there would have been no way to enforce that. With national park status, a management plan for the island will be drafted in the next five years and the process will be an open one, she says. "Everyone will be able to be involved."

Sable's new status, however, would still not rule out a grey seal cull. In the spring of 2012, the project manager for Sable Island National Park, Julie Tompa, said that DFO was still the lead agency with respect to seals, that there were no plans for a cull on the island and that any recommendation on the part of the fisheries minister to do so would trigger an environmental assessment and involve public consultations. However, since then, in very short order, the federal government under Prime Minister Stephen Harper changed more than seventy laws in the so-called Omnibus Bill C-38 and essentially dismantled decades of environmental protection. Two crucial environmental laws that received drastic alteration were the *Canadian Environmental Assessment Act* (CEAA) and the *Fisheries Act*. It was unclear at the time of writing whether changes to these laws may negate the requirement for either an environmental assessment or public involvement in Sable matters.

---

* It is being called a reserve pending the outcome of land claims negotiations with the Mi'kmaq, who have asserted aboriginal rights and title to all of Nova Scotia.

If pressure from a small number of renegade sealers on Hay Island was enough to change a provincial statute and allow for the commercial hunt of a relatively small number of grey seals in a protected wilderness area, what is standing in the way of opening up the wild heart of the grey seal population to sealing? In other words, does Hay Island set a precedent that could affect the future of Sable Island? For answers I spoke to Howard Epstein who was against amending Nova Scotia's *Wilderness Areas Protection Act* to allow sealing on Hay Island. "Precedent is a tricky word in the legal context," he says. "It's usually used in the context of cases decided by judges." Epstein says that in the case of Hay Island a law was changed and no other jurisdiction is bound by that change. But, he says, it could affect other protected areas in the province. It also doesn't bode well for other protected spaces. "Once this kind of activity is allowed — commercial activity inside a protected area — it questions the idea of a protected area in the first place." However, it was the following point that was most worrying: "Wilderness areas, like Hay Island, usually have even more protection than national parks." If, as some contend, Hay Island was really a test to see what might be possible on Sable Island and given the recent draconian changes made to important hard-won federal environmental legislation, the future of the largest, and last, grey seal refuge may not be as secure as some may think.

Chapter 3

The New Normal

I don't know what was around hundreds and hundreds of years ago. I was not around then … [Grey seals] are showing up in areas that they traditionally have not been, at least in the recent hundreds of years. They're an invasive species.

— John Levy, President, Fishermen and Scientists Research Society, March 29, 2012

I love animals, and I would love to see that little seal herd down there of fifteen to twenty-five seals that I used to go down and feed as a child, I would love to see that again. It was normal. Today, what is going on in the seal herds of Atlantic Canada is not normal.

— Harold Theriault, MLA, Digby-Annapolis, *Hansard*, April 18, 2006

Ever since he was big enough to get over the side of a boat, Danny Arsenault has been in one. He bought his first fleet when he was eighteen and for forty years he's been fishing. "When I started fishing, I didn't know what a grey seal was," he says. "I had never seen one back then in our area." Arsenault lives in the fishing village of Tignish, on the northern tip of Prince Edward Island. He fishes in the southern Gulf of St. Lawrence known as fishing district 4T. "In the spring I would start fishing as soon as the ice was gone. We would fish groundfish, cod and hake. There was lots of it and we would fish right until the ice came," he says. When the herring was running, he would switch to that — then mackerel, then back to groundfish. "I'd fish lobsters in the fall season too," he says. "Everything was great. We always had a fishery."

Today, Arsenault spends three or four of the winter months in Alberta driving a mulcher in the forest industry to supplement his fishing income. His boat sits on the land much of the year except for when he takes it out lobster fishing in the fall. The rest of the time he gets hired on as a mate with his brother-in-law and other fishers in Prince Edward Island and in Nova Scotia.

Arsenault says the grey seals started showing up in the Gulf about twenty years ago. "We have a big reef here and in the fall, especially when the herring season is on, there's thousands of them, you couldn't even count them." Arsenault says it only takes the fishers a day or two of fishing before they reach their quota for halibut and "every second fish is taken away by the seals." Arsenault doesn't dispute that there was overfishing in the past, but he says once that stopped the seals took over. "Now there's another predator out there besides us," he says.

Arsenault is not alone in his view. As we have seen, many fishers and politicians have likened the grey seal presence to an invasion. Recently, some scientists have also challenged the view that grey seals were abundant historically by pointing to the lack of quantitative or numerical data for grey seals before 1960, suggesting that current population numbers must therefore be unprecedented.[17] This argument is an important one for cull advocates because if the current grey seal population size can be deemed abnormal, then it's much easier to argue that human intervention in the form of a cull may be necessary. But as we shall see, while it's true that in the last fifty years — well within Arsenault's lifetime — the grey seal population has swelled, there are reasons for this, and for why the population levels four decades ago were not at all "normal" for the species. As we'll see, reconstructing ecological history can be a very complicated and sometimes controversial endeavour.

Scientists first began counting the grey seals born on Sable Island in 1962. That year marks the first year of quantitative data and in that year there were 13,000 seals whelping on the island and between 200 and 300 pups born. Back then the pups could be counted individually but, as the population increased and the breeding colony spread along the long stretches of beach and inland onto the grassy dunes, tagging the pups became impractical. Today the Sable, Gulf and Eastern Shore herds are estimated by counting the number of pups born using digital aerial photography. These aerial counts, carried out every three years, are combined with a complicated set of modelling assumptions to come up with an estimate of the total population.[18]

In 2010 — the most recent year DFO estimated the grey seal populations — there were 62,100 pups born on Sable Island, and the total population amounted to somewhere between 260,000 and 320,000 animals depending on the model used. For more than four decades, the population growth trend has been exponential, increasing about 13 percent per year. In other words, pups were being born at a nearly constant rate, and the total population was doubling every seven years. In the last decade, however, scientists have discovered that the exponential growth has stopped: they attribute this to the high mortality of juvenile grey seals — a subject we'll return to.

Since the DFO has been counting pups, the Gulf herd estimates have been much more variable than those for the Sable herd. Scientists say that is because of a history of culling and scientific "harvests" in the Gulf and the greater chance that a Gulf pup will die because of poor ice conditions. In 2010, it was estimated that 11,228 pups were born in the Gulf.[19]

But estimating the number of pups born is no easy task. On Sable Island, it is complicated by the fact that the aerial pictures may not pick up those pups that get covered by sand, or have died or haven't been born yet that year. In the southern Gulf of St. Lawrence, estimating the numbers is even more daunting because the grey seals are not concentrated in one discrete area, as they are on Sable. Instead they whelp in small groups of a few hundred animals, some on the pack ice but increasingly they've been spotted on islands and shoreline beaches. According to Mike Hammill, the head of the department's marine mammal section, who leads the federal government's population surveys for the Gulf herd, the breeding locations of grey seals in the Gulf are highly variable. For instance, if the pack ice is unstable, they might breed on land the following season. This lack of fidelity to a whelping site makes it difficult to predict where the rookeries will be, and to know where to fly the reconnaissance surveys. Coming up with an accurate pup estimate becomes even more uncertain if the ice breaks up too early and pups drown because they are not yet able to swim. The aerial survey would miss these ones. The issue of poor visibility in severe weather conditions makes surveying even more difficult; for example, pups may often be covered by snow.

As we have seen, when Canadian scientists started counting grey seals fifty years ago, their population had already been severely depleted, leading some to believe they were already extirpated. In other words, their population in 1960 was far from either normal or natural. While actual numbers are not known, it is believed that at one time they were historically abundant and widely distributed along the eastern seaboard of the U.S and in Canadian waters. It was after the Europeans decimated the walrus populations that they turned their sights to the grey seal, which was subsequently hunted extensively for oil. Their numbers were depleted by the mid 1800s, but even when they were considered rare they continued to be hunted. Federally sponsored cull and bounty programs continued until 1990. These practices all kept their numbers unnaturally low.

The Complexity of Reconstructing History

Daniel Pauly, arguably the world's most prolific and influential fisheries scientist today, is a professor at the University of British Columbia's Fisheries Centre. In 1995, he coined the term "shifting baseline syndrome" to describe the phenomenon where "each generation of fisheries scientists accepts as a baseline the stock size and species composition that occurred at the beginning of their careers, and uses this to evaluate changes." When Pauly was writing about this he was referring mainly to the fact that fish stocks were generally in decline and, as the baseline shifted with each generation of scientists, there was "a gradual accommodation" of the creeping loss. He explains that with the baselines shifting our perception of what is natural shifted too, making it impossible to evaluate the true social and ecological costs of fisheries.

This could just as easily be applied to grey seals. Because there are no quantitative data for grey seal abundance before 1962, that year tends to be used as a baseline for comparing current population estimates. By doing this we focus on recent history and, when we do this, the current population looks like it's a deviation from the "norm," when in reality it was the size of the population in 1960 that was abnormal. This myopic perspective also ignores what may have been extraordinary losses in the past — long before scientists began measuring them. Pauly says one of the failings of fisheries scientists is that they have not incorporated "earlier knowledge," or anecdotes into their present models, which he says would "have the effect of adding history to a discipline that has suffered from lack of historical reflection."[20]

According to Pauly, one of the dangers of this short-term thinking is that species can more easily be lost. "When the fish are there, the knowledge that the First Nations or the fishers have — the local traditional knowledge — gets passed on reasonably well because it gets renewed by every encounter with the animal in question. But when the animals are gone, the knowledge becomes superfluous and it passes away." Pauly says that when change is incremental over several generations, species can disappear without us even noticing because we have "rendered it rare first."[21] This is nearly what happened to the grey seal.

Heike Lotze is one scientist who is trying to inject some history into fisheries science. She is part of an emerging field called marine historical ecology that contends the key to understanding how the marine ecosystem functions today is in knowing about its past: not just the last twenty to fifty years — equivalent to the lifespan of some long-lived fish and marine mammals — but the historical past, dating back thousands of years. Lotze tells me that, when viewed from this perspective, the recent increases in grey seal populations "is not an unnatural increase, it is just the normal recovery of a population, which should be seen as a positive sign." She says that grey seals, like many marine mammal populations, hit their low point in the early to mid-twentieth century because of a long history of exploitation.

The kind of reconstruction work Lotz and her colleagues are engaged in involves using a lot more than standard fisheries statistics. Palaeontological and archaeological evidence, molecular markers and historical records are all gleaned for clues. For instance, historical ecologists would mine what are called kitchen middens, or old domestic garbage heaps, for a wide assortment of items including animal remains such as bones and shells. These artifacts tell them about the diets of past societies, about the variety and quantity of the marine species that were being eaten and what impact this might have had on the exploited populations.

In one 2009 study, Lotze and Worm describe how the information gleaned from middens can be used in this case to reflect the local abundance of a marine species. In the southern Baltic Sea, for instance, between the seventh and ninth centuries, the European sturgeon accounted for 70 percent of all the fish consumed. Three hundred years later it accounted for only 10 percent. Its decline continued into the 1900s when annual catches numbered less than 500 fish. The fishery finally ended in 1915; today the European sturgeon is locally extinct and endangered across its range.

A similar reconstruction is possible for Atlantic cod. In a fascinating 2001 paper that appeared in *Science,* marine ecologist Jeremy Jackson, along with eighteen co-authors, reported that archeological evidence of cod backbones showed that for nearly 5,000 years, the average size of cod fished in the Gulf of Maine was about the same: about one metre in length. We've all seen the pictures of fishers holding up what now seem to be fantastically huge fish, half the height of the men themselves. Later in the twentieth century, fisheries data paint a very different picture and the average Gulf of Maine cod today measures only thirty centimetres long — marking a three-fold decline in average body length.[22] Similar studies have reconstructed the historical abundance of cod stocks on the eastern and western Scotian Shelf; they estimate that, in 1852, there were nearly 1.3 million metric tonnes of cod there, compared to less than 40,000 metric tonnes 150 years later.

To date, this kind of detailed reconstruction has not been undertaken for grey seals in eastern Canada although it is known that the earliest fossils of the family *phocidae* — to which grey seals belong — were found in the north Atlantic dating back to the mid-to-late Miocene period, or twelve to fifteen million years ago. Grey seal bones have also been found in midden sites in Maine and Massachusetts dating as far back as 6,000 years and in the Quoddy region of the Bay of Fundy from about 4,000 years ago. But when it comes to estimating actual numbers the task becomes much more challenging.

In 2012, Michael Sinclair, former director of the Bedford Institute of Oceanography, a DFO research facility in Dartmouth, Nova Scotia, co-authored a paper with Robert O'Boyle on seal-cod interactions on the Scotian Shelf that came to the conclusion that seals account for the high natural mortality of cod and are impeding their recovery. We'll be discussing this study in greater detail later in the book, but it is important to note that Sinclair said he wanted to find evidence that grey seals were actually abundant in earlier times and that seals and cod coexisted at these high population levels. While Sinclair had no difficulty locating quantitative evidence of past cod abundance, finding this for grey seals wasn't so easy. "We just can't find the evidence," says Sinclair. DFO scientist Don Bowen, who has been studying the population dynamics of grey seals on Sable Island for thirty-one years, says drawing any kind of conclusion about grey seal past abundance is "premature," because there just aren't any good estimates. Despite this, he tells me, it is possible to make inferences. "I can see no fundamental reason why

there shouldn't have been hundreds of thousands of grey seals historically."
Bowen points to cull data from the United States which suggests that there
had to be harbour seal populations that were in the order of hundreds of
thousands along the eastern seaboard and into Canadian waters. "They paid
bounties on tens of thousands of animals so for that to happen they had to
have fairly sizable populations," he says. "And we know that we drove those
harbour seal populations down to the point where they were considered
uncommon." Bowen says that harbour seals have a slightly more southern
distribution than grey seals, but that there's also a broad overlap in the
geographical distribution of the two species. Where they co-occur now, at
least, grey seals typically have the upper hand competitively. "Where we had
hundreds of thousands of harbour seals it's hard for me to imagine that there
weren't also large populations of grey seals," he says.

Sinclair and others have characterized the exponential growth of grey
seals on Sable Island over several decades as being an unusual and "unique"
phenomenon. "This sort of order of magnitude change hasn't been observed anywhere else," he says. But Jeff Hutchings disagrees. "I don't think
it's unusual. It's actually the predicted response." Hutchings says that both
the harp and grey seals have increased in an exponential fashion and this
kind of growth is expected. "When you stop exploiting something and it's
at very low levels of abundance, you expect an exponential rate of growth.
If it doesn't do that then you wonder why not."

In a 2003 paper on the exponential growth on Sable Island, Bowen and
his colleagues pointed out that the rapid growth of the colony was actually
expected given its severely reduced state, but that there are relatively few
examples of this exponential growth phase in pinnipeds and other marine
mammals in the world, mainly because long-time series data have been difficult to collect.[23] But some examples do exist. For instance, although northern
elephant seals, found in the eastern Pacific Ocean ranging from California to
Alaska, were hunted extensively for their oil-rich blubber and thought to be
extinct in 1884, remnant populations were discovered later and the species
was legally protected in 1922 by both the Mexican and U.S. governments.
Their numbers have now recovered to more than 170,000.

The Antarctic fur seal is another species that was heavily hunted for two
centuries for its fur, and by the early 1900s it too was brought to the brink
of extinction. A small remnant colony continued to breed on Bird Island
and the species has now recovered, recolonizing a number of islands in
their former range in South Georgia. Recent estimates put that population
at more than six million.

In spite of the fact that exponential growth is the predicted response
in species that have been pushed to (and released from) the margins, some
scientists have argued that the extirpation of the Atlantic walrus and the

precipitous decline in sharks have contributed to the grey seal's meteoric rise from the ashes since they no longer keep grey seal populations in check through predation. There is no question that removing one species from a marine ecosystem has effects elsewhere in the food web but the question here is, how important were the walrus and the shark in the life, and death, of a grey seal in the distant past?

When it comes to the walrus, little is known about its historical abundance or its diet and life history, let alone how the species may have interacted with grey seals. Without knowing this, understanding the ecological fallout from its loss is extremely challenging.

Perhaps the only person who has made any serious attempt to reconstruct the historical abundance of terrestrial and marine life on the northeastern seaboard is Farley Mowat. In 1984 he published a seminal book titled *Sea of Slaughter*, exploring the idea of shifting baselines before the term even existed, and documenting, in often harrowing detail, the exploitation and drastic declines of a diversity of wildlife. The book was hailed at the time and soon after became the subject of a CBC *Nature of Things* television episode. Since then, it has been cited in a number of scientific studies, and one in particular used the historical accounts provided in the book to conclude that the biomass of fish and other exploitable organisms along the northeast coast of Canada now represents less than 10 percent of what existed two centuries ago.[24]

In his book, Mowat estimated that in the Gulf of St. Lawrence walrus numbered 250,000, with colonies of almost as many from Sable Island south to Cape Cod. The North Atlantic Marine Mammal Commission (NAMMCO) corroborates this and estimates, based on recorded observations by early explorers and traders, as well as known records from commercial walrus hunting, that they must have numbered "at least in the hundreds of thousands" before the Europeans hunted them for oil and ivory.

Some believe that in the past walrus would have competed with grey seals for haul-out space on places like Sable Island and that therefore with the loss of the walrus more space became available to the grey seal, allowing the population to increase. Evidence from the Arctic suggests that walrus are very sensitive to human disturbance, and loud noises can result in a panic-induced stampede. Once they are hunted at a haul-out site, it's been observed that those that survive may never return to that spot. Grey seals are also sensitive to human disturbance, so it is possible that the two species sought out similar locales. However, this line of argument assumes that, prior to European discovery of North America, safe haul-out spaces were as scarce as they are today. Given the historical evidence about the plenitude of such locales, referenced in Mowat's book and elsewhere, one would be hard pressed to conclude that haul-out spaces were at a premium or that the grey seal received any net benefit from the loss of the walrus.

There is evidence, however, that individual walrus would have occasionally eaten seals, as well as small whales and seabirds, even though the mainstay of their diet is bottom-dwelling creatures: clams, worms, shrimp and slow-moving fish. In the Arctic, it is believed that walrus eat seals when they don't have access to shallow water, the domain of their preferred prey. Hunters say they can identify a seal-eating walrus by its yellow tusks. Apart from this, little has been done to quantify walrus predation on seals and precious little is known on the subject.

Another species that some argue would have been a formidable predator of grey seals in the past is shark. They argue that because there are now fewer sharks, not much is keeping the grey seal population in check. Of the twenty shark species that have been recorded off Nova Scotia, only the Greenland, shortfin mako, blue, and white sharks are known predators of marine mammals such as grey seals. Killer whales have also been known to prey on pinnipeds, particularly harbour seals. But quantifying shark or killer whale predation on grey seals and how it may or may not have kept past populations in check is largely uncharted territory. We'll return to this topic later in this chapter, but for now, the one thing we do know for sure is that, like the cod, there are a lot fewer sharks today than there were in the past.

In 2003, the late Ransom Myers and Boris Worm, both Dalhousie University fisheries biologists at the time, reported that 90 percent of all large fish, including tuna, marlin, swordfish, sharks, cod and halibut are gone. In addition to analyzing historical abundance, their study, which appeared in the prominent journal *Nature*, also looked at the historical size of predatory fish in four continental shelf and nine oceanic systems. They found the average sizes of once fantastically large fish had been reduced to one-fifth or one-half their former glory. Echoing the view of others like Pauly and Jackson, the study authors say that any attempts to restore present ecosystems to so-called "healthy levels" have to be based on an understanding of what an unexploited system would have been like.[25] In other words, rebuilding efforts had to take into account the pre-industrial abundance of these species, not just the more recent, and already badly degraded, snapshot in time.

Myers and Worm also found, remarkably, that it typically took industrial fisheries about fifteen years to reduce a fish community to only 20 percent of what it was before it was fished. Management schemes for fisheries are usually only undertaken well after industrial fishing has begun, they said; often, by this point, it is too late. The cod is an obvious example of this, but so too is the shark fishery.

In Canada prior to 1994 there were no restrictions on fishing for sharks. Before the groundfish collapsed, little domestic interest in sharks existed, and of the twenty species reported in Canadian waters — there are about five hundred species of shark worldwide — most were commercially unattractive. But porbeagle shark was an exception. Targeted intensively on the other side of the Atlantic since the 1920s for its high quality meat, liver oil, fishmeal and leather-quality skin, the porbeagle population collapsed there in the 1960s, and the effort shifted here: twenty-eight Norwegian freezer longline vessels, as well as a few from the Faroe Islands, fished a "virgin" population of porbeagle from Georges Bank and the Gulf of Maine to the Flemish Cap, just east of the Grand Banks. But this wouldn't last for long: landings plummeted to only two hundred tonnes in 1970, after peaking at nine thousand tonnes just six years earlier.

Around the same time a technological change took place within the fishery for swordfish that would create significant unintended consequences. Traditionally, swordfish were caught with hand-held harpoons, a highly selective technique which inflicts little harm on non-target species. However, this was replaced by pelagic longlining, where fishing lines as long as one hundred kilometres are suspended near the surface of the ocean and set each day with several thousand baited hooks. Ever since, sharks, as well as sea birds and sea turtles, have suffered: caught on the hooks intended for swordfish — and discarded at sea.

Shark "bycatch" — a term used to describe the creatures caught unintentionally in fishing gear — has become a serious issue. In 1983, DFO scientists Paul Brodie and Brian Beck reported that the bycatch estimates of porbeagle, hammerhead, and mako sharks, even though very high, were likely underreported and that the "swordfishing industry would have been better classified as a shark fishery with a bycatch of swordfish."[26] For instance, Brodie and Beck report that in the 1980s, shark bycatch was estimated to be two to three times higher than the catch of swordfish by the fleet off the U.S. coast. Today, according to the EAC, for every one swordfish landed by Canada's east coast longline fishery, five sharks are landed.

In 2011, DFOs shark specialist, Steven Campana, reported that in the previous year the swordfish/tuna fishery accounted for 58 percent of all porbeagle discards, 70 percent of all mako discards and nearly 100 percent of all blue shark discards. Despite this less than stellar track record of sustainable practices, the swordfishery was granted eco-certification from the Maritime Stewardship Council (MSC) in 2012. This certification scheme targets consumers but it has come under increased scrutiny lately by prominent fisheries biologists.[27] In response, several environmental groups including the David Suzuki Foundation, the Sea Turtle Conservancy and the EAC, which all participated in the consultation process held by the certification firm hired by the fishery, filed a formal objection, which was ultimately ignored by the adjudicator. In a media release, the EAC stated that the MSC label — a stylized blue fish and a check mark — is supposed to identify fish caught in well-managed and sustainable fisheries. It went on to say that Nova Scotia's entire longline fishery was responsible for catching 100,000 sharks and killing 35,000 of them every year, along with 1,400 sea turtles, of which 200 to 500 were endangered leatherbacks.

In the late 1980s and 1990s alarm bells started ringing about another practice in the east coast swordfishery when it was discovered that the bycatch of blue sharks were being "finned" — a wasteful and cruel practice whereby the shark fins are cut off and kept while the carcasses are discarded at sea. For a number of reasons, reliable estimates of the extent of the finning that took place are not readily available.[28] For one, prior to 1994, shark bycatch data recorded in swordfish longline logbooks were not considered reliable and bycatches were usually not even recorded unless the sharks were brought aboard the vessel. As well, there was little coverage of the swordfishery fleet by fisheries observers — independent technicians who stay on board fishing boats and collect data for the DFO on fishing effort, catches and discards at sea. So, it was hard to verify what was happening on these boats.

By 2012, things hadn't improved that much. By then, less than 10 percent of all swordfishing trips had observers on board, despite calls by environmental groups for a substantial increase in coverage. "We know that fishermen have vastly different behaviour when there are observers on board," says Susanna Fuller, the marine conservation coordinator with the EAC. In order to get a better picture of the true quantity of shark bycatch, Fuller tells me that the EAC has asked the DFO to provide 100 percent observer coverage for two years in the swordfish longline fishery. "We'll never get that, but we've asked," she says.

According to the Shark Specialist Group of the International Union for Conservation of Nature (IUCN), "finned" sharks are often still alive when they're tossed back into the ocean, but without fins they are unable to swim and sink to the bottom where they are eaten alive by other fish. The burgeoning demand for shark fins — in a soup that has become a status symbol in Asia as well as in traditional medicines — fuelled a global and largely unregulated multi-billion dollar trade in which as many as seventy-three million sharks, including blue, hammerhead, silky, shortfin mako, and great white sharks, are killed annually. Today, the IUCN says that this demand, coupled with the fact that shark fins are one of the world's most expensive fisheries products, is driving shark mortality.[29] In markets in Malaysia and Thailand, shark fins can fetch between US$200 to $400 per kg; it has been reported that US$57,000 was paid for a single basking shark fin. A fish that has survived at least four mass extinction events on the planet and has been around for 450 million years is now on a fast track to oblivion.

In 1994, well after industrial shark fishing began, the DFO implemented its first management plan for sharks, establishing catch levels, setting gear restrictions and attempting to prohibit shark finning. According to Robert Rangeley, Vice President of the Atlantic Region for the World Wildlife Fund

(WWF), the practice of finning is prohibited in Canada, but how it's controlled depends on the fishery in question. In the pelagic longline fisheries, fins do not have to be attached to the sharks they land; however, they have to abide by the 5 percent rule: landed fins on board cannot exceed 5 percent of landed shark "dressed weight" — the weight after the head and guts have been removed. In the groundfishery, any sharks landed must have fins attached.

According to Shannon Arnold, a marine coordinator with the EAC, if Canada really wanted to curb the practice of shark finning it would adopt a "fins attached" rule, which many countries, including developing ones, have imposed. She says the longline industry doesn't want it because they say it's impractical to have the fins attached. She thinks the longline swordfish industry has a lot of sway with the DFO managers and that it has argued against the "fins attached rule" saying they couldn't fit whole sharks on the boat. Arnold says U.S. fleets out of New England use exactly the same boats and have learned how to deal with the fins attached rule. "The National Oceanic and Atmospheric Administration ran training courses for all fishers on how to store the sharks with their fins partially cut, folded against the body and tied on for transport. Really not a big transition. Just a bit more post-harvest handling." Arnold says she doesn't understand why there is so much reluctance among fisheries managers to address the issue of shark bycatch and shark finning. "The [DFO's] current regulations are so lacking that once they open the door to a review they will really have to face up to their lagging bycatch and shark protection," she says.

Fuller says she's been told that despite the prohibition there is a small shark fin industry on the east coast of Canada — "they call it beer money and they sell it for nine dollars a pound, but it's not huge."

By the time the first management plan was put in place for sharks, some say the damage had already been done. Once the groundfish collapsed in the early 1990s, shark suddenly registered on the commercial radar screens in Canada and a directed fishery by Canadian vessels expanded. Between 1988 and 1994, shark landings in eastern Canada, by Canadian fleets, jumped from one hundred tonnes to nearly two thousand tonnes — a twenty-fold increase — mainly of porbeagle, shortfin mako and blue sharks. Landings of porbeagle peaked in 1994 at 1,545 tonnes but then collapsed again, by 90 percent, to 146 tonnes in 2003. A decade later, porbeagle was declared endangered by COSEWIC and recommended for listing under Canada's *Species at Risk Act*, a move that would require its protection. But the proposal to list the shark was rejected by the DFO, citing economic reasons.

Once sharks are overfished, they have a very difficult time recovering. This is partly because they can live to be very old — some species up to one hundred years, though it is reported that the elusive Greenland shark may live to be two hundred years of age.[30] Sharks are also slow to mature and have few offspring, and when they do reproduce they have gestation periods of up to twenty-two months. For instance, according to the IUCN's Shark Specialist Group, even if fishing for porbeagle were closed and strict limits were placed on its bycatch, it could take thirty to sixty years for the population to recover.

In a 2010 interview on CBC radio, Paul Brodie, who's now retired from the DFO, said that since the late 1950s the swordfishery has captured millions of sharks. He said intensive fishing coupled with the bycatch problem reduced shark populations so much that it essentially removed the one natural predator that would prey on juvenile grey seals and therefore control their population. Brodie says he raised this issue back in the 1970s but there was little attention paid at the time by the DFO to what he called "species interactions." He said that back then the department was only interested in numbers and managing the fisheries. The department had a lot of skilled people who understood seals, he says, but the correlations were not being made. Now, Brodie argues, the seals require "predator intervention," and that, since the sharks can't do it anymore, maybe humans should. But what Brodie did not acknowledge on radio, but did in his 1983 paper, was that there are no data indicating that shark predation ever held grey seal abundance at low levels or that the decline in shark populations has reduced that controlling effect.

According to Bowen, while there is very little known about predation rates, past or present, existing data do not support the position that the decline in sharks has contributed to the exponential growth of grey seals on Sable Island. He says that, while there has been a significant decline in the Atlantic population of the blue shark and the white shark, which is now endangered, little is known about their diets off eastern Canada and how much grey seals would have factored into them. The food work that has been done on sharks on the Scotian Shelf indicates they mostly eat large groundfish and other fish populations and that pinnipeds are an uncommon part of their diet. "We know sharks are in the area, we know occasionally they do consume pinnipeds, but we have no way of estimating their importance," he says. Estimating the historical importance of sharks in terms of grey seal population dynamics is even more difficult, says Bowen, because there's absolutely no information on what they ate historically.

The lack of research and data on the subject is something that frustrates Fuller. She says sharks may never have kept grey seal populations at a low level, but they could have kept them in check. Fuller says there's been no focus within the DFO to look at predators. "There's this assumption that the seals are on top of the food chain, but they're not." She says it's not just about what the seals are eating, but what are (or rather aren't) eating the seals. "The ecosystem is out of whack and it's not just a cod-seal issue. There's a bigger story and picture there. I don't know what it is exactly but we haven't spent any time or money looking into it."

Fuller says we need to go back to a time before we nearly extirpated the grey seal, and "figure out what the balance was" then. She says recent studies done elsewhere may provide some clues. "We do know from other places in the world where they have done work on shark residency at seal rookeries [that] there is a significant amount of juvenile predation." She says the white shark population in California, for instance, spends six months basically eating baby seals. "They have feeding grounds and that's actually resulted in a lot of control of some of the seal populations." She says that, because Sable Island is within the range of two known seal predators, the Greenland shark and the white shark, they might have had an impact on seal populations at one time when their numbers were plentiful. Fuller wonders why so little research has been done here to look at these predator-prey relationships. "Why hasn't DFO started asking these questions?" she asks. "Maybe it's not an issue, but we have to rule it out."[31]

Bowen agrees that more needs to be learned but he says there are other much more compelling reasons for the recent success of the grey seal population. He says reduced bounty hunting and favourable environmental conditions including increased breeding habitat and greater food availability since the collapse of the cod all account for the population's rapid growth. Overexploitation by humans, not shark predation, accounted for their rarity in the recent past, he says.

Estimating Past Grey Seal Abundance

In *Sea of Slaughter*, Mowat uses maps, charts, and written accounts of well-known English and French explorers and settlers, dating as far back as the 1500s, to reconstruct what the historical abundance and distribution of grey seals would have been. He includes the writings of Jacques Cartier, Sir Humphrey Gilbert, Nicolas Denys, Samuel de Champlain, and the Sieur de Diereville. He writes:

> Gregarious and polygamous, horseheads used to gather in January and February in enormous numbers on myriad islands and even mainland beaches from Labrador to Cape Hatteras, there to whelp and breed. Some of these colonies were so large that, as late as the mid-1600s, the lupine howling from them could be heard several miles away.[32]

It was likely this lupine howling, referred to by Mowat, led to the naming of a cluster of islands in the Gulf of Maine as the "Isles aux Loups Marin." In his 1672 two-volume book *Description and Natural History of the Coasts of North America (Acadia)*, Nicolas Denys makes particular note of these islands, how the grey seals used them for whelping in the winter, how the adult grey seals were driven off into the water by hunters with clubs and how the young were then killed: "There are days on which there have been killed as many as six, seven, or eight hundred."[33]

In the 1630s, Denys, a French aristocrat, was a lieutenant on an expedition to the New World, where he founded various settlements in what we now refer to as the Maritimes. Considered to be one of the first naturalists to write about Nova Scotia and its surrounds, Denys provides some of the earliest written accounts of the natural abundance that existed here nearly 400 years ago. "A kind of inexhaustible manna," is how he described the cod, which was the foundation upon which everything was built. But cod were not alone. The salmon were so plentiful, he says, that the noise of them entering the river at night, "falling upon the water after having thrown or darted themselves into the air," made it impossible to sleep. He also writes of the "great quantities of birds," such as fulmars, petrels, guillemots, and great auks "as to be almost unbelievable." He noted that the smallest salmon were three feet long and that some mackerel were caught "of monstrous bigness."[34]

Four centuries later, two of the most celebrated fish in history — the cod and salmon — are teetering on the edge of extinction and the population of the great auk, a flightless bird that some say once numbered in the millions, was effectively destroyed when the last breeding pair, incubating an egg, were found and killed on a small Icelandic island in the summer of 1844. According to the IUCN, the last sighting of a live bird was on the Grand Banks of Newfoundland in 1852.

Based on accounts like these, by Denys and others, Mowat tried to reconstruct the grey seal's past. With historical evidence of more than two hundred whelping rookeries extending from Cape Hatteras, North Carolina, to Hamilton Inlet on the Labrador coast, Mowat estimates that the total grey seal population prior to European contact was somewhere between 750,000 and one million animals — two to three times higher than the population estimates of today.

Yet, despite the apparent rigour and the fact that several scientists, including ones working for the government at the time, were enlisted by Mowat to review his book,* his historical abundance estimates for grey seals are not entirely believed by some DFO scientists today. If one were to take

---

* Scientists with the Canadian Wildlife Service — D.N Nettleship with the Seabird Research Unit, Steve Wendt, Chief of the Populations and Survey Divisions, and Nick Novakowski — all reviewed chapters on sea birds as well as other birds and land mammals. D.J. Scarratt, from the Department of Fisheries and Oceans reviewed the fish chapters, and Edward Mitchell from the Arctic Biological Station reviewed chapters on whales and porpoises. Lavigne, then professor of zoology at the University of Guelph, reviewed the chapters on seals and walrus.

the time to check, many of Mowat's other numbers are corroborated by DFO science as well as by non-government sources. For instance, in his book Mowat says the historical abundance of harp seals was in the vicinity of ten million, which is actually lower than DFO estimates of eleven to fourteen, based on modelling catch data from records dating back to 1723 as well as recent harvest numbers.

Mowat's estimates of historical levels of cod population are also congruent with official historical estimates. Based on historical accounts as well as the science available to him in at the time, Mowat concludes that by the time Canada had extended economic control to two hundred miles offshore the Atlantic cod had been reduced to less than 2 percent of its historical abundance. There's no shortage of studies, including ones by DFO scientists, corroborating the same magnitude of loss. For example, in 1995, Myers, a DFO scientist at the time, said that in 1962, the biomass of cod off Newfoundland and Labrador capable of reproducing was 1.6 million tonnes, whereas by 1992 it was reduced to 22,000 tonnes, or 1.3 percent of what existed just three decades earlier.[35]

So, why is there an issue with the grey seal abundance? Bowen tells me he's uncomfortable with not knowing how the numbers were derived. "As far as I can tell that's a number picked out of the air," he says. "We know grey seals were broadly distributed and it's very likely they were an abundant coastal predator, but how abundant we simply have no idea."

Mowat acknowledged openly in his book that although it is not possible to estimate the historical abundance of any species with any degree of certainty, he still wanted to hazard a guess. His grey seal estimates were almost solely based on early accounts, or what is viewed as anecdotal, because historical quantitative data, as discussed earlier, don't exist for grey seals. Many of the other abundance estimates in his book are at least in part based on commercial catch data, fisheries data and other more accepted quantitative measures. There is still reticence among scientists to embrace the value of pure observation as a means to reconstruct the past despite the fact that a number of globally renowned fisheries scientists are trying to change this. Jackson and Pauly, for instance, have been laying the groundwork for a shift in the way information is judged. They argue that anecdotes, or earlier knowledge, can be as factual as any other type of record and can provide important insights into the deep historical causes of our current problems.[36]

But this shift in thinking will take time: meanwhile, the recent past still dominates the scientific and public discourse around grey seal populations. The world of plenitude that Denys described more than three centuries ago, of monstrously big fish, skies dark with birds, and beaches and reefs alive with walrus, no longer exists. These are now ghosts from a not too distant past — one that is nearly impossible for many of us to even imagine.

Chapter 4

The Devil Is in the Details

Gerald decapitated the [seal] carcass with the axe and severed the two hind flippers. He tossed it into the stern corner and threw the head and flippers overboard. "You'll eat no more of our fish!" he said.

— Michael Dwyer, *Over the Side Mickey*

The biomass of fishes that eat cod is much bigger than seals. But seals are physically much bigger — they lie on the beaches and we can see them. It's like looking for a key under a street lamp.

— Daniel Pauly, Fisheries Scientist, University of British Columbia

The early 1990s didn't just mark the collapse of cod. It marked a gigantic shift in the structure of the ocean ecosystem. Almost all groundfish species with any commercial value were wiped out: haddock and pollock took a big hit and so did the flatfishes like Atlantic halibut, Greenland halibut (turbot), American plaice and yellowtail flounder. Thorny skate, cusk, grenadiers, silver hake, white hake, wolffish, redfish, lumpfish and monkfish didn't escape the draggers either. Industrial fishing ravaged the biological structure of the marine ecosystem to such an extent that scientists are still trying to understand the fallout.

As we have seen, two decades after the crash, the cod stocks, as well as other fish stocks, still remain at very low levels, while the grey seals are enjoying a conspicuous recovery. No matter where one stands on the issue, one has to admit the optics are not very good. Proponents of a cull have boiled the intricacies of the marine food web down to one simple mathematical equation: less seals equals more cod. Key to implicating the grey seals has been to show that they are eating enough cod to affect the cod recovery. These diet data are also used to work out how many grey seals should be killed, should a cull be authorized. But as we shall see, not only are there limitations to the methods used for analyzing what individual grey seals eat, but seal diet experts argue that using these data to then come up with a diet for the whole population is nothing short of misleading.

Our Quest to Understand an Invisible World

Rachel Carson may be best known for her seminal 1962 book *Silent Spring* — a call to action against the pesticides that were devastating bird populations — but she was first and foremost a naturalist. Her early career began as a marine biologist with the U.S. Bureau of Fisheries and her love of the marine environment and the life it contained was never more evident than in her 1941 book *Under the Sea Wind: A Naturalist's Picture of Ocean Life*. In this book, Carson presents a vivid and beautifully written narrative of the rich and interconnected lives of a myriad of creatures found in and around the Atlantic Ocean off the northeast coast of the United States. About a third of the way into the book, she introduces us to a mackerel she calls Scomber, which is the scientific name for the genus that includes the Atlantic mackerel, a schooling fish that lives in the open ocean. Carson takes us on Scomber's journey, starting from the time it was one of the forty or fifty thousand eggs released by its mother during the spring spawn to the moment it is born in the surface waters of the open sea, and ending with its transformation into an adult fish:

> On the journey up the coast, the heavy, unmoulded lines of a larval fish had been sculpted to a torpedo-shaped body with a hint of power in the shoulders and a speed in the tapering flanks. Now he had put on the sea coat of the adult mackerel. He was clothed in scales, but they were so fine and small that he was soft as velvet to the touch. His back was a deep blue green — the colour of the deep places of the sea that Scomber had not yet seen.[37]

What is perhaps most remarkable about Carson's narrative about Scomber's life, and indeed the individual lives of all the fish in her book, is how beautiful and visible she makes it. She shows us how Scomber's life, hidden from view beneath the ocean, is intertwined with that of the sea birds, as well as with the tiny one-celled organisms and of course, with other fish. She shows us part of an ocean food web, its complexity and, when intact, its stability. We relate to Scomber and we even root for him. We become worried when he encounters a two-hundred-pound, six foot cod, hiding on a ledge among some rockweed:

> The cod had grown old and very large because of his cunning. He had found the rock ledge above the deep pit of the sea years before and, knowing it instinctively for a good hunting place, he had adopted the ledge for his own, fiercely driving away the other cod.... Many fishes met their death in his jaws, among them cunners and hook-eared sculpins, sea ravens with ragged fins, flounders and sea robins, blennies and skates. Sight of the young mackerel roused the

cod from the semi-torpor in which he had lain since the last feeding time and kindled his hunger. He swung his heavy body out of the ledge and climbed steeply to the shoal. Scomber fled before him.[38]

Cod was definitely king among fish at that time: some scientists have hypothesized that it was dominant for a reason. In 2001, fisheries scientist Carl Walters of the University of British Columbia (U.B.C.) and zoologist James Kitchell of the University of Wisconsin said that adults of a dominant fish species are abundant predominantly because they "crop down" forage fish — the term used for the small fish on which they prey — which are also potential competitors and predators of their own juveniles. So, for example, the monster cod hiding in the rockweed in Carson's book has to eat Scomber, because Scomber is a forage fish, feeding mainly on drifting communities of life: tiny crustaceans called copepods, and fish eggs, including that of cod. As Scomber gets older he adds small fish, including codlings and even young mackerel, to his diet. If the big cod eats Scomber — and he doesn't in Carson's book — it removes a fish that would potentially prey on or compete with its young, reinforcing its dominant position in the ocean ecosystem. Walters and Kitchell call this a "cultivation effect."

However, there is a flip side. What happens if the numbers of the adults in the dominant species, in this case cod, are reduced by overfishing? Essentially, when there are no cod, the condition of the ecosystem turns against the cod. It's called the depensation effect, which in ecological terms simply means that when there are very low numbers of a species, their chances of survival are much reduced.

When it comes to the current situation, where the cod have not bounced back, some scientists say the problem has to do with the high natural mortality of the adult fish. They argue that the cod are in a "predator-pit," and that their population is being kept low by other predators — in this case, grey seals. These scientists say the growing grey seal population is the most likely cause for the non-recovery in the southern Gulf of St. Lawrence — a subject and a particular set of circumstances to which we'll return in the next chapter. Another possible explanation for the cod non-recovery, which is still consistent with the hypothesis put forth by Walters and Kitchell in 2001, is that, on the eastern Scotian Shelf, in the vicinity of Sable Island, there's been a "predator-prey reversal," so that, when cod lost its place as a top predator, its prey populations increased in abundance, with the result that these fish, which are predators of cod eggs and young cod, have held back the recovery. While each of these hypotheses is fervently advocated by some and attacked by others, there is no question that something is going on.

In 2011, DFO scientist Ken Frank and his colleagues reported in *Nature* that the groundfish collapse on the eastern Scotian Shelf resulted in a restructuring of the entire food web, with evidence of what's called a "trophic cascade," a phenomenon that occurs when a succession of fundamental changes make their way through the trophic levels of the food web, eventually to the tiniest life forms — the plankton.* In this case, Frank and his colleagues reported that the loss of the cod set in motion two key patterns. One involved the invertebrates and the other, the forage fish.

Invertebrates, such as shrimp and small crab, were reported to have surged by 200 percent compared to pre-collapse years — a boom that was reflected in their commercial landings. This is because, in a marine food web, the lives of cod and invertebrates, such as shrimp, are connected. Hatched-out shrimp eggs drift in both the deep and surface layers of the ocean; once they are a few months old they move into deeper waters, finally settling on the ocean floor, the primary domain of the cod. However, when the cod collapsed, this freed the shrimp from predation, and their numbers increased. Since shrimp will eat the egg and larval stages of cod during their nocturnal migration up the water column in search of small crustaceans, this played a role in keeping the cod down.†

Frank and his colleagues also argued that the population of the forage fish — namely herring, capelin, and sandlance — erupted in the mid-1990s, reaching levels 900 percent higher than pre-collapse levels. These were also implicated in the sluggish recovery because they eat the egg and larval stages

---

* Trophic levels are essentially the layers of a food web: an animal's rank depends on how many steps it is from the primary producers — the phytoplankton at the base of the food web or trophic level one. These microscopic, single-celled, free-floating plants take nutrients in the ocean and combine them with carbon dioxide and sunlight to manufacture their own food. All other ocean creatures need to eat other organisms for food. Depending on what they eat, they occupy a certain position, or trophic level, in the food web. This is further complicated by the fact that some consumers eat at multiple trophic levels, some organisms change their diets as they grow, and some species, such as cod, are cannibalistic. Most marine mammals, such as grey seals, occupy trophic levels three to five.

† Retired DFO shrimp expert Peter Koeller agrees, but he argues colder water temperatures in the late 1980s and early 1990s also contributed to the shrimp boom. In fact, so dependent are shrimp on water temperatures, that the international research project led by Koeller concluded in a 2009 study published in *Science* that shrimp stocks, now the mainstay of the east coast fishery, may be vulnerable as oceans warm as a result of climate change. Debbie MacKenzie of the Grey Seal Conservation Society has a different hypothesis for the surge in shrimp. She says that as we've fished out the open-ocean fish — the plankton-eaters — more un-eaten plankton rains down onto the bottom layers and gets eaten by shrimp.

of cod. But recently, the forage fish complex, a key element of the trophic cascade hypothesis, has come under some scrutiny.

In 2009, DFO scientist Ian McQuinn raised concern about the way in which forage fish — particularly herring — abundance was being measured. He wrote that the trophic cascade linkages could not have been made without the forage fish abundance data from the DFO's annual bottom trawl survey data. According to McQuinn, these data are misleading for a couple of reasons. First, herring and other forage fish such as sandlance and mackerel are open ocean fish — "pelagic" is the scientific term used — and their abundance really should be measured, for the sake of accuracy, with hydro-acoustic surveys, a method in which underwater sound pulses are used to detect objects — such as fish — in the water column: the echoes produced provide information on fish size, location, abundance and behaviour. But very little hydro-acoustic data have been gathered here, and then only sporadically.

Second, pelagic fish, like herring, don't normally occupy the ocean bottom. However, according to McQuinn, around the same time that the cod collapsed, herring started behaving differently — occupying the bottom ocean layers, which had been "vacated by their diminishing groundfish predators" instead of forming their signature schools in the water column.[39] As a result, DFOs bottom trawl survey was picking up an unusually high number of them: when this was extrapolated to come up with an overall abundance, it made it appear as though their numbers had spiked. McQuinn also pointed out that if the forage fish population had grown as much as was indicated by the bottom trawl, there should have been other signs of this explosion, like huge increases in landings (the quantity of fish caught) — as was the case with shellfish. Instead, landings in the herring fishery declined, despite higher quotas. In fact, when the bottom trawl survey was showing a two-hundred-fold increase in herring, the fishery was experiencing the opposite. Similarly, since grey seal diets are thought to reflect local prey abundance, then evidence of increases in forage fish would likely show up in seal diet studies; however, analysis of seal diet did not show any increasing trend in forage fish consumption.

Some of McQuinn's misgivings about using the trawl data were echoed in 2012 by two other DFO scientists, Doug Swain and Robert Mohn. They also said that a focus on forage fish was irrelevant since the main factor causing the delay in recovery on the eastern Scotian Shelf was that too many adult cod were dying, not that too few codlings were surviving.

When it comes to the complex of forage fish on the Scotian Shelf, no estimate is reliable — it's mostly speculation, says DFO population ecologist Jae Choi. He tells me that questions surrounding the forage fish data do weaken the trophic cascade hypothesis, but certainly don't discredit it. He says the controversy highlights the uncertainty associated with our understanding of marine food webs and how we're inclined to favour simple, even sensational, explanations that provide "a smoking gun" over more complex ones.

For instance, in 2004 Choi co-wrote a paper with Ken Frank and others reporting that over the last forty years on the eastern Scotian Shelf, dozens of groundfish species have been getting smaller and thinner and are in progressively poorer condition. The authors hypothesized that this was caused by "energy depletion in the system," or a problem with food supply, probably as a result of decades of intensive fishing, which has removed an enormous supply of biomass — the organic matter that eventually breaks down and feeds the food web cycle. Choi says we have been "strip mining" for centuries and that "trawling has decimated the bottom cover to the point where there's almost no substrate left." He says that "there's no complexity, essentially we've mined an area and expect it to return, but for that to regenerate it could take hundreds of years."

Choi says we are now witnessing some of the cumulative effects. "When you remove the biomass, you're removing the availability of elements that compose the animals — carbon, nitrogen, phosphorus, silica, iron, the key things," he says, altering the quantity and quality of what's available to the phytoplankton at the base of the food web. In his view, it is not unlike clearcutting a forest. In other words, the large-scale cumulative removal of fish, coupled with other changes in the system, might have led to a whole suite of pathological effects, including one that is difficult to fathom: that most large-bodied fish are physiologically stressed and some are even starving.

Choi's hypothesis is rooted in an alternative view of how the food web is controlled. Unlike the "top-down" approach, which focuses on predation and basically says that species lower down in the food web are regulated by one or more predators higher up, this alternative view of the ocean ecosystem — from the "bottom-up" — contends that overall productivity is dependent on its tiniest parts, including the plants producing the food, and the precious supply of nutrients required to do so. In other words, changing the abundance of the tiny plant life called phytoplankton affects the abundance of the zooplankton, which would lead to changes in the abundance of prey fish and then of their predators.

Every marine species is influenced by a combination of forces, some of which we have yet to identify. Choi says the system is too complicated to even comprehend but the top-down approach provides some of the easiest answers. "You look for the smoking gun, and you try to control it. It's a very reductionist western tradition — European and North American — to try to control things in that way, to engineer things to try to achieve a certain outcome. But it doesn't always work." In other words, pointing a finger at one culprit, whether it's the forage fish or the grey seal, is easy and tempting but not likely to solve the cod's problem.

Delving into Seal Diet Studies

The calculation of the importance and amount of cod in the grey seal diet is a key piece of evidence in the attempt to implicate the species in the cod's non-recovery. In fact, on both sides of the Atlantic where grey seals have come into conflict with fishers and are believed to be competing with commercial fisheries, diet studies are almost an obsession with some scientists. But grey seal diet studies are fraught with shortcomings and tell us little if anything about how grey seals interact with cod.

Sara Iverson is a researcher in physiological ecology at Dalhousie University: she has worked with Don Bowen for years studying the diets of grey seals on Sable Island using a technique which was developed to analyze the fatty acids in seal blubber. This technique provides information about what the seal has eaten over a period of weeks or several months. "Fatty acid signature analysis is based roughly on the principle 'you are what you eat,'" she says. Iverson analyzes a small piece of blubber, taken from a live seal, and calculates both the mixture and amount of prey the seal has eaten.

In one ten-year study of seal foraging behaviour and diet, published in 2006, Iverson and Bowen and three other scientists found that cod are not a staple food for grey seals that breed on Sable Island. "Cod make up a very small proportion of their diet," she says. Looking at twenty-seven species of fish including invertebrates, the scientists found that between two and five species accounted for more than 80 percent of the diet by weight. "By far the largest diet items for grey seals on the Scotian Shelf are northern sand lance, redfish and other forage species such as capelin and herring." Iverson says seals prefer eating these fish because they are abundant and have a high fat content — 5 to 14 percent — compared to cod, which is only 1 percent fat.

Bowen says this is because grey seals make decisions on what to eat "based on economics" and on what's "profitable" for them to eat. "There's simply a large amount of candy bars on the Scotian Shelf," he explains, and the candy bars are the redfish, sand lance and herring, which he says are abundant. "Even if there is a cod population, seals may not eat them." In fact, Iverson's fatty acid analysis found that cod accounted for only 1.8 percent of a seal's diet.

However, when seal diets are measured in other ways, by looking at the scat, stomach, or intestine contents, there are often very different results: by these measures, cod appears to be a much more important component. Bowen says that unlike the fatty acid analysis, the other methods are not as representative of a grey seal diet. He also points out that the other methods are notoriously "biased" — a term used in science to mean that the method systematically results in an error inherent to the method itself. Because of this, identifying what a seal may or may not have eaten using any of these techniques is very challenging, to say the least.

"One of the biggest problems is that a very large fraction of the parts of fish completely disappear and we never see them because they get digested," says Bowen. For instance, one way to know for sure the kind of fish that has been eaten is to find its otoliths, or ear bones, somewhere in the seal's digestive tract or in its scat. Otoliths normally rest in fluid-filled chambers in the fish's inner ear and are used for sound detection and for balance, pulled by gravity so their movement helps the fish tell what's up from down. Depending on the shape of the otolith, it's possible to tell what species of fish has been eaten. Otoliths also have growth rings of calcium carbonate, protein and various trace elements, so counting the rings, just like you would in the trunk of a tree, can tell you the fish's age, and from that scientists can estimate the fish's size.

Cod otoliths tend to be robust and can withstand the process of digestion better than the hard parts of other fish species, such as herring and sand lance, which have small and fragile otoliths that tend to get digested. So, for instance, when scientists look at a seal scat, they may find cod otoliths but no evidence that herring was eaten. But this doesn't mean herring wasn't eaten. So, through experiments, scientists have learned that they typically only see evidence of 5 to 10 percent of herring and sand lance otoliths; based on this they have developed crude ways to "correct" for this so that the data are not biased toward species such as cod and haddock. "When you apply the correction factor, for example, to the Sable Island data, the proportion of cod in the diet [based on otoliths] drops by 50 percent to 7 percent," he says.

The other problem, according to Bowen, is that these correction factors are for fecal or scat samples only — the most widely used technique — and that no one really knows how to correct for stomach or intestine samples. "By the time you get to an animal, unless it's just eaten that food, you've already lost a lot of these otoliths," he says. The other problem with using stomach samples is that it may contain no information at all: "If the seal ate six or twelve hours ago, the stomach is empty." Getting information from a stomach that is representative of a seal diet is extremely difficult, he says. Stomach samples may have information on what a seal just ate, and fecal samples, which are collected from haul-out sites, only shed light on the last meal a seal has eaten, typically close to the site. "Meals that we can sample, whether we use stomach or fecal analysis, are vastly less than 1 percent of the meals that are actually eaten," explains Bowen.

While DFO scientists attempt to correct for the overestimation of cod in a seal diet, the fishing industry has long argued that cod is actually underestimated because they say there's no accounting for "biting" or "belly-feeding" of the large fish. They argue that seals often prefer eating just the cod's belly, in which case the otoliths, which occur in the head of the fish, would not be ingested. In this way, they argue, some predation could be overlooked.

Belly-feeding is about as contentious an issue as you can find when it comes to seals and cod. In Newfoundland, the DFO has documented eyewitness accounts, by fishers and divers, of dead cod with holes bitten out of their middles, strewn on the ocean bottom. These reports, however, have more often than not been associated with cod die-off events — where overwintering cod enter icy shallow waters. The largest documented event of this kind took place one morning in early April 2003 when the villagers of Smith Sound, Newfoundland, awoke to a sea brimming with cod. They rushed out in their boats, scooping the fish up in nets and buckets and in three days, they hauled hundreds of thousands of cod aboard their boats, in the end totalling 780 metric tonnes — roughly the combined weight of five hundred average-sized cars. It was reminiscent of the days when the fish were so abundant off their shores that they could be caught in baskets lowered over the sides of boats — except for one glaring difference: these fish were dead. At first, fishers and even some scientists blamed harp seals for chasing cod into water that was too cold for them. A federal investigation eventually showed that the subsurface water in the entire Sound was colder than it had been at any time during the previous decade, causing the cod to freeze to death. So, if seals were eating the bellies out of slow-moving, cold-stricken or dead fish, could we really blame them?

David Lavigne says there is anecdotal evidence that belly-biting does occur, but only around fishing gear: "If you have cod caught in a gillnet, so that the cod is suspended in a water column, the seal will bite away and it could very well bite the belly out," he says. "But seals don't have the time or inclination, or the teeth, to bite the bellies out of free swimming fish. He says seals usually eat their fish whole and head first. "They don't go swimming at high speeds chasing fish and nipping at their bellies.... I think this is the general consensus of scientists," he says. But not all scientists.

Doug Swain is DFO's cod expert in the Gulf of St. Lawrence region. He says belly-feeding isn't out of the ordinary: "When prey are locally abundant — in areas of dense cod aggregations during migrations and on the over-wintering grounds — the optimal foraging strategy is often to consume only the most energy-rich portions of the prey." Swain points to other examples of this: bears feeding on spawning Pacific salmon, and sea turtles feeding on jellyfish. He says the most energy-rich portion of the cod is the liver, located in the belly, where the cod store their energy reserves.

Lavigne argues that if belly-feeding was a common practice, we would find — given the thousands of grey seal stomachs that have been examined — evidence of belly-feeding. "To my knowledge none has ever been found," he says. One recent DFO study of seal diets that used DNA testing to double-check results corroborates Lavigne's view. It found that when otoliths were not present in the seal stomachs, neither was cod, "suggesting that if seals were feeding on soft parts of cod (i.e., 'belly-biting), it was not common."[40]

Instead there was evidence that the opposite could be the case. Some grey seal stomachs with cod otoliths actually lacked DNA for cod. Scientists say this could be due to the rapid breakdown of DNA or it could mean that otoliths might actually accumulate in a seal's stomach over time, which could result in an overestimation of the amount of cod eaten in the short term.[41]

Bowen says that even after all the diet estimates from the various techniques are derived and corrected for, they are still "misleading." He explains using this analogy: "If we came up with an average diet of Halifax, you might find you don't eat any of those foods as an individual or might eat them in very different proportions. That's the same as what we see in seals." Bowen says the "average" isn't telling us what we might think it is. He says sometimes averages can be meaningful. For instance, if you took the average height of ten-year-old boys, the average is meaningful because heights are normally distributed with an obvious peak at the centre of the distribution. "So, in fact most of the population of boys will be near the average height." But when it comes to grey seal diets, averages are "a mythology," he says. "A ten percent average value [for cod] in the diet *could* mean that most seals eat about ten percent of cod," explains Bowen. But it doesn't actually mean that. It actually means that most seals eat no cod while a small number eat quite a bit of cod. "The average really does not represent the diet of the grey seals sampled, and by inference therefore cannot represent the whole population."

According to Sara Iverson, pointing a finger at grey seals is also overly simplistic. "Grey seals are only one small cog in a very large wheel," she says. The "very large wheel" she is referring to is the complex marine food web, which features an overwhelming number of evolving interactions, the majority of which we know precious little about. Food webs also involve feedback loops that are themselves complicated by the fact that fish rarely eat the same foods as they grow and develop. For instance, a juvenile cod dines on a cornucopia of floating life: copepods, small crustaceans, and plankton, so it eats at a *lower* trophic level than an adult cod, which will eat just about anything, including other cod. The adult fish are so cannibalistic that cod jiggers — a baitless piece of lead used to attract cod by anglers — are often shaped to resemble a young cod. In one stock it was estimated that large cod were the most important predators of small cod and that cannibalism accounted for 44 percent of the juvenile mortality.[42] So when a seal eats an adult cod, for instance, there can be a number of spin-off effects because it's also eating a predator of small cod and other potential prey such as capelin, herring, sand lance, turbot, crabs, shrimp, and brittle stars, to name a few. In other words, when all the possible interactions are factored in, there's every possibility that grey seals could be doing more to help cod than to hinder it.

Debbie MacKenzie says the grey seal is basically taking over the position that the big fish once had: "Fish like hake and cod, the ones that got big enough to be forces to be reckoned with, *they* were the predators of the small fish." Mackenzie points to the fact, surprising to some, that the biggest predator of fish is other fish. She says that the collapse of the fish-eating fish — the groundfish — resulted in there being only one predator species left. "There used to be millions of predators. Now we only have one predator left, the grey seal, and there's more than enough fish for 400,000 of them." She says that even a large grey seal population has considerably less impact than a large cod population would have had and that overall intensity of predator activity has decreased. "It looks like increased predator activity because they pop their heads up and they crawl out."

Although Mackenzie is not a trained scientist, her intuitive grasp of fisheries science and her passion for ocean life are remarkable. Her background is in nursing, but fish and the ocean were never too far away. She worked as a public nurse in the fishing community of Shelburne, Nova Scotia; she says she was "married to a family of fishermen." Her father also worked as a scientist for the DFO. For MacKenzie there is nothing simple about the marine food web or the way the ocean systems work. She seems comfortable with this complexity and has been working tirelessly against the pressure to reduce it to meaningless sound bites. When Mackenzie talks about the fish or the seals she talks about them like they are real, living things. She describes how they behave, and shows a great interest in their life histories and in their true nature. And it's not just the seals and the fish she's interested in, it's the barnacles and the seaweed and the copepods and the plankton. Mackenzie has an encyclopedic knowledge about them all, from reading and researching but also from paying attention — observing them and trying to make sense of patterns over time and of how things fit together.

This way of seeing ocean life — in qualitative descriptive ways — stands in sharp contrast with what Dean Bavington calls "the quantitative abstract ways that involve instruments and experiments but little experience of wild animals." Bavington grew up in Newfoundland and is a professor at Memorial University in St. John's. His PhD thesis led to his recent book, *Managed Annihilation: An Unnatural History of the Newfoundland Cod Collapse*, in which he focuses on the cod fishery and the rise of what he calls "scientific management" — a turning point he links to the rise of industrial capitalism. We'll explore Bavington's ideas in greater detail later, but at this juncture the relevant point is that in the past, cod, or seals for that matter, were not seen as something within the realm of control by humans. Bavington says this shifted when "fluctuations, the ebb and flow of codfish themselves, [became] a problem seen as solvable through some form of intervention, as opposed to something that is just given."[43] Because of a whole range of forces, many of them economic, there was pressure to catch more fish and a demand for fish landings that were at least steady and predictable. Bavington says the agency that was expected to solve this problem was science.

"There's been a split in fisheries biology," he says. "There are the natural historians: those looking at the life history of fish, or looking at the acoustic ecology of cod and how they find mates through sound, or how they need old fish to learn the migration routes and what happens when you take the old fish out." Then there are the "quantified modeler types." Bavington explains: "It doesn't matter if they're talking about fruit flies, cod, or caribou, it's the same approach, the same models. We're now in the world of statistics." Bavington says this approach reflects a world-view where animals of all kinds are just seen as resources to be managed. "Fish are just swimming inventory," he says. "A certain type of science is now required for political and economic reasons."

Assumptions In, a Scapegoat Out

In early 2012, a study about seals and cod made the headlines in Atlantic Canada — one that would be cited by cull advocates for months afterwards. The news reported that the study confirmed what the fishing industry had been saying all along: the seals were to blame for the cod non-recovery. The authors of the peer-reviewed study that appeared in *Fisheries Research* estimated that in 2010, grey seals ate more than 688,000 tonnes of fish — including cod — and that they "could well be the primary source of the unaccounted for natural mortality" of adult cod on the eastern Scotian Shelf and the lack of recovery since 1993.[44]

Just after their study was published, I met with Robert O'Boyle and Michael Sinclair, the two retired Bedford Institute of Oceanography directors who wrote the study, and discovered that in person they weren't nearly as conclusive about their findings as the media had initially reported. They were both refreshingly candid about the fact that there were still a lot of unanswered questions. For instance, O'Boyle explained quite openly that the study couldn't account for the fact that the very cod stock the seals were said to be decimating — the one in the vicinity of Sable Island — was at the time showing preliminary signs of recovery, at least according to Ken Frank's 2011 study in *Nature*. Frank and his colleagues reported that the cod stock on the eastern Scotian Shelf was about one-third of the way back to historical levels and that an increasing number of cod at an increasing number of locations had been observed in the DFO bottom trawl survey since 2005. This caveat appeared prominently in O'Boyle and Sinclair's study: O'Boyle explained to me that if the recovery on the eastern Scotian Shelf was in fact a real one, it would mean their model was "wrong" and would "need adjusting." He felt, however, that it was still too early to tell if cod were recovering because the increase could be the result of what he called "noise in the survey," referring to the DFO annual groundfish survey. O'Boyle explains: "You've got such low [cod] abundance and if you hit an aggregation you'll get a big spike. You see this in lots of surveys, it could be the conditions are conducive to cod being on the bottom during a survey, so you get a big spike." The scientists needed a few more years of data showing an upward trend before they would be convinced.

The authors also openly stated that their study didn't reflect the tenor of scientific consensus at the time and that they were "going against the grain from a scientific perspective." This is because nearly all the literature on the impact of grey seals on cod to date, including the bulk of it conducted by their own colleagues at DFO, did not implicate grey seals in the failure of cod to recover. For instance, in 2006 a study by DFO scientists Kurtis Trzcinski, Robert Mohn, and Don Bowen looked at seal diets analyzed using fatty acid and fecal sample data and concluded there was "little evidence" that grey seals were the cause of the failure of cod to recover. "Even the complete removal of the grey seal population would not assure the recovery of the cod, given the high levels of other sources of mortality."[45]

But O'Boyle and Sinclair didn't agree with this previous work and decided to embark on their own study using different modelling assumptions. They said none of the earlier papers accounted for the high level of natural mortality. "If you look at the same information from a different angle you might get a different answer and that's all we were doing."

One of the areas where their study diverged was in regard to seal diet. Even though the previous work on Sable Island seal diets concluded that seals were eating small or juvenile cod, and even possibly avoiding the adults altogether, O'Boyle and Sinclair said there was "growing evidence" based on the belly-biting accounts by fishermen, as well as the recent DFO work in the southern Gulf, that seals were eating big cod too. We'll return to this subject in the next chapter. For modelling purposes they decided to see what would happen if seals ate in proportion to what's in the ocean? "So if the size structure of the cod population changes [the seals] will eat proportional to that size composition. If there aren't any big cod out there, they're not going to eat them but if there are big cod they'll eat them, in proportion to their abundance," explained O'Boyle. So, as cod increase (as was reported by Frank in *Nature*), O'Boyle and Sinclair's model makes seals eat more cod. They argue that by making the relationship proportional it is possible to explain a lot of the natural mortality of the adult fish and the recovery slump.

But according to Bowen, who has studied the diets of the Sable Island seals for years, their model just doesn't reflect reality. He says there's very little scientific justification for the assumption that grey seals eat in proportion to what's in the ocean. "[O'Boyle and Sinclair's study] is little more than a 'what-if' scenario," he says. What if seals ate more cod? When you plug into the model that there's more cod, the fraction has nowhere to go but up. "So one needs to take their conclusions with much more than a grain of salt," says Bowen.

Where previous studies had relied predominantly on the diet studies of the Sable Island grey seals, O'Boyle and Sinclair favoured the use of a hypothesized "global average," which worked out to be 10 to 15 percent cod in the seal diet: this was estimated from a variety of studies, many from the other side of the Atlantic. According to Bowen, the problem with doing this is that most of the studies they used had not "corrected" in any way for the biases that are known to overestimate the fraction of cod in the diet. This, of course, resulted in increasing the amount of cod seals were eating.

O'Boyle and Sinclair also opted not to use the locally derived fatty acid analysis data in their modelling because they said it "underestimated the impacts of seal predation on cod population trends."[46] They base this view on the work of a small group of Norwegian scientists led by Otto Grahl-Nielsen at the University of Bergen and the Norwegian Polar Institute who have challenged the work of Sara Iverson and her team at Dalhousie University, going so far as to call the use of fatty acid analysis as an estimation of prey consumption "unreliable."[47] But according to Iverson, Grahl-Nielsen's critique is unfounded because it's based on poorly executed studies using questionable sampling and statistical analyses. She says the use and study of fatty acids has been around since the 1930s and that it should not be dismissed based on conclusions that are not adequately supported. She tells me that O'Boyle and Sinclair cite Grahl-Nielsen because "it's the one thing that can support their non-use of the fatty acid data," and therefore their use of other much higher cod consumption estimates.[48]

Another modelling assumption made by O'Boyle and Sinclair raises important questions about the assumptions themselves, ones that are often used and go unchallenged. In 1999, the Fisheries Resource Conservation Council (FRCC) urged David Anderson, the Minister of Fisheries and Oceans at the time, to "expedite efforts to quantify the effect of seals' predation on groundfish," and recommended that the models used to do this treat the seal population as a "fishing fleet."[49] O'Boyle confirmed that this was how their model worked, that "the foraging of seals is analogous to a fishing fleet's operation" and that this approach was common practice even before the FRCC recommendation. "A fishing fleet consists of a number of vessels operating in a specific area using a specific gear which causes them to catch a certain tonnage of fish consisting of an age distribution based on the selectivity characteristics of the gear," he explains.

Ian Boyd is a biology professor at the University of St. Andrews in Scotland and director of its Sea Mammal Research Unit and the Scottish Oceans Institute. He tells me there are huge differences in the way marine mammals forage for food and the way fishing fleets catch fish. For one, fishing fleets have very powerful fishing units — large trawlers capable of cleaning up a sea bed or pelagic area of fish — while seals will only continue to exploit a fish species until the fish density is at such a level that it is uneconomical for the seals to continue feeding. "That density is likely to be a lot higher than what's left by a large pelagic trawler," he says.

Seals are also able to switch their diet very quickly and easily, whereas, he says, "we've designed our fishing industry to very targeted fisheries, for cod, capelin, or other species." If the density of a particular species goes down, seals will move to another species and will only feed on what's most abundant at the time. "This is not how the fishery operates."

Boyd says the other big difference is that seals are not subsidized: "When a fishery collapses, or when it becomes uneconomical, because of local political pressures, very often a subsidy is put on to keep that fishery going." He says that if the fishery were really behaving like a natural predator, the fishery would simply die. "That's why you get overexploitation of fish stocks and it's also why animals like seals cannot overexploit their food source."

If one critique of O'Boyle and Sinclair's study dominated scientific circles in early 2012, it was with respect to the way their model simplified the food web. They used what's called a two-species model, one that only considered the interactions between seals and cod. To be fair, their approach was consistent with what a number of other DFO studies involving seal-cod interactions had done previously, but many scientists argue that this model is overly simplistic and fails to recognize that marine systems are complex and unpredictable. As a result of this failure, the findings of these studies are often highly questionable.

Alida Bundy, a fisheries scientist at DFO, tells me that the two-species model ignores the complexity in the system. "They reduce all the other predation, for example, on cod into a single number, and often it's not considered what might make up that other predation or the dynamics of the other species that are causing the predation and it also ignores the environment." Bundy says it can be dangerous to ignore the complexity. "The more we ignore the more risk there is that our predictions will be less, I won't say accurate, less realistic, less useful."

Boyd describes the model as being a fairly "standard classical fisheries-type model," but adds that such models "have proven repeatedly not to be useful when managing fisheries, let alone seals." Boyd illustrates the "inexactitudes" of some of this modelling work by telling me the story of his colleague, who, using the same methods used by O'Boyle and Sinclair, tried to calculate the amount of cod eaten by the part of the European grey seal population found on the west coast of Scotland. The modelling work showed that "grey seals were probably eating most, if not all, of the cod

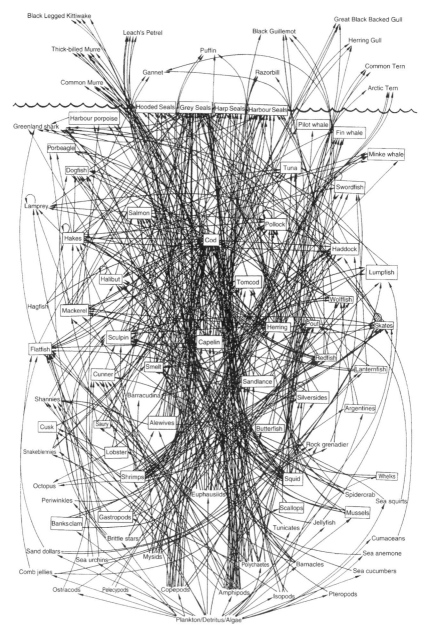

A partial food web for the Scotian Shelf in the northwest Atlantic off eastern Canada. Species enclosed in rectangles are also exploited by humans. This food web is incomplete because the feeding habits of all components have not been fully described. Further, all species — including some of the marine mammals — do not spend the entire year in the area. Reprinted with permission from David Lavigne (2003).

that was reckoned to be present in the region," he says. "There was even a suspicion that the data showed they were eating more cod than was present, which is clearly ridiculous. It shows there are some major inaccuracies within the system." Boyd says the inaccuracies stem from our inability to really know how much cod is there. "The mismatch between the apparent amount of cod eaten by seals and the amount of cod 'present' according to stock assessments," suggests we don't know as much about the cod stocks as we think we do, and that fisheries scientists might be deluding themselves into thinking they do know this quantity quite accurately. "It's far from an exact science," he says.[50]

Seeing the Forest for the Trees

The key to scientific uncertainty is not to remove the uncertainty, advises Daniel Pauly. "When physicists don't see something — when a process is a bit uncertain — they don't develop statistical tools to cancel out the noise, which we do in biology. We develop statistical tools to see it better. The physicists build a bigger machine and then the process that was fuzzy becomes clear."[51]

Pauly is referring to the Large Hadron Collider (LHC) built by CERN, the European Organization for Nuclear Research, a scientific organization located near Geneva whose mandate is to find out what the universe is made of and how it works. The LHC is the largest machine in the world — a scientific instrument that spans the border between Switzerland and France and lies about one hundred metres underground. Physicists use the LHC to recreate the conditions just after the Big Bang, by colliding two beams of the smallest known sub-atomic particles called hadrons head-on at very high energy. They are trying to understand the sub-atomic world, one that they can't see. Some fisheries biologists are trying to do the same thing.

In the early 1990s, Pauly and his colleagues developed a tool to understand the ocean ecosystem better: Ecopath and Ecosim — modelling software able to take a static snapshot view of an ecosystem but also able to describe changing things and simulate through time.* Bundy did her PhD thesis at U.B.C., has worked with both Pauly and Walters, and uses Ecopath and Ecosim in her work.

Bundy says there's a whole range of models from simple, conceptual ones like flow charts to more complex models that try to quantify different relationships in a system. "An Ecopath with Ecosim model attempts to model

---

* The Ecopath and Ecosim modelling software was first initiated by Jeffrey Polovina at the National Oceanic and Atmospheric Administration (NOAA) but in the early 1990s was further developed and made available by Daniel Pauly, Villy Christensen and Carl Walters at the Fisheries Centre at the University of British Columbia.

the whole system so everything is in there from primary producers, such as phytoplankton right through to your top predators," she says. "There's fishing too, and all the different steps in between. It can also include bacterial cycles to a certain extent."

Bundy points out that as you add in more information, you also add in more uncertainty. But she says all models, even the more complex ones, are reductionist: "The system out there is extremely complex, and so, by developing a model, you are reducing that complexity into something that's understandable and something you can work with." As a result, she says, "no model tells you the truth." But some reflect reality better than others.

Bundy used Ecopath and Ecosim to develop models of four northwest Atlantic ecosystems including Newfoundland and Labrador, eastern Scotian Shelf, and the northern and southern Gulf of St. Lawrence in order to compare the structure, function and key species of these ecosystems before and after the cod collapse. In the 2009 study, Bundy and her colleagues found that since the collapse of the cod, all the ecosystems had shifted to an alternate state: "Cumulative removals by fisheries over ten, twenty, thirty years, longer, has changed the structure of the system and has removed the larger fish and older fish and by taking those larger and older fish out it's changing the predation patterns within the system," she says. In some of her earlier work, Bundy found that cod on the eastern Scotian Shelf were "trapped in a vicious circle" — their numbers were being kept low because of competition and possible predation on larval and juvenile cod by a high abundance of forage fish: this resulted in the cod's inability to compete for a decreasing amount of prey (small zooplankton). The result was that the small cod that did survive were in poor condition and this, carried through to adulthood, caused high adult mortality.[52]

Bundy says that the "cultivation-depensation" hypothesis — discussed earlier in this chapter — is supported by models and some evidence elsewhere, but there isn't really any data to support that it happens here: "We don't have empirical concrete evidence that our forage fish species are eating young cod, or young white hake, or any of these young species. We don't have the diet data. It's been seen in other places, and it's a working hypothesis." Bundy says that getting the diet data isn't easy because the DFO research survey doesn't go out at the time of year when the cod or haddock are at the larval stage: "It's quite a short window and then also because they're so small, they get digested very quickly and they're harder to observe. So you'd have to have a dedicated survey going out at exactly the right time of year to do this."

I asked Bundy this question: "Given that it's a complex ecosystem, does it make sense to say one marine species is responsible for the demise of another?"

"I wouldn't make that statement," she answered.

Chapter 5

The Case of the Missing Fish

> People are far too interested in the trigger and the smoking gun and not in the multiplicity of processes that brought the gun into play and the actors into alignment. Ecological systems and change are fundamentally multi-causal systems.
>
> —Jae S. Choi, Population Ecologist, Fisheries and Oceans Canada

> The greatest obstacle to discovery is not ignorance — it is the illusion of knowledge.
>
> — Daniel J. Boorstin, Historian

On the surface, the Gulf of St. Lawrence is a semi-enclosed body of water surrounded by five of Canada's ten provinces. But below the membrane-thin interface between air and water lies a submarine landscape of deep fjords and plateaus, slopes and cliffs — remnant carvings of two-million-year-old glaciers — where currents and tides combine with nutrient-rich upwellings in a synergistic gusto to create one of the world's most productive and diverse ecosystems. It's really a combination of estuary and ocean — technically, an estuarine environment, which comprises a unique and complex three-dimensional world where fresh water from the St. Lawrence and Saguenay Rivers flow, draining a giant 1.8 million square kilometre watershed into the salt water of the north Atlantic. These waters, which swirl and mix in a complicated pattern influenced by temperature and currents, as well as the depth and contours of the seabed, support a dazzling variety of marine life.

The Gulf was at one time the home of a legendary population of Atlantic cod. Northern and southern Gulf cod — the two populations or stocks that inhabit the Gulf — have been commercially exploited for five hundred years; as well they sustained the First Nations — predominantly the Mi'kmaq — for thousands more. These cod populations, along with all the others in the waters of the northwest Atlantic, are what first attracted the attention of the early European explorers and traders.* It's now a familiar narrative of

---

*   The Northwest Atlantic Fisheries Organization (NAFO) fishing areas were originally delineated for the purposes of collecting fisheries statistics, but, where possible, attempts were made to match these areas with real stock boundaries. A "stock" is understood to be a self-sustaining population of a

almost mythical proportions: the cod were so plentiful and prolific that they could be scooped up in buckets; so thick that you could hardly row a boat through them. It was thought to be inexhaustible. But time proved otherwise.

The collapse of the cod stocks is a story of how rapacious fishing interests, ruinous factory-fishing technology, government mismanagement and wonky science all combined to catastrophic effect. As we have seen, the fishing industry, the federal government and some of its scientists are blaming seals for the cod population's failure to bounce back. While blaming the seals may be politically convenient, it glosses over many unwelcome, little-known facts — facts that also point to a lack of enlightened political leadership. For one thing, endangered cod stocks have continued to be fished even after temporary moratoriums. For another, cod are still being caught accidentally in other fisheries such as those for shrimp and lobster. Add in the disastrous effects of climate change and it becomes obvious that the seals are merely convenient scapegoats.

Doug Swain is the DFO's cod expert in the Gulf region. In 2008, he and his colleague Ghislain Chouinard reported in the *Canadian Journal of Fisheries and Aquatic Sciences* that what they termed the "productivity" of the southern Gulf stock was no longer viable. Basically, the population was doomed. This is not just true of cod in the southern Gulf. It's also true of white hake — a lesser-known species, also seriously depleted by overfishing — as well as winter skate and possibly other species. Southern Gulf fish in general have been reduced to extremely low levels. The scientists stated in no uncertain terms that at the current level of productivity, this cod population would be extirpated within forty years without a cod fishery and in half that time with one. The report warned that, "even small fishery removals will substantially hasten its demise."[53]

Swain and Chouinard also reported that the natural mortality rate of the adult fish — the number that die from causes other than fishing — was unusually high and that this was holding back a recovery, because adults

species: a biologically discrete reproductive unit. Stock structure influenced the creation of fishing area boundaries, particularly in the case of cod, which held a very high profile when it came to commercial importance. According to the DFO, the cod stocks, and corresponding NAFO fishing areas within the two hundred mile fishing zone are: West Greenland (NAFO IA-IF); Northern Labrador (2GH); Southern Labrador-Eastern Newfoundland (actually a "stock complex," composed of several large interrelated stocks; also called the northern stock) (2J and 3KL); Southern Grand Bank (3NO); Flemish Cap (3M); St. Pierre Bank (or Southern Newfoundland) (3PS); Northern Gulf of St. Lawrence (4RS and 3Pn); Southern Gulf of St. Lawrence (4T); Sydney Bight (4Vn); Eastern Scotian Shelf (4VsW); Western Scotian Shelf (4X); Georges Bank (5Z); and Gulf of Maine (5Y).

produce the next generations of fish. In other words, big cod seemed to be disappearing, not showing up in the DFOs annual bottom trawl surveys as expected. The cod in this stock are not alone. Big cod seem to be disappearing from many of the dwindling stocks of the northwest Atlantic.

George Rose, a former DFO scientist and current head of Newfoundland's Fisheries Conservation Group, says that the Newfoundland cod stocks are also experiencing high levels of natural mortality. He writes:

> All we know is that cod with poor livers are disappearing at an unprecedented rate and that few cod older than five or six years of age can be found from the outer Grand Banks to Labrador, where, historically, cod normally lived for 15–20 years. It is impossible for this stock to increase quickly or at all with such elevated death rates — with every gain through fish born into the population, there is nearly as much loss.[54]

According to Swain, it's "normal" for about 18 percent of adult cod to die every year of natural causes, meaning that each year after reaching two or three years of age, every cod has an 18 percent chance of dying from natural causes before the end of the year.* But in the southern Gulf cod stock, the rate was now closer to 45 or 50 percent, and it's been this way for nearly twenty years. Swain and Chouinard hypothesized that the "missing" fish in the southern Gulf could be linked to the growing grey seal herd. But this hypothesis, they noted, was "inconsistent" with the available science on seal diets, which, as we've seen, showed that for the Sable Island herd at least, cod make up a very small proportion of the diet and what they do eat tends to be young fish. The amounts could not explain the increase in mortality among adults. Further work was "urgently needed," they wrote.[55]

In June 2009, before that work could be done, Gail Shea, the fisheries minister at the time, announced the closure of the southern Gulf cod fishery and, at the same time, directed her department "to ensure the targeted removal of grey seals."[56] Incredibly, Shea issued her directive without any scientific evidence supporting the hypothesis that seals were holding back the cod recovery.† Some critics, including prominent academics and scientists,

---

*   This so-called "normal" rate for natural mortality (M) was first derived in the 1960s, based on data from the 1950s. It's against this rate that the current levels of natural mortality are considered to be "unusually high." But it's worth noting that in the 1950s, the marine environment was far from pristine and what was considered to be "normal" for cod then may not necessarily have been "natural."

†   You will recall that in 2009 Shea also commissioned a study to examine the costs and logistics of "managing" the Sable Island grey seal population, and

say that federal scientists were then pushed to justify a cull of seals in the Gulf. Politics, not science, was in the driver's seat.

Circumstantial Evidence Implicates Grey Seals

In the autumn, southern Gulf cod form dense aggregations and migrate great distances from their summer feeding grounds — up to 650 kilometres for some — to the deeper and warmer waters on the southern slope of the Laurentian Channel, a nearly three hundred metre deep underwater valley that extends for 1,250 kilometres from the estuary to the edge of the continental shelf south of Newfoundland. It's here that they mix with other stocks in the area, where they feed less, use up the energy stored in their livers and muscles, and wait for spring, when they make their way back into the Gulf to spawn. According to information from satellite transmitters attached to some grey seals, it is also here — on the overwintering grounds — where the two species overlap. Some grey seals spend time in the vicinity of St. Paul's Island, northeast of Cape Breton during the winter months: it is here that some scientists say the adult cod are being eaten.

In the winter of 2008, DFO hired sealers to kill grey seals that were foraging near St. Paul's Island in the Cabot Strait near the cod overwintering areas. Scientists analyzed the stomach and intestinal contents of ninety seals and found that cod made up a significant portion of the diet of a few of the grey seals — mainly the males — foraging in the overwintering area. After having examined, and rejected, all other alternative hypotheses, DFO scientists were still working on the grey seal predation hypothesis: they say that, even though the sample size is small, grey seal predation is still likely the greatest contributor to the high natural mortality of cod. The other explanations for the "missing fish" include unreported catch, emigration, disease, contaminants, poor fish condition, parasites and changes in their life-history, including maturing and aging prematurely — all subjects we'll return to later in this chapter.

At the same time, DFO scientists also state cautiously that the evidence implicating the seals is mostly circumstantial, and that, even if there are correlations, they don't prove cause and effect. However, Swain argues that, even if large cod are a small component of an individual seal's diet, it could still account for much of the increased natural mortality of cod, given the relatively small number of cod and the large number of seals. But this argument doesn't sit well with his colleague, Don Bowen, who has studied grey seals and their diets on Sable Island for more than thirty years: he says that with 300,000 grey seals, either a small fraction of the population eating all cod

---

hired CBCL Ltd., a Halifax-based engineering firm. Shortly thereafter, Shea announced a TAC of 39,000 grey seals on Sable Island.

or most of the population eating very few cod can generate high mortality. "There are enough seals that you could do a calculation to show that seals *could* generate all the mortality required to explain the non-recovery. So, it is feasible," he says. "But the question is, is it happening?"

According to Jeff Hutchings, while it's within the realm of possibility that grey seals are contributing to the high natural mortality of cod, "this says nothing about what you do about it," he says. "This is only happening because of what we did. We are at fault. We're at fault for making cod an endangered species. We're at fault for reducing these populations to levels where cod appear to be unable to sustain the natural mortality levels that they're currently experiencing."

The Politics of a Fishing Moratorium

The cod collapse is mostly associated with the northern stock and with Newfoundland, since this was the largest cod fishery in the world, where the magnitude of job losses was highest. However, the cod population declined significantly everywhere in Atlantic Canada: the Gulf was no exception. According to the DFO, the average annual landings of southern Gulf cod exceeded 60,000 tonnes in the 1980s — in 1986 the stock's total biomass was estimated to be 511,000 tonnes. When combined with the northern Gulf stock, the biomass of Gulf cod in the mid-1980s exceeded one million tonnes. But by 1993, the year the cod fishery in the Gulf was shut down, the spawning stock biomass (SSB) of the southern stock, which is a good indicator of stock health, had plummeted to 61,200 tonnes, from 375,500 tonnes just seven years earlier. In 1993, nearly four decades after a record landing of 100,000 tonnes of southern Gulf cod, only 5,300 tonnes could be found.

In 2010 the Committee on the Status of Endangered Wildlife in Canada (COSEWIC) designated all cod in Canadian waters from the tip of Labrador south to Georges Bank as endangered. In other words, since the collapse, most of the stocks have gone from bad to worse and are now teetering on the brink of biological extinction: something COSEWIC attributes, at least in part, to the fact that some stocks continue to be fished — something that might come as a surprise to most people.

While directed fishing on all the cod stocks was closed at some point during the 1990s — for the northern stock in 1992, Grand Banks cod in 1994, Flemish Cap cod in 1999, and all other stocks in 1993 — not all of these have remained closed. The moratorium on the northern stock was maintained in the offshore areas, but fisheries have been allowed in Newfoundland's inshore cod stocks for many years. This has undermined a recovery of the stock. However, there have been recent reports that the northern stock has shown preliminary signs of a resurgence, partly as a result of warmer waters and rebuilding plankton and capelin stocks,[57] but it remains to be seen whether this "recovery" will be sustained. The fishery for the southern Grand Bank cod has also stayed closed, but, according to the DFO, recovery there has been impeded because cod are being caught as bycatch in the skate, yellowtail flounder and Greenland halibut fisheries. The southern Newfoundland stock, which had shown some recovery in the early years, reopened to fishing in 1997 and has more recently shown considerable signs of decline.

The eastern Scotian Shelf cod fishery, which has been shut since the moratorium was first announced, at first continued to decline; however, more recently it has shown some positive signs of recovery, which, as we've seen, were reported by Ken Frank in 2011 in the journal *Nature*. At the time of writing, however, I received some unpublished and non-peer reviewed data that indicated there was some question emerging about whether there has been some reversal of these reported gains.

Directed fishing for cod in the Gulf has actually been the norm since the moratorium. Following the closure in 1993, the two Gulf stocks showed positive signs of recovery, but small directed fisheries have been allowed since then and have erased any of these gains. The first groundfish closure — the moratorium most people think remained in place — held initially for about four years, but even during this time a recreational cod fishery was allowed, and cod continued to be caught as bycatch in other fisheries. In 1998, directed fishing resumed with cod quotas set at between three thousand and six thousand tonnes until 2003, when it was closed again because of poor cod recovery. Fishing was reopened the following year, with quotas ranging from 2,000 to 4,000 tonnes a year. By the time Shea (Minister of Fisheries and Oceans) shut it down in 2009, some say it was already too late. Today the southern Gulf cod population is endangered and will be considered officially extirpated if the spawning stock biomass dips below 1,000 tonnes or less than 0.3 percent of historical levels.

Understandably, hopes had been pinned on a quick recovery; at first it was thought two years of no fishing might be sufficient. But this didn't happen. By the mid-1990s one DFO scientist was already saying that a full recovery of the severely depressed stocks would require a much longer moratorium than initially thought.[58] In fact, there was very little scientific evidence that a rapid recovery was even possible with fish as slow-growing and late-maturing as cod. As early as 1996 the IUCN had listed Atlantic cod as vulnerable; two years later COSEWIC followed suit by assessing cod throughout its Canadian range as "special concern." By 2000, in a paper published in *Nature*, Hutchings reported that, after analyzing ninety marine fish stocks, he found that many of the gadids, including cod and haddock, had "experienced little, if any, recovery as much as fifteen years after 45–99 percent reductions in reproductive biomass." He went on to write: "Although the effects of overfishing on single species may generally be reversible, the actual time required for recovery appears to be considerable."[59]

The decisions to resume fishing for cod in the inshore area of Newfoundland, on the western Scotian Shelf and in the Gulf were clearly not based on scientific evidence, but on political considerations. Some have pointed out that the opening of some directed fishing coincided with the end of nearly $2.5 billion in income support and retraining programs, as well as with the 1997 federal election.[60] Indeed many critics of the discretionary power held by the Minister of Fisheries and Oceans argue that governments are simply unwilling to risk political capital and that fishing quotas as well as many other fisheries management decisions are essentially vote-buying exercises that put short-term socio-economic considerations ahead of real stock recovery. Others say the reopening was also a result of pressure from the fishing industry because a few stocks were showing some improvement. In any case, some cod fisheries were reopened, contrary to scientific advice. As one insider put it: "As soon as the gopher sticks his head out of the hole you shoot its head off."

Science and Its Positive Feedback Loop

In a circuitous chain of events, in the fall of 2011, two years after Fisheries and Oceans Minister Gail Shea announced there would be a cull of grey seals, the Fisheries Resource Conservation Council (FRCC) — a fifteen-person council made up of members from both science and industry, whose role is to advise the minister — urged the minister to approve one.* They recommended that 73,000 grey seals in the southern Gulf be killed in the first year, and another 70,000 over the next four years.

At the time, six prominent scientists including Boris Worm, Hal

---

* According to Dean Bavington, before the establishment of the FRCC, fisheries management discussions were the domain of DFO science and industry: "Scientific data from offshore scientific surveys and the commercial dragger fleet were reviewed exclusively by fisheries scientists to determine cod stock status. Once the stock status was agreed upon, TAC levels were secretly negotiated by DFO officials and hand-picked representatives from the fishing industry." In other words, the fishing industry and DFO scientists had always met behind closed doors before a recommendation of fishing quotas was given to the minister — who always has the final say. Bavington says the FRCC, which was founded in the wake of the groundfish collapse "opened that up" and "represented a significant departure from past practices." For the first time there was a mechanism for fishers themselves to have a say in fisheries management decisions. He says council members are selected "based on merit and standing in their respective communities, and not as representatives of organizations, areas, or interests." In October 2011, the Harper government cut all future funding to the FRCC, and the federal fisheries advisory body was disbanded.

Whitehead, Sara Iverson and Lindy Weilgart, all from Dalhousie University, as well as IFAWs David Lavigne and Sidney Holt — the father of fisheries science — sent an open letter to Fisheries and Oceans Minister Keith Ashfield about the FRCC recommendation saying the announcement about a cull was made before the science was even heard, that the outcome was predetermined and that it was the "antithesis of how science should function in the fishery management process." They said that following the 2009 directive by Minister Shea, some scientists "dutifully set out to provide a rationale for the previously announced cull," and that workshops that followed only examined negative impacts of grey seals on cod, not positive ones, which amounted to nothing more than a "self-fulfilling prophesy."[*][61]

Debbie MacKenzie wasn't surprised. She says, "Whoever controls the terms of reference for the DFO workshops, also controls what science gets studied." In this case, she says, it's the fishing industry that wields power. As a result, issues like the effects of trawling on habitat, the ecological impacts of removing biomass from the ocean by fishing and the ecological role of having a healthy seal population generally don't get looked at by DFO's science branch. This raises an important question. What happens if the scientific questions being put forward and subsequently studied by federal scientists with regards to the cod non-recovery are coming from vested interest groups? Can this science be trusted?

The question was posed to Daniel Pauly, arguably one of the world's most renowned fisheries scientists. He says the published science isn't wrong but it's important to look at it in context. "The [DFO] is trying to protect industrial fishing interests — policy that comes from the top down. It trickles down gently and when it reaches the people on the ground there is no *scientific* distortion really — you just don't get money or funding for studying this, but you get money for studying that." He says that in the case of the cod non-recovery, a great deal of time, effort and money have gone into studying the impact of the grey seals and not the other possible explanations for the non-recovery. He concludes, "This is how you can distort findings without ever being caught."

The Alternative Hypotheses

Today, the Gulf of St. Lawrence is a marine oasis in decline. A plethora of human pressures pose significant threats to its integrity and ability to function as a healthy ecosystem. In recent years the DFO has reported that a number of major "impact issues" are affecting the Gulf and its marine life. Among

---

*   The letter signatories are referring to a four-day DFO workshop held October 4–8, 2010 — a Zonal Assessment Process (ZAP) on the potential [negative] impacts of grey seals on fish populations in eastern Canada.

them are noise disturbance from seismic and exploratory drilling, commercial fishing activity, invasive species, chemical contamination and — the most daunting one of all — climate change and its related horrors of ocean acidification, dead zones and loss of seasonal sea ice cover. While each of these has serious effects individually, studies warn that when they interact, as they will do in the real world, there are likely to be "significant cumulative effects," but that because these are poorly studied, they are not known.[62]

In trying to explain the "missing" fish in the southern Gulf of St. Lawrence, DFO scientists did entertain half a dozen other "alternative" hypotheses — in addition to grey seal predation — but as noted, these were all flatly rejected. This decision was based on what is called a "weight of evidence approach." Essentially, the hypotheses, or proposed explanations, were "weighted" by the evidence, explains Swain. "We looked at all the evidence relevant to each of the hypotheses. The hypotheses that were most strongly supported by the evidence were considered to be the most likely hypotheses, those that were inconsistent with the evidence were considered unlikely or rejected."

Don Bowen was also present at the meetings that led to choosing the grey seal predation hypothesis and he was not impressed. "There is a reasonable concept called 'weight of evidence' but it's not being applied in this situation," he says. "We can't figure out what is [causing the non-recovery], but we know grey seals eat some cod and therefore grey seals are the problem. That's the 'weight of evidence.' That's the logic." Then he adds, "It's basically the blind man looking where the light is brightest."

Bowen says that some of the hypotheses were dismissed because little was known about them. "We don't know anything about pesticides: what we know about pesticides and pollutants and contaminants and their effects on these cod populations you can summarize in one sentence, which we did basically," he says. The DFO argued that if cod were going to be dying anywhere in the world from a high contaminant load it would be in the Baltic and North Seas, since both are severely toxic semi-enclosed seas. However, scientists found that while cod in the Baltic Sea, for instance, had a higher contaminant load than southern Gulf fish, it did not seem to result in high natural mortality there. Based on this, scientists ruled out contaminant-induced death as a possible cause of high natural mortality here — a questionable conclusion, since different geographic locations are involved.

Bowen says the DFO also rejected disease as a possible culprit because very little is known on this subject. Since there were no reports of sick or diseased cod from fish harvesters or processors or from sixteen years of cod sampling on the DFO annual bottom trawl surveys, it was not seen to be an issue.

As far as other potential predators of cod, Bowen says little time was spent on that subject as well. "We know a lot about grey seals and we know nothing about most of these other predators." When I approached Dalhousie University whale expert Hal Whitehead on this issue, he said sperm whales are also known to frequent the Cabot Strait area while the cod are overwintering. "They weigh a hell-of-a lot more than a grey seal and they eat cod!" said Whitehead. But one DFO scientist who worked on the various hypotheses said they had no data for sperm whale diets in the Cabot Strait, only data for grey seals. In other words, if there were no data available to support a hypothesis then the hypothesis was not on the list.

One possible explanation for the "missing" cod that the DFO did seriously entertain was that cod are dying because they are now maturing earlier. Doug Swain explained to me that otter trawling in the 1950s targeted the bigger adult cod at such intensity that it favoured the evolution of early-maturing cod. Scientists first began noticing in the early 1960s that cod were maturing smaller and younger, and they hypothesized that this was because only those fish that matured and reproduced before being caught would be able to pass their genes onto the next generation. Swain says that while these changes may have increased the probability of cod surviving to spawn, it also meant fewer offspring since smaller females have fewer and usually smaller eggs, which in turn produce lower quality larvae. Another predicted consequence of early maturation, says Swain, is a shorter life span. Reproduction comes with heavy energy requirements and an increased vulnerability to predation, he says, and "many of these costs are expected to be greater in smaller individuals."

For a while, some scientists suspected that early maturation, and the increased natural mortality associated with it, could be behind the sluggish recovery, but they argued that, if this was so, there would be a strong genetic push for a return to maturing later. They argue that the current high natural mortality of southern Gulf cod is a cause, rather than a consequence, of the continued early maturation of this population, and thus rejected it as possible explanation.

Scientists also considered the possibility that the missing fish were not actually dead but had emigrated to the neighbouring northern Gulf, eastern Scotian Shelf or the Sydney Bight areas. Any possibility of a mass defection to the northern Gulf was ruled out by tagging and stock mixing studies conducted in the mid 1990s. DFO bottom trawl survey data indicated that if there was emigration to the Sydney Bight area, it was negligible and they could find no evidence that there had been an influx of cod aged five and older into the eastern Scotian Shelf area either — where natural mortality of adult fish is also estimated to be very high.

Another possibility was that elevated death rates were due to poor condition — an indicator of fish health — but this too was rejected because they said poor condition in southern Gulf cod was related to seasonal cycles as well as low bottom water temperatures and that, while condition was poor in the 1970s and 1980s, it had improved and was near average levels in the last two decades.

One of the things the DFO didn't assess, says Bowen, was the change in ecosystem structure and functioning. "We know there have been large-scale changes in the ecosystem but how does that affect cod at the level of individual stocks? I don't think anyone knows." It will be recalled that the cumulative removals of fish over many decades and the resulting groundfish collapse resulted in a shift in the marine ecosystem to what some scientists refer to as an "alternate state," whereby the structure and the predation patterns shifted. To ignore the role this might play in the recovery of a fish species seems a monumental oversight. For instance, while it may be true that condition among southern Gulf cod has improved in the last two decades, this clearly has not been enough to lead to a recovery. DFO scientist Jae Choi says that, given the magnitude of the changes that have taken place, good condition would not be sufficient for a recovery. "A relic population that is now more 'healthy,' does not mean it will be able to out-compete the other species that are now resident and dominant," says Choi. "In other words, the [cod's] ecological role and function and position has been displaced or replaced by other species."

To help illustrate, Choi provides a market analogy using Blackberry, the once dominant phone manufacturer:

> Blackberry has gone through some lean times and after consolidating and trimming excess are now in better "condition." But their numerical superiority — their market share — is far lower than their market dominance in the last decade. Just because they are in better condition does not mean they will automatically dominate the phone world. However, if they were in poor condition, they would not even have a chance at dominating and would most likely collapse.

Similarly, the cod, perhaps in better condition, are now living in a very different marine ecosystem than what existed twenty years ago.

Bowen says the DFO also neglected to seriously look at cumulative effects and whether any of the potential threats, once combined, may be causing the cod's high mortality. "You talk to any ecologist and they will say we should be combining them to see whether there might be synergistic or unanticipated effects, but we really don't know how to do that even though we know it's the right thing to do."

When it comes to cumulative effects, one 2006 study out of the U.S. about the effects of contaminants provides a case in point. The study found that cod on George's Bank and Stellwagen Bank were found to have low levels of various contaminants, including PCBs, organochlorine pesticides and trace metals, such as cadmium. Since the level of each contaminant was considered "fairly low" (except for cadmium), the scientists concluded that these levels posed little risk to reproduction and development of the fish. However, they went on to explain that little is known about the cumulative effect of combining small concentrations of many different chemicals "particularly in stocks that may already be stressed." They called it a "neglected area of research."[63]

Another area of research that has been largely ignored is the effect of bottom trawling and dredging on ocean habitat and sea life. We know from one of the first studies ever done on the subject that trawling has been practised with such intensity that in just one year — 1985 — trawlers and dredgers fishing off Canada's east coast plowed a length of track estimated to total more than 4.3 million square kilometres, an area twice the size of Greenland.[64] The magnitude of destruction that would take place over many decades at this unrelenting pace can hardly be contemplated. We do know, however, that trawling decimates biodiversity and that fragile marine life, particularly those that attach themselves to the ocean bottom, such as sponge colonies and coral reefs, are most vulnerable. When trawling occurs in these sensitive habitats, the effects may even be irreversible.

One recent DFO study looking at the "recovery potential" of cod in the southern Gulf as well as on the eastern Scotian Shelf noted that habitat structure means the difference between life and death for a juvenile cod. In the early stages of development, cod require, and indeed select, bottom habitats that display certain characteristics: they tend to be complex, which means they might include corals, eelgrass and macroalgae and they include a substrate — or seabed material — with rocks and gravel of a certain size. In other words, these habitat structures provide hiding places that protect the codlings from predators. But if these habitats are disturbed by fishing gear or by other types of human activity, then their value in protecting the fish is also diminished. According to the study: "Juvenile cod mortality rate is very high in non-complex habitats, compared to complex habitats nearby. The ecological significance of complex habitat on survival of demersal juvenile cod cannot be overstated."[65] Despite this stated significance, quantitative data on the areas of different habitat types impacted by fishing are not available for Canadian waters. Nor are there benchmarks set for acceptable impacts of fishing. The most the DFO has done to date is identify that there is a need to establish these objectives.[66] Trawling and dredging, or threats to seafloor habitat in general, did not make the DFO list of possible explanations for the missing adult cod, perhaps because loss of habitat is only known to directly impact the juveniles. But this is precisely the point: to the degree that it affects juvenile survival rates, habitat loss is definitely known to be a threat to the recovery of the species; yet it has garnered none of the attention that grey seals have.

Another subject that the DFO has downplayed is unreported catch. During the meetings that delivered the grey seal verdict, unreported catch in both the Gulf and on the Scotian Shelf was also ruled out as a contributor to the cod non-recovery. It falls under the broad category of bycatch — a term, it will be recalled, used to describe those fish taken by accident in trawl nets, gill nets, longlines and even traps. Some accidentally caught fish are allowed to be kept and sold: these fish are recorded in fishers' logs and verified by dock-side observers. But the rest are wasted and discarded, either dead or in poor condition, and never reported.

DFO scientists believe that catch misreporting was "substantial" leading up to the groundfish collapse — to the extent that, after reported landings, unreported landings made up a "significant portion" of the rest of the mortality in cod.[67] But since then, because fishing for cod is limited and dock-side monitoring is said to have increased, they believe it is low.

However, in 2007, one Nova Scotian politician made it sound like discarding was still a very serious issue. During hearings at the legislature, Harold Theriault complained about the illegal dumping of cod bycatch on George's Bank, between Cape Cod, Massachusetts and Cape Sable Island in southwestern Nova Scotia. "There's hundreds of tonnes of codfish going over the side, dead, not being reported, because they can't report it, they can't bring it in, they can't dump it, so they can't report it even being dumped," Theriault said.[68]

Ronnie Wolkins has been the president of the South West Fishermen's Rights Association based out of Clark's Harbour on Cape Sable Island, Nova Scotia, since 1996. He has fished with a hook and line for thirty-one years. A vocal advocate of the technology, he claims that it is a more sustainable way to fish since it doesn't damage fish habitat or needlessly kill juvenile or unwanted fish. He points to "destructive fishing practices" as the reason why the cod haven't recovered. He says the large-boat halibut fishery in his district is discarding a lot of dead cod. "They haven't changed their ways. Right now there's so much thrown overboard." Wolkins explains to me that fishers were using the dead codfish as bait for the halibut, but that the DFO doesn't allow this. The DFO "wants them to chuck it overboard," he says.

Susanna Fuller and others at the EAC have spent a lot of time studying and writing about bycatch. "There is cod that gets discarded at sea, mostly on the Scotian shelf and George's Bank, not so much in the Gulf, because there just isn't that much cod there, but we don't have a good handle on the discards." She says a groundfish fisherman catching cod under his haddock quota does have a motive to misreport. "This would be happening in the groundfish trawl fishery and the bottom longlining fishery because they have a cod bycatch limit. If they've already caught their cod but haven't caught their haddock, they would just dump their cod."

It's a point that's hotly contested by many in the fishing industry. They argue that government monitoring of the number of cod taken accidentally shows that bycatch is not the reason why the stocks are failing to recover. But can these data be believed?

Information about discards at sea from the at-sea observer program indicates that the opposite might be true.* One 2010 DFO study aimed at identifying the gaps in discard information overall looked at the data that were available from Canadian commercial fisheries between 2002 and 2006. The study concluded that current levels of at-sea observer coverage for the main fisheries were too low and sporadic to provide any reliable information on discard estimates. For example, in the offshore bottom-trawl groundfishery over the five-year study period, Gavaris and his colleagues reported that for the most part observer coverage of fishing trips was less than 10 percent and sometimes as low as zero. One exception was in 2006 when observer coverage was reported to be as high as 42 percent in fishing district 5z. The study recommended that coverage should be improved immediately on the scallop dredge, lobster trap, groundfish longline and swordfish longline fisheries.[69]

Sara Quigley is a senior advisor in resource management with the DFO. She says we estimate fairly accurately the bycatch that is landed, or kept, but not those that are released or discarded. "The percentage of at-sea observer coverage varies with each fishery," she says, "and if you have very low observer coverage and then you take from those trips the discard data and you extrapolate that up to one hundred percent of the fishery, well, there's a lot of room for error there."

Despite the obvious role that wasteful discarding of fish has had on the devastation of sharks, sea turtles, and a number of groundfish species, it remains largely ignored. Fuller says twenty years have passed since the groundfish collapse and Canada still doesn't have a national bycatch policy. At the time of writing, Fuller said a draft policy existed but it still hadn't been finalized. "I have no idea why it takes so long. But it tells you something," she says. Fuller says the problem is systemic within DFO. "Typically, because of the influence of industry, and I mean big fishing industry, the way it works is that management asks the questions. If management doesn't ask questions about bycatch, science doesn't respond."

A case in point is the shrimp fishery. Fuller says that juvenile cod are definitely getting caught in the shrimp trawls. She also says that shrimp and

---

* At-sea observers are independent technicians accredited by DFO but employed by a private-sector contractor. They stay aboard Canadian fishing vessels to document catches at sea. Their presence also serves as a deterrent against illegal fishing activity. The program was originally cost-shared between DFO (one-third) and the fishing industry (two-thirds) but in 2013, industry ws scheduled to assume full costs of the program.

crab have become very lucrative, and that most fishers don't even want the cod to come back. "They're making more money now on shellfish fisheries," she says. "They're all geared up for shrimp and crab, and it's more money per pound and it's been twenty years. There's a whole generation of fishermen who've never even fished cod."

Since the collapse of the cod, the landings of shrimp in the Scotia-Fundy region alone increased by 470 percent, from only 3,996 metric tonnes in 1990 to 22,733 metric tonnes in 2010. In Atlantic Canada overall, landings increased by 340 percent in that time period, peaking in 2007 with 178,500 metric tonnes. In Newfoundland, the situation was the same. In his book *Lament for an Ocean,* Michael Harris chronicles the years before and after the collapse of the Atlantic cod fishery. He writes that, between 1989 and 1996, revenues from the shellfish industry — shrimp, crab and lobster — had basically replaced, even exceeded, those of the groundfishery. "While the total groundfish revenues for Newfoundland fishermen had collapsed from about $155 million in 1989 to only $26 million in 1996, shellfish revenues for crab, shrimp and lobster had jumped from $51 million to $192 million during the same time period."[70]

There's no doubt that shrimp is now a booming industry and, for the most part, everyone is grateful that a new fishery has filled the groundfish void. But few have stopped to ask about its collateral damage. The shrimp trawl fishery worldwide has been the most notorious of bycatch offenders: catching only 2 percent of the global weight of all fish but producing more than one-third of the total bycatch. Another way of looking at it is that shrimp trawlers usually discard 90 percent of their actual catch. But today, at least in Canada, the shrimp fishery has cleaned up its act enough to gain the blue Marine Stewardship Council (MSC) eco-label: in 2008 for the inshore northern prawn fishery and in 2011 for the offshore fishery.

Part of the reason for the certification is that, since 1993, Canadian shrimp trawls have been fitted with a bycatch exclusion device called a "Nordmore grate," which was originally designed to reduce the capture of jellyfish but was also found to reduce the accidental capture of other fish. Proponents of the grate say it works because it allows bigger swimming fish to escape from the net through an opening above the grate while the smaller, passive shrimp pass through it. However — and these are the relevant points — it's not known how well the creatures too large to pass through the grate, such as adult cod, actually survive the escape process. Furthermore, the grate does not exclude those fish that are about the same size as shrimp, such as small codlings.

SeaChoice, another seafood certification scheme endorsed by the David Suzuki Foundation and the EAC, cites conservation concerns with the northern shrimp fishery despite the MSC labelling. It says that bottom trawling for shrimp damages seafloor habitats and that trawls are among the most damaging gear types in use. It also explains that even if the levels of bycatch are actually reduced by the grate, a low bycatch of small endangered Atlantic cod is still a major conservation concern.

Pauly describes the Nordmore grate as "a bandaid on a gangrenous leg." He says that it only removes the adults: when you actually count the number of small cod caught in the trawl it could be quite substantial. For example, Pauly says a six-centimetre cod weighs about one gram. So one kilogram of these, which doesn't sound like very much in terms of bycatch, represents the loss of 1,000 cod. "So what seems like very little can be thousands of fish, which don't become adults," he says.

Adult cod is also a common bycatch species in the lobster fishery, although it is not known what the levels of bycatch are or to what degree they are impacting the adult population. Fuller says that in the past if fishers caught groundfish in their lobster traps they would just cut them up for bait.

> They're not supposed to do that now. Juveniles can get in and out of the traps and don't get caught but the adults get caught and when you haul up the trap their swim bladders explode so they don't live. I would say that is also an adult cod mortality issue, but no one likes to talk about it.

Fish and Seismic Testing

As we have seen, when scientists were entertaining the various hypotheses to account for the sluggishness of the cod recovery, the only explanations considered were those for which there was supporting data. But what if certain scientific questions have not been studied sufficiently — for whatever reason — and therefore little or no data exist?

Seismic testing is one area where there appears to be a scientific vacuum. Since the 1960s, oil and gas companies have collected roughly 60,000 kilometres of seismic data in the Gulf of St. Lawrence, probing deep beneath the ocean floor and using sound to create a picture of the rock formations — some of which are associated with oil and gas. The sound explosions are produced by what are called air guns, which emit blasts at regular timed intervals — every ten seconds or so for twenty to thirty days. Underwater microphones receive the sound when it is reflected by the undersea rocks.

The sound pulse generated by an air gun array from a distance of one metre underwater is 255 decibels (dB) — louder than a lightening strike on water but quieter than a seafloor volcanic eruption.[*]

---

[*] There is no simple way to compare the intensity of an underwater sound with its equivalent in air because the standard reference pressures used in underwater and in-air acoustics are not the same. In other words, 140 dB

Since few studies have been done on this topic, little is known about the effects of the noise produced by seismic operations on the behaviour and health of marine organisms, including marine mammals, fish and invertebrates. But studies that do exist suggest that marine animals, especially those that can hear, can experience permanent physical damage if they happen to be near an air gun blast.[71] Whales navigate and communicate by echolocation — essentially a natural form of sonar. Studies indicate that extreme noise can cause hemorrhaging around the ears. Over the years, a number of mass strandings of whales have occurred in the vicinity of navy sonar exercises. It is believed that air gun noise is actually more damaging than navy sonar.

Fish with swim bladders — such as cod — are particularly vulnerable to underwater explosions because the gas-filled organs used to control buoyancy can rupture in response to shock waves. Internal injuries, stunning, egg and larval damage and death are all possible effects, studies report. Farther away from the blast they might experience hearing loss and changes in behaviour that might affect their ability to find food or a mate. For instance, cod have been described as versatile vocalists, producing a variety of sounds, some of which are used to court their mates. Given the magnitude of oil and gas exploration in the Gulf, it is reasonable to ask what effect air gun noise might be having on cod's spawning behaviour and reproductive success. It is also reasonable to wonder whether the underwater blasting might explain why some adult cod are "disappearing." However, according to the DFO, information on these and other impacts is scarce because the research has not been undertaken. You could say that the subject is virtually unexplored.

The prospect of future research in this field has been even further stymied by the recent drastic changes the Canadian government made to the *Canadian Environmental Assessment Act* (CEAA), which eliminate federal regulations for both exploratory drilling and for seismic blasting.* Critics of the move say the changes are an effort to fast-track offshore drilling in the Gulf, which will have dire consequences in what is already a compromised ecosystem.

At the time of writing, the Halifax-based energy company Corridor Resources was in the midst of a seven-year exploration licence granted by the Canada-Newfoundland and Labrador Offshore Petroleum Board for exploratory drilling of the "Old Harry Prospect," which is located in the

---

in air (where sound becomes painful to the human ear) is not the same as 140 dB in water. A jet engine, for instance, is 140 dB at one metre. When a conversion factor is applied, it is equivalent to 202 dB in water.

* It should be noted that not all "exploratory wells" are benign. The BP Macondo Deepwater Horizon well in the Gulf of Mexico that gushed oil unabated for three months in 2010 was one of these. It is believed to be the worst marine oil spill in the history of the petroleum industry.

Laurentian Channel about eighty kilometres from Newfoundland. The Old Harry Prospect area is the principal spawning ground for both the Gulf cod and the redfish. The company itself has acknowledged that no less than forty-five "at risk" species and populations of marine mammals, fish, turtles and sea birds are thought to occur in the project area.

According to Isabelle Perrault, a senior communications advisor with the Canadian Environmental Assessment Agency, since the Environmental Assessment (EA) for the project was already underway when the CEAA was amended in 2012, the "Old Harry" project is still subject to the requirements of the earlier Act but that the regulator is now required to complete its review of Corridor's EA by the summer of 2013. As this book was going to print the EA was still in progress. However, a recent report in the *Globe and Mail* revealed that one aspect of the review — which was to gauge public opinion from those living in the Gulf region, in the vicinity of the exploratory well — has been terminated. While it remains to be seen what form a public consultation will take, the news report suggested it would not be one that provides an additional hurdle to the project proponent.[72] If the project is approved, Corridor plans to drill a 2.5 kilometre exploratory well beneath the seafloor for natural gas and light oil in 2014.

The "Evil Troika" of Climate Change

In the mid-1980s scientists with the DFO began noticing serious changes in the ocean's underwater chemistry, particularly in the Lower St. Lawrence Estuary (LSLE), spanning the area from the entry of the Saguenay River onto the St. Lawrence to the waters of the northwest Gulf. They found severe hypoxic conditions. The lay term for this is "dead zone": it describes areas where the oxygen level is so low that it doesn't support life. In technical terms it means there is less than two milligrams of dissolved oxygen per litre. These lethal and life-less "blobs" are widespread, the most infamous one located in the Gulf of Mexico, which, in 2011, was estimated to cover 17,500 square kilometres — an area slightly smaller than Lake Ontario. Today there are more than four hundred dead zones around the world, but few people have heard about the one right here in Atlantic Canada — one that some believe might be spreading.

By 2003, roughly 1,300 square kilometres of the LSLE — equivalent to a quarter of the size of Prince Edward Island — was bathed in hypoxic waters. Like the one in the Gulf of Mexico, it has been around for a while — many decades in fact. According to the DFO, the dead zone in the Gulf is caused by a combination of two things: the bottom waters of the Channel have been getting progressively warmer as a result of climate change, and, at the same time, there has been an increasing amount of nutrient pollution from human activities. Scientists say municipal sewage, chemical fertilizers and manure from agricultural land inject large quantities of nitrates and phosphates into the ocean, which fertilize the ocean plants — the plankton — and fuel their rapid growth. When the uneaten plankton die, they sink to the bottom and the process of bacterial decomposition takes oxygen out of the water.

It has been shown that very low oxygen levels can be lethal to fish and other sea life, causing large-scale mortality. However, at higher levels — that is, not lethal but still not good — hypoxic conditions can cause physiological stress and what are called sub-lethal effects, such as reduced growth and reproduction. Fish have also been known to abandon low-oxygen areas altogether.

Today, part of the Laurentian Channel — the submerged 1,200 kilometre-long gully frequented by both the northern and southern Gulf cod — is a dead zone. Small pockets of the deep Channel are so oxygen depleted that laboratory studies show the low level of oxygen would cause 5 to 50 percent of cod to die after a four-day exposure. But much of the Channel has oxygen at levels that would fall in the sub-lethal category for cod: high enough not to kill them, but low enough to slow their growth.[73]

In 2002, DFO scientist Denis Chabot explored the effects of hypoxia on northern Gulf cod — a stock that has to deal with severe hypoxia levels for a large proportion of its range. He found that cod are not able to swim for as long, or as fast, in hypoxic conditions, making them more vulnerable to predation, or fishing, and less able to hunt for food.[74] He reported that hypoxic conditions also slowed digestion, which caused the cod to eat less. The study also looked at the distribution of northern cod in relation to oxygen-depleted areas and found that cod avoided areas that were lethal but that a large proportion (nearly half the stock) still frequented areas with sub-lethal conditions.

MacKenzie says the information about the hypoxic waters in the Gulf has to be linked to the depletion of the cod stocks there.

> The northern Gulf cod have been forced to abandon part of their former range and the DFO has even admitted that. The southern Gulf cod overwinter around the Cabot Strait area — in a deeper spot, where it's warmer — but this spot is less oxygenated than the open ocean. So this could be part of the increased vulnerability of these fish.

MacKenzie poses an important question: If the hypoxic waters — or any other factor or combination thereof — has made the cod more vulnerable to predation by grey seals, then are the seals really the cause of the mortality? MacKenzie says the role of top predators is to enhance the health of its prey by removing the weakest members. But it can't be held responsible for whatever made them weak in the first place.

According to the DFO, another stressor that is believed to work synergistically with hypoxia is ocean acidification — which is occurring in the Gulf of St. Lawrence but currently thought to be weak and affecting only the surface layer. In her 2009 book on the plight of the global ocean, *Sea Sick: The Global Ocean in Crisis,* Alanna Mitchell describes the molecular exchange that takes place at the thin membrane between the air and the sea. She says that here not only does excess carbon in the atmosphere from burning fossil fuels get absorbed by the ocean, but also oxygen, produced by plankton, gets released into the atmosphere. "Every other breath you take comes from the ocean," she says.

Once the carbon is in the ocean it reacts with water to form carbonic acid, which causes a decrease in ocean pH. "It's the part that scientists are most concerned about because as the water becomes more acidic, it's less able to support the kind of life it has evolved to support," she says. Calcium, which is needed to build shells, bones and teeth, is less available to creatures to use when the ocean becomes more acidic, and shells start to erode — a phenomenon that is already happening in the Arctic and Southern Ocean where the water is colder and absorbs more carbon dioxide. She says, "The pH is a fundamental descriptor of a life system, and when it alters, it's like a knock-on effect, a cascading effect. We're not exactly sure what else will shift. Some creatures are going to do fine, but there are many — and it's unclear which ones — that are not going to survive."[75]

While there are still many unknowns about how acidification will affect marine life, a great deal of literature dating back to the 1960s exists on what it has done to freshwater fish. In lakes and rivers, acid rain — from sulphur dioxide and nitrogen oxide emissions — resulted in a whole chain of unforeseen events that eventually killed fish, reduced their numbers or eliminated them as a species altogether. We know that at a certain pH, females won't spawn and fish eggs cannot hatch: even if they do, the hatchlings cannot survive the acidity. We also know that some fish — smallmouth bass, walleye, brook trout and salmon — cannot tolerate high acidity and tend to disappear first.

But what happens if you have both acidification and hypoxia in a marine environment? Although nobody knows with certainty what the cumulative effects are, it is possible that when they exist at the same time, as they do in the Gulf, the process of obtaining oxygen from the water — also known as respiration — is even more difficult for fish like cod.

Hypoxia and acidification are two parts of the "evil troika" of global climate change, says Mitchell. The other is temperature. "The ocean contains the switch of life. Not land, not the atmosphere, the ocean. And that switch can be flipped off," she says. Life in the ocean could survive the dying of everything on the land, "but if everything in the ocean were to die tomorrow, everything on land would die as well because we're fully dependent on the chemical systems of the ocean to give us life."

Chapter 6

Limiting Factors

> We don't actually value anything unless it's rare.
>
> — David Johnston, Marine Scientist, Duke University

Once it was discovered that the grey seal population on Sable Island was growing exponentially, alarm bells began to go off. It will be recalled that the multiplying herds were characterized by some as being virtually unstoppable and were soon going to be spilling onto the streets of Halifax! Of course not all cull proponents resorted to such absurdity, but many did argue that the population growth was evidence that human intervention was needed to stabilize the population. They also argued that, in the absence of this, disease or some other catastrophic agent would inevitably set in, forcing the population to crash. But according to experts, there are a number of factors that naturally limit the growth of populations without a resulting collapse: there is good evidence this is already occurring on Sable Island. There is also evidence that even without a cull, human activity is already negatively influencing the survival of grey seals. Climate change and the loss of sea ice as well as our contamination of marine environments are already effecting pinniped populations around the globe, as well as here on the Atlantic coast.

Population Growth Slowing Down

Exponential growth cannot go on forever; sooner or later any population will run into limits. Ecologists call this the carrying capacity: it is basically the maximum stable population size that a particular environment can support over a long period of time. As a population becomes more crowded, each individual has access to an increasingly smaller share of food and space, which are finite resources. The DFO calls these "density-dependent factors": it looks like they're kicking in on Sable Island.

Zoe Lucas has spent several decades living much of the year on Sable studying its flora and fauna. She has also been studying the garbage. On any given day, Lucas might travel its length on her ATV doing beach surveys, collecting rubbish the waves have washed ashore. She's noticed a change over the years.

> I have to do the beach surveys even when the seals are there, and during the breeding season for grey seals it's become increasingly more difficult to do that because of the crowding on the beaches. But, during the last couple of years, I found I had less problems and there seemed to be more space between the animals.

Lucas says that either the seals are spreading inland or there are fewer animals. DFO staff and scientists, who also make their way around the seals on ATVs while doing their research, had the same impression.

"Over the past couple of years it has been easier to navigate the beach," says Don Bowen, who heads up the population studies for the Sable Island seals. But he says drawing any conclusions from these observations is tricky: "Essentially, you've got a fifty kilometer island that's covered from stem to stern with seals," he says. "It wouldn't take a huge redistribution of animals up into the dunes a bit more to skew our perception." Bowen describes how the island is colonized each year: "Hundreds of pregnant females will arrive on the beach together and they'll leave together and then they'll arrive on the beach somewhere else together," he explains. "If there are already animals on the beach, it's as if they'll move preferentially into that region and so you get these little seeds starting to grow out." The way the island is colonized by the seals is different every year but the broad scale pattern is the same.

Adult grey seals hauled out on the beach, west spit, Sable Island, late December.
Photo courtesy Zoe Lucas.

Grey seals and Sable Island's wild horses, east end of the island, mid-January.
Photo courtesy Zoe Lucas.

Bowen says the acid test of the numbers will be the next population survey, scheduled for 2014.

According to Bowen, the fact that population surveys occur only every three to four years makes it difficult to pinpoint when the shift happened precisely, but he says that sometime in the early 2000s the exponential growth of the Sable Island seal herd stopped. The population is still growing, he says, but as of 2010 the annual growth rate was only 4 percent. As we have seen, the growth rate during the exponential growth period was 13 percent. During this phase, pups were being born at a nearly constant rate, and the total population was doubling every seven years. In the last several years on Hay Island the rate of increase has slowed as well, indicating that populations there may have reached their carrying capacity. In the Gulf of St. Lawrence, where pup production is much more variable, grey seal pup numbers peaked in 2004 at 14,200 and since then seem to have stabilized in the 11,000 range.

For the most part, pinnipeds, such as grey seals, require predator-free islands, sandy beaches, or stable ice floes to breed and flourish. But as their numbers increase, these pupping locales can become crowded, with a scarcity of food. In response, fewer pups are born, and those that are, have a higher chance of dying through injury, disease or starvation. Bowen says the growth of the Sable herd is clearly slowing down; he is pretty certain he knows why.

Starting in the 1960s, Bowen and his team began permanently marking or branding a random sample of grey seal pups. "It's almost like a tattoo and you can identify the individual for its entire life." This has been done periodically, over the years, so that today a total of 7,200 grey seals, both male and female, have been branded. For each of these animals you can then develop what Bowen calls a "sighting history," which is unique to each individual and provides a good way to tell if a seal is still alive. The first "sighting" of the seal is recorded when it is branded as a pup. After that, juveniles typically don't come back to Sable Island until they get pregnant, which means several years can go by before the seal is sighted again on the beach. As soon as this occurs, a sighting history develops. "We do a census every week [during the breeding season] of the entire island to look for these animals," Bowen explains. "So, over the course of time we keep track of these sightings." Bowen uses a blackboard to illustrate an example of a sighting history. He jots down the number one — representing the first sighting when the pup was branded — followed by a series of zeros. This means the seal wasn't seen again on the island and is probably dead.

On the basis of this long-term study, Bowen and his colleagues are able to estimate the juvenile survival rate. They found that, during the exponential growth phase of the population, about 70 percent of juveniles were surviving to the age of six or eight, when they'd return to the island to give birth. However, between 1998 and 2011, survival dropped substantially to only 33 percent. He says the most likely cause is food scarcity: he postulates that the young animals are losing the competition for food to the more experienced ones.

Drawing on clues from another study that is currently underway, Bowen is trying to make sense of why the juveniles might be running out of food. At one time, scientists used to study grey seals the same way they study nesting birds — only during the breeding season — when large groups of relatively sedentary animals are easy to observe. But this shed little light on what grey seals were doing the majority of the time, hidden from view beneath the ocean surface. In an attempt to get a glimpse of their mysterious, subaquatic lives, in 2009 fifteen randomly selected grey seals were equipped with satellite transmitters so that their whereabouts could be continuously tracked. Bowen and his colleagues wanted to find out more about their social behaviour and whether these "instrumented" seals interacted with each other when they were at sea. Bowen describes some of the data he's seen so far as "extraordinary" and says it has "transformed" his perception of what the ocean looks like to a grey seal.

With only fifteen seals tagged from the Sable Island population — estimated to be at least 260,000 — the scientists thought the chances of two of these seals running into one another was "astronomically small," says Bowen. It had also been assumed up to now that grey seals were solitary foragers. But instead, the study found they were running into each other all the time — this usually happened on the shallow offshore banks when they were foraging for food. "This is because there are so few supermarkets," Bowen explains. He discovered that submarine areas, previously thought to be good grey seal feeding grounds, actually were not. "There are large sections of the Scotian Shelf that they don't use because it's not a profitable place to feed," he says. "There's no point in eating something if it costs the seal more to eat it than it gets out of it," explains Bowen. Scientists are now trying to figure out whether the interactions are just coincidental or if the seals are actually helping each other to forage. If they are, then there may be some kind of social structure at sea so that the seals "receive greater benefit from being part of a group than being alone."[76]

As a way to determine, independent of seal diet, whether grey seals and cod interact, the same seven-year study has also tagged about six hundred cod in the southern Gulf and on the eastern Scotian Shelf. "Do these animals ever bump into one another in the open ocean and, if they do, how often do grey seals appear to eat them?" While the study is ongoing, Bowen says the data so far indicate that "seals and cod are feeding in the same areas but are not necessarily interacting as predator-prey."

When it comes to understanding the juvenile mortality of grey seals, Bowen says that the satellite data show that the seals concentrate in these more profitable areas. "If you look at where the juveniles are feeding, they're pushed to the outer areas that are less profitable." He says this could be affecting their survival.

Bowen says that sometimes when populations reach food or space limits, all the individuals in the population do poorly: this can lead to what he calls "overcompensation." When overcompensation happens, the population rises above the carrying capacity, until the "bubble bursts," at which point the population drops rapidly, then eventually works its way up again. Bowen says that this doesn't appear to be the case on Sable Island, where the juveniles are losing out and being out-competed by the adults. "When there are clear winners and losers, you tend to reach carrying capacity smoothly."

Mystery Wound Raises Questions

While food scarcity appears to be the leading cause of the high mortality of juveniles from the Sable Island herd, there is another, more puzzling, factor that is also contributing to it. Since 1993, Zoe Lucas has been studying the seals that have been washing up dead on the island's beaches. Over a seven-year period, Lucas found nearly 5,000 seal corpses, 2 percent of which displayed a slash — characteristic of a white shark attack. These have some tell-tale signs: marks left on the seal bones as well as shark tooth fragments and bite wound patterns that have been identified on white shark victims elsewhere. But for the other 98 percent, which display a "corkscrew" wound, the cause of death is somewhat of a mystery.

A "corkscrew" wound, like the name implies, is a long, smooth, clean-edged cut running from the chin of the seal spiraling around it's body, like the stripe on a candy cane, and ending at some point between its shoulders and pelvis. These wounds almost always cut into the hide and blubber but leave the muscle intact. Lucas, a vocational scientist, has been working with Lisa Natanson, a scientist from the U.S. National Marine Fisheries Service; in 2010 they published a paper in which they hypothesized that the Greenland shark was responsible for the signature wounds.[77]

According to Lucas and Natanson, the Greenland shark is the most likely predator, based on what it likes to eat, its foraging behaviour and its jaw and tooth morphology. This shark's distribution and range also seem to fit the bill. While mostly a cold and deep-water shark — with a predilection for the frigid waters of the Arctic — Greenland sharks are found in the Gulf of St. Lawrence, on the Scotian Shelf and in the Gulf of Maine. They are also known to frequent the colder, shallower waters of the Scotian Shelf in the winter months — when the grey seals are gathering to breed.

Trying to reconstruct the feeding event that leads to the gruesome injury is challenging, and controversial. Lucas and her colleague believe that the large and sluggish shark likely ambushes the seal, biting it head first. The shark's lower teeth cut into the hide while the upper teeth, which are not cutting teeth, hold the seal, and this piece of hide tissue with blubber attached is pulled and torn off the body, presumably as the seal tries to escape. Lucas and Natanson say the characteristic corkscrew path of the tear is explained by the way the collagen fibres in the skin and blubber of marine mammals is wound around the body — so as the tissue is pulled, the tear runs diagonally around the seal.

Bowen imagines it happening differently. He says the only way he could see the wounds occurring is if the pup actually goes into the shark's mouth: "So the animal goes in, about half a body length into the shark's mouth, before it realizes it's in there and then as it's being bitten, it spins its way out." Bowen says this spinning response could be an anti-predator response among pinnipeds and has been observed in harbour seals. "It's got to be the shark teeth that are making the cut because it *is* a cut, like someone took a scalpel. It's not a tearing."

In the last few years, there has been a spate of seals washing up on the east coast of the U.K. and in Northern Ireland with wounds that are remarkably consistent with the corkscrew injury on Sable Island seals. However, scientists from the Sea Mammal Research Unit at the Scottish Oceans Institute hypothesized that the injury was anything but natural. They argue the laceration is caused by the seals being drawn headfirst through a ducted propeller, common to a wide range of ships including tugs, self propelled barges and rigs, and various types of offshore support vessels and research boats. In 2012, this was the conclusion reached by six scientists in a study published in *Aquatic Mammals*, who also suggested the injuries were associated with the increased ship traffic associated with the building of offshore wind farms in their area. The authors postulated that the female seals may be lured to their deaths by the low frequency hum produced by the propeller blades — resembling the mating calls of male seals — where they are then sucked up by the powerful pull.[78]

Lucas says she and her colleague were able to eliminate the possibility of involvement by vessels at Sable Island because of evidence that some kills occurred close to the beach. In 1996 two pups were found wearing time-depth recorders, which are used to monitor foraging and diving behaviour. The recorder registered that they were killed in two metres of water, just thirty metres from shore — a depth and location not accessible to ships. But the U.K. scientists aren't swayed by the evidence and say that the presence of ExxonMobil just offshore of the island — the closest platform being five kilometres away — would result in a great deal of shipping traffic, and potential danger for seals.

Bowen says he doesn't buy into the U.K. hypothesis. Propellers may be the cause of the U.K. seal deaths, but he doesn't believe they have anything to do with the Sable Island seals, mainly because the wounds are different. "The Scottish wounds almost invariably start at the nostril, or the mouth area, and go all around the body, sometimes the whole length," he explains. "The ones at Sable usually start at the neck and wrap around and stop at the thorax. There's also much more variability in the extent of the wounds," he says. "We've looked at vessel traffic and there's a big wide swath around Sable, and because of the navigability of the waters there are very few ships, at least certainly around the time of year when we see these wounds on grey seals," he says.

Lucas says the number of grey seals with the corkscrew kill increased over the period of her study, from a few dozen to five hundred a year. Bowen says that while it may sound like a lot, from a population dynamics perspective the numbers are not significant. "If sharks are killing a few hundred or even a thousand grey seals a year, it's trivial," he says. Bowen explains that even when the grey seal population on Sable was growing exponentially, 30 percent of juveniles were dying from a variety of causes. He says shark predation was still low enough to allow for the exponential growth to happen. "We do know that the sum total of all the various sources of mortality — disease, starvation, shark predation — were small enough to allow this population to grow exponentially," he explained. "You can't get a grey seal population to grow any faster than that."

Lucas, who is currently working with Natanson on a follow-up report to clarify some of the outstanding issues, is well aware of the controversy in the

U.K. but says the role of the Greenland shark will remain pure speculation until someone is able to witness and document what is actually happening under water.

Marine Mammal and Ocean Health Linked

Disease can also play an important role in the population dynamics of marine mammals. In fact, as seal populations recover, there is a greater chance of what are called "density-dependent" diseases, as a result of crowding, which creates conditions in which diseases can establish themselves and be more easily transmitted. But according to Bowen, in the last fifty to seventy years, grey seals here have been pretty resistant to those kinds of influences. To date, diseases have not been a limiting factor for grey seals, although there is always that possibility.

In the winter of 2012 Rebecca Aldworth, head of Humane Society International, was on Hay Island, but this time it wasn't to observe the grey seal hunt. She heard the hunt wasn't going ahead because there were no markets for seal products, so she had taken the opportunity to film the seals that were alive. She found half the pups were already dead. "We checked for skull compressions and bullet holes and we didn't find anything and it doesn't seem to have been human-induced." Aldworth says what was unusual about the dead pups was that they weren't starving but appeared to be perfectly healthy seals. At the time, Aldworth speculated that the deaths could have been caused by a virus, since some seal species are susceptible to both distemper and influenza, which have killed seal pups elsewhere.

A virus did strike in the summer of 1988 and again in 2002 when a mass die-off of more than 50,000 harbour seals in the North Sea wiped out more than half the population. The cause of death appeared to be the phocine distemper virus; in both cases the outbreak was thought to have started on the small Danish island of Anholt, between Denmark and Sweden, but then spread to other colonies in the Irish Sea and in the Dutch Wadden Sea. Since the harbour seal is a relatively sedentary species during the breeding season, scientists who were trying to understand how the disease might have spread hypothesized that the grey seal, which tended to share the same haul-out spaces with their smaller relative and was known to move long distances, could be a vector or a carrier of the disease, but wasn't as susceptible to it. It is estimated that three hundred grey seals died in 1988 from the virus and that female carriers, while not showing clinical signs of the disease, might have lost their pups and suffered from a weakened immune system.

Shortly after Aldworth's grim discovery, DFO scientists visited Hay Island and counted more than four hundred dead grey seals — the majority of them weaned pups in good shape, showing no physical signs of trauma, as well as five adults. Based on current estimates of pup mortality rates in the Sable herd — where it's normal for 3 to 10 percent of pre-weaned pups to die — it is expected that as many as 250 of the 2,500 pups born on Hay Island will die from a variety of natural causes before being fully weaned. According to Bowen, from this angle, four hundred pups is certainly a higher fraction, but still not high enough to raise any red flags or to affect the population dynamics of the Eastern Shore herd. But the fact that the dead pups looked otherwise healthy was considered noteworthy.

At the time, samples were taken for testing to the Atlantic Veterinary College in Charlottetown, Prince Edward Island. A few months later they had narrowed down the cause. DFO seal specialist Mike Hammill says a protozoan parasite was to blame, but that scientists needed to know more before they could figure out how the seals got it. He says seal pups have weak immune systems because of their young age, and that while the source and the mode of transmission are still unknown, he speculates the mother seals may have picked up the parasite by drinking the swampy island water, which is full of feces, and transmitted it through their placenta or milk. Alternatively, an insect or fly might have carried it.

Another possible explanation involves water-borne pathogens, such as protozoan parasites, known to be carried in ship ballast water. In late September 2011, just a couple of months prior to the seal die-off, a 230-metre derelict cargo carrier called the *M. V. Miner* ran aground on Scatarie Island, impaled in shallow waters on the northern side of the island, in the vicinity of Hay Island. The ship was being towed to a Turkish scrap yard when it broke free of its tow-line in heavy seas. At the time, although 10,000 litres of marine diesel oil, lubricants and oily, likely contaminated, bilge waste were removed from the ship, the coast guard reported sheening at the stern of the wreck, which raised concerns that some had escaped from vessel. The provincial government also expressed concern at the time that the carrier was a threat to local fishing grounds because of possible contamination from lead paint crumbling from the deteriorating hull as well as from electronic gear housed inside. But little was said about what was done with the ballast water.

John Harwood, a professor at the Scottish Ocean's Institute, reported in the *Journal of Mammology* in 2001 that discharge of ballast water can be extremely dangerous for marine mammals. Cargo ship discharge has resulted in the widespread distribution of toxin-producing marine organisms; in 1997, the toxin produced by one such organism — a dinoflagellate called *Gymnodinium catenatum* — was implicated in the mass mortality of 70 percent of the Mediterranean monk seal population on the coast of the former Spanish Sahara.

When Gary Andrea, a spokesperson with the province's Department of Natural Resources, was asked what was done with the *M. V. Miner's* ballast water he said that within the first week of the ship being grounded, the ballast water was dumped into the ocean at Scatarie Island to try to float the ship higher so the vessel could be towed off. But he said he didn't think the ballast water could have been contaminated. "The ballast tanks were cleaned, inspected, and refilled with fresh water prior to the vessel being discharged in Montreal for towing." He also says that because the ship spent all its time in Canadian waters, moving bulk ore through the Great Lakes and down the St. Lawrence River, the discharge was deemed clean, though it was never actually tested.[79]

A growing body of evidence now indicates that marine mammals may become more susceptible to diseases because of exposure to contaminants found in the marine environment. In other words, as ocean health deteriorates so too may the health of marine mammal populations. Although it is not known to what extent contaminants currently pose risks to the grey seal populations here, they should nevertheless be acknowledged as a potential risk. For example, oceans are known to be the eventual destination of what are called xenobiotics — the invisible chemicals, pollutants and substances that are not supposed to be there. A compelling body of evidence now indicates that toxic waste, particularly from industrial sites worldwide, can physically weaken seals, affect their immunity and make them more susceptible to disease. One 2007 study, for instance, looked at trends in marine mammal disease and mass strandings and found that the annual number of mass mortality events in the U.S. doubled between 1980 and 1990 and that since 2000 there have been seven to eight events a year, linked to biotoxins, viruses, bacteria, parasites, human interactions, oil spills and changes in oceanographic conditions due to climate change. The study also noted that persistent organic pollutants (POPs) — compounds like DDT and PCBs that accumulate in animal tissue — can weaken the immune systems of marine mammals and that exposure to these chemicals may have played a role in the mass die-off events.[80]

The Gulf of St. Lawrence on Canada's east coast, for instance, contains a vast assortment of these toxins, the result of industrial and municipal waste, agricultural runoff, shipping, dredging operations, aquaculture and oil and gas development. Many made their way there via the St. Lawrence River from the heavily industrialized and populated Great Lakes region. Once in the Gulf, xenobiotics disperse and settle, then travel through the marine food web, from tiny organisms to fish, and eventually into the organs and tissues of long-lived predators near the top of the web, such as whales, seals and humans, where they biomagnify or become more highly concentrated.

For instance, we have long known that some of these xenobiotics have taken a terrible toll on beluga whales in the St. Lawrence Estuary. Beluga whales are considered a species at risk and currently listed as threatened. According to the DFO's 2012 *Recovery Strategy for the St. Lawrence Beluga*, belugas are dying from infectious diseases caused by parasites or bacteria, and from tumours — typically in the older animals — partly attributed to eating fish contaminated by the cocktail of carcinogens carried downstream.

A telling indication of the persistence of organochlorine compounds is that while some have been banned in Canada for more than thirty years, they are still found in high concentrations in both adult and baby belugas, who are exposed in gestation as well as through their mother's milk. For instance, high contaminant loads of PCBs, DDT, Toxaphene and Mirex — just to name a few — have been found in dead belugas; the concentrations of some of these toxins in the St. Lawrence whales were found to be one hundred times higher than their Arctic counterparts.[81]

While attention has been paid in Canada to the plight of the beluga, there is much less known about the presence of contaminants and their possible impacts on other marine animals.* However, if belugas in the St. Lawrence estuary are being harmed by contaminants, then it stands to reason that other predators high up in the food web, dependent largely on fish for food, are as well.

A 2001 DFO study out of the Maurice Lamontagne Institute in Mont-Joli, Quebec, found polychlorinated biphenyls (PCBs) and organochlorinated pesticides, such as DDT, in the blubber samples of harbour seals from the St. Lawrence Estuary, and grey, harp and hooded seals from the Gulf of St. Lawrence. More recently, in 2011, polybrominated diphenyl ethers (PBDE) — flame retardant compounds used to reduce product flammability — were also detected in the blubber and blood of harbour, grey and harp seal pups. The levels of contamination varied and were attributed to a variety of things. For one, contaminants accumulate with age, so older seals had higher contaminant burdens. Since nursing mothers transfer some of their contaminant load to their pups through their milk, reproductive females had lower levels than males and non-reproductive females. Levels also depend on migration

---

*   Despite the importance of monitoring and understanding the effects of xenobiotics in the ocean ecosystem, in 2012 the Conservative government, under Stephen Harper, cut funding for DFO science and technical staff who were working on contaminants. Government scientists who have worked for years on long-term databases showing trends and patterns in contaminant levels, as well as those who have discovered the presence of new contaminants, like flame retardants, in marine animals, have been cut. Databases will likely be turned over to universities, but it's unclear if they will be able to get the funding required to carry on routine monitoring. So, for instance, data showing contaminant levels in beluga whales, which have been monitored for nearly three decades, will now have such gaps that trends will no longer be apparent. The cuts also mean a loss of expertise, or internal capacity, within government to inform policy.

and feeding patterns and proximity to sources of industrial and agricultural pollution. In other words, what they eat and how long they spend in the Gulf seems to make a difference.[82]

Perhaps not surprisingly, the highest POP levels were found in harbour seals, the least migratory species, residing and foraging year-round in the highly contaminated St. Lawrence Estuary. But hooded seals also had relatively high levels, which presented a bit of a mystery to the researchers since these seals spend much of the year foraging in waters off southern Greenland. However, despite its distance from industrial or agriculture activity, the Arctic is not as pristine as we'd like to think. Its ocean acts as a sink for contaminants that have in some cases been discharged half a world away. Transported via ocean and atmospheric currents, these toxic chemicals bioaccumulate and biomagnify in the Arctic marine ecosystem, as well as in the bodies of northern Indigenous people, who eat fish and marine animals at or near the top of the food chain.

Hooded seals also feed mainly on long-lived deep-water fish that would have higher levels of contamination. Diet also helps explain why harp seals, which spend much of the year in the Arctic, had the lowest POP contaminant levels: they feed largely on short-lived and therefore less contaminated, invertebrates. Grey seals in the study were somewhere in the middle, spending at least seven months of the year residing and foraging in the waters of the northern and southern Gulf. Although a small portion of the herd disperse to waters off eastern Newfoundland, Nova Scotia and the northeastern United States, a significant number remain in Gulf waters year round.

The issue of contaminated seal blubber raises serious questions about whether products such as seal oil, marketed as an Omega-3 supplement, is actually safe for human consumption. It also points to other health safety issues that Debbie MacKenzie has been raising with government officials since 2006. She says that because seals have been erroneously classified as "fish" they are not bound by the same rules and directives as other mammals that are butchered and sold for their meat and hide. For example, she says all other exports of animal products must be accompanied by Veterinary Health Certificates, which essentially indicate that the animal was "healthy at the time of slaughter." However, because seals are classified as seafood they are regulated under the *Fish Inspection Act*, and subject to the same requirements applicable to fish. "Certificates attesting to the wholesomeness of 'fish' are not generated by veterinarians but by fish inspectors, who have been trained to screen for food threats to humans that might be found in fish," she writes.[83]

MacKenzie has expressed particular concern in recent years over the presence of brucellosis in seals: an infectious bacterial disease that is present in many marine mammal species and has been positively identified in Canadian harp, hooded and grey seals. Called a zoonotic pathogen, which can cause illness in animals and be passed to humans through contact, brucellosis manifests as flu-like symptoms that may be chronic and last for years. It is not transmissible between humans. It's known to affect farm animals like cows, pigs, sheep and goats. What concerns MacKenzie is the potential for brucellosis to spread to those who are at higher risk of contacting infected seal tissue and blood — the sealers. But little, if any, study has been done to assess the risk to sealers, to determine the incidence of the illness in this group or to educate them about the risks.[84]

Seals and the Loss of Sea Ice

One factor that we do know is profoundly affecting seal populations is climate change. While the ramifications of this on the ocean and its ecosystems and on life itself, are daunting to say the least, we are already seeing its impact on seal species that depend on ice to breed, including grey seals in the southern Gulf of St. Lawrence.

In January 2010, the ice in the Gulf of St. Lawrence was not normal. It had formed late in the season and was thin and fragile. According to ice specialists, when sea ice forms it starts out as what are called "frazils" or needle-like crystals. In a process of thickening and clumping these eventually become slushy balls called "shuga," which adhere to form pancake ice. This consolidates and thickens and becomes a thick piece of continuous ice — first-year ice — the kind certain species of seals in eastern Canada need for birthing and nursing their young. However, in 2010 the first year ice was scanty at best; what little there was didn't last very long.

On January 26 a rainstorm with strong westerly winds swept across the region, destroying most of the ice in the Northumberland Strait between Prince Edward Island and Nova Scotia. Mike Hammill, who was working on the grey seal population survey at the time, had flown over the area a few days before and after the storm. He says the pup mortality was "extensive" and that an estimated seven hundred pups had drowned — or about 16 percent of the seals born on the ice that year.

The following two winters weren't much colder. According to Rebecca Aldworth, who was in the area to observe the harp seal hunt in the Gulf in the spring of 2012, by the time the hunt was set to begin there was so little ice remaining as a result of the warm temperatures, rain and wind that the sealers opened the hunt four days early. "When the killing commenced, there were very few live seal pups left in the southern Gulf," she says. "In an area where there are supposed to be hundreds of thousands of seal pups, we found only a few thousand." Weeks later, reports of dead whitecoats washing up on the western shores of Cape Breton emerged.

Gulf ice is used by three species of seal: harp, hooded and occasionally grey seals. According to Hammill and his colleagues, in the last century the ice floes in the Gulf provided a refuge for breeding grey seals trying to escape harassment on the coastal and island beaches. At one time, in the not too distant past, less than 1 percent of the pups in the Gulf would have been born on land and ice availability wasn't much of a concern. In 1955, ice build-up in the Gulf was increased by the construction of the Canso Causeway linking the island of Cape Breton to Nova Scotia. Prior to this, ice would drift out past Port Hawkesbury through the channel and into the Atlantic, where it would be readily destroyed, along with the pups, by the rough seas. However, once the causeway was built, this exit of Gulf ice was blocked; instead it moved north, building up in the Canso Strait and St. George's Bay areas, which allowed stable ice to form in the southern Gulf as well, creating prime pupping habitat for grey seals.[85]

Ice data from the Canadian Ice Service show that, since 1981, the most ice encountered in the Gulf in a single season occurred in 1989–1990, and the least occurred in 2009–2010. While the ice charts show that ice coverage fluctuated considerably from year to year, starting in 1968 (the first year data were provided), prior to 1994–1995 conditions were above normal. However, since then, they've been below normal; in the last several years, ice quality and coverage have deteriorated. For seals that need it to breed, good ice has become hard to find.

According to Hammill, in the last twenty years, there have been some years when 60 percent of the grey seal pups were born on land. "New" colonies have recently appeared on quiet, predator-free islands. "For a long time we had the impression that poor ice would have a negative impact on grey seals in the Gulf," he says. "In one sense we still think that way, but the grey seals have the same problem as harp seals. If the ice is good enough for pupping, the seals are 'tricked' into pupping on the ice, then a storm comes through and the animals are thrown into the water and drown because the pieces are too small for them to haul-out on again or they're crushed or re-peatedly thrown in." In other words, the back-to-the-land movement by some grey seals might be what saves them. He says grey seals are now colonizing islands they weren't using in the recent past either because there was good ice, or because it was too cold or there was too much disturbance. He says Brion Island, for example, had several families living on it at one time. "Now, there are only one to two families, and they are people that don't wander around or make a whole lot of noise so the seals are not threatened." Another island that has been recolonized is Pictou Island in the Northumberland Strait. For the last several winters, thousands of grey seals have found refuge there from the deteriorating ice floes. But, in 2006, a storm surge wiped out three-quarters of the pups on the beach, who were still too young to swim. According to news reports, one eyewitness, a resident on the island, said the mother seals kept pushing the pups with their noses, trying to keep them on the beach, but eventually the force of the waves swept the pups out to sea, where they drowned. Some of the herd had made it to higher ground.[86]

Hammill says that, because it can take about a month before a grey seal is able to swim, how long the ice will last is crucial to the pups' survival; yet reliable predictions about this factor are impossible to make. So, if there's no ice, the seals will whelp on land, but if we have this in-between ice, the seals may be fooled into using it. "While we're in the transition, there are going to be years with low pup survival," he adds.

Apart from some of the Gulf herd of grey seals, there are four other seal species in the north Atlantic that depend on ice for breeding: harp, hooded, bearded and ringed seals. Except for the ringed seal, which breeds primarily on land-fast ice inside subnivian lairs — burrows dug out of snow drifts — pups of these species are born on drifting ice floes. Since grey seals breed on both land and ice, they may be less vulnerable to the loss of sea ice due to climate change, unlike the dedicated ice-breeders, who cannot whelp on land. For them the loss of ice is nothing short of devastating.

According to Lavigne, seal breeding behaviours are the result of millions of years of evolution. It will be recalled that female seals generally produce milk that is so rich in fat that they only need to nurse for a short time: four days in hooded seals, twelve days in harps and about fifteen days in the ice-breeding greys. From an evolutionary perspective, this brevity reduces the likelihood that they will encounter predators — historically, polar bears in the case of harp seals — and increases the likelihood that pups will be weaned before the ice breaks up. He says that, because the milk is so rich, the mother seals use up their own stored energy quite quickly, a condition compounded by the fact that they generally fast while they nurse. But once the pup is weaned, mother seals return to foraging and replenishing their own energy reserves. They also come into estrus at this time and turn their attention from nursing to mating.

Once the pups are weaned they need between seven and ten days more of stable ice because they don't yet know how to swim. During what's called the post-weaning fast, pups of most species undergo their first moult and, in the case of the grey seals, shed their white coat. During this time they stay on land, or on the ice, drawing on their own energy stores — their thick blubber — to continue developing organs and tissues. Lavigne explains, "Basically, the mother seal packs her kid a lunch bucket in the form of a blubber layer to tide it over until it can swim and forage on its own."

Unlike grey seals, harp seals depend exclusively on ice for a pupping platform, and its disintegration, particularly at peak pupping periods, doesn't only result in higher pup mortality by drowning and injury but could also mean an increase in disease due to overcrowding on the stable ice patches that remain. According to the DFO, there are a number of ways that harp seals might respond to the lack of ice. They might use whatever ice is available, including unstable ice, or they might change location and travel further north than usual, or delay giving birth until suitable ice is found. There is no evidence to suggest females would give birth on land, though a few thousand harp seal pups were found on a Newfoundland coastline in 2010, after their floating ice platforms were driven there. These seals, separated from their mothers, eventually died of starvation, disease or predation by coyotes.

It will be recalled that in 2011 the DFO had set a record TAC for the harp seal hunt at 400,000 animals. At the time, Hammill argued this number was too high because it didn't account for the last two years of poor sea ice conditions in the Gulf, which resulted in the drowning of harp seal pups, which need stable ice on which to nurse. As it turned out, the loss of pups due to poor sea ice alone exceeded the catch quota. Of the 580,000 harp seal pups born in 2011, nearly 80 percent of them died due to poor ice: when you factor in the ones killed in the hunt, not many pups survived at all that year.

If all the pups born one year were to die, this would mean that five or six years down the road, there wouldn't be any seals entering the breeding population. In other words, it's possible that entire year classes could disappear, says one recent study, the first of its kind to look at the decrease in seasonal sea ice and how it might affect harp seal populations into the future. The 2012 peer-reviewed study, funded by Duke University's Marine Laboratory in North Carolina and IFAW, found that seasonal ice cover in all harp seal breeding regions has been in decline as much as 6 percent per decade and that climate-related changes, along with hunting and other environmental factors, could be responsible for the dramatic changes in the trajectory of harp populations across the North Atlantic over time. The study found that harp seal populations appeared to fluctuate in sync with trends in ice conditions and that "these animals may not be well adapted to absorb the cumulative effects of human influences," such as hunting, short-term climate variation and climate change.[87]

David Johnston, the study's lead author, tells me that harp seals have evolved to live in a place where the ice is ephemeral. "Under normal conditions, having a bad year every now and then isn't necessarily a bad thing for harp seals." Johnston says that's just part of their relationship with the environment. "Using sea ice is a way to avoid predation and so the risks of having a bad year of sea ice are outweighed by the benefits of not having a bad year every year due to predation," he says. "What becomes concerning is when you have a string of bad years. You don't have to be an actuarial scientist to know that if you burn the candle at both ends that eventually the candle no longer burns. That's how I feel with having a commercial hunt and the high pup mortality. You're taking from the bottom and the top," he says.

Lavigne, one of the study co-authors, says, "The one thing we can do immediately would be to reduce non-climate-related causes of seal mortality. This would involve reducing quotas dramatically or placing a moratorium on hunting all together." He says IFAW has argued in the past that it is necessary to protect abundant species from various risk factors such as over-exploitation and climate change before they actually become threatened or endangered. "Once species become endangered, it may actually be too late to do very much," he says. "Zero quotas for harp, hooded and grey seals would indeed be a precautionary step," he says. "The problem is that harp seals, not to mention grey seals, are seen to be very abundant at the present time, and the traditional conservation community will never see the need to provide them with any significant protection, at least not until it becomes painfully obvious that they are in trouble."

While DFO managers and our elected politicians may not be willing to take such precautionary measures, their U.S. counterparts aren't waiting around for catastrophe to hit. In December 2010 the National Oceanic and Atmospheric Administration (NOAA) announced that four subspecies of ringed seals and two distinct population segments of bearded seals be listed and granted protection under the country's *Endangered Species Act*, because the Arctic ice and snow they depend on is vanishing. At the time of writing, a decision about whether to list the ribbon seal was still pending.[88]

While all three seal species require sea ice, the ringed seals also need deep snow into which they burrow to give birth. In 2008, when these species were last assessed by the IUCN, bearded and ringed seals were listed as "least concern," because of their abundant populations. The population and status of the ribbon seal was unknown because there were so little data available on the species overall. Given the warmer winters of the future, the fate of all three species is worrying.

Back on Canada's east coast, there should be similar concerns. The hooded seal, like the harp seal, breeds on pack ice in the Gulf and on the "Front," east of Newfoundland, but breeds later in the season, when ice is even less likely to be available. The IUCN says the population of the northwest Atlantic stock appears to be stable, but the northeast Atlantic herd, which breeds off the east coast of Greenland, is already listed as vulnerable, having declined by 85 to 90 percent in the last forty years. Harp seals, though currently abundant and listed as "least concern" by the IUCN, also have a very uncertain future. In 2008 the agency warned that "climate change poses a serious threat to this species" and that its population should be reassessed within a decade."[89]

Despite the need to at least address this uncertainty, Canadian fisheries ministers and managers are not rushing in to protect either the harp or hooded seals from what appears to be an inevitable future without seasonal ice. Instead, DFO seems to be downplaying the issue: It could be years before the impact can be truly assessed, they say. Seals are a long-lived species, and females can breed for a number of years, so one or two bad years may not have too much of an effect on the population.[90]

But when continued hunting and loss of sea ice are coupled with another worrying trend — that harp seal pregnancy rates have declined from 56 percent in 2009 to 22 percent in 2011 — the spectre of a population collapse is within the realm of possibility.[91] According to the DFO, this is because of the lagged effects of pup losses. Not much would likely happen if there were great pup losses for a year or two because there's a large group of mature animals that are still breeding; but if it were to happen for several years in a row, then the impact could be much worse. "You should think of it as a mortgage," explains Mike Hammill. "In a mortgage you spread your house payments over many years." But as the number of year class failures increase then you start to see an impact on the population. "It's like increasing your monthly mortgage payments, and at some point the payments become punitive." He says that over time, with that many pups dying, the population would decline — having reached a new environmental carrying capacity — unless the animals find a more northerly habitat for pupping.

"It's not inconceivable that there won't be harp seals in the Gulf of St. Lawrence or on the Front in fifteen years or so," says Johnston. "Without the ice, there might not be any reason for those animals to come here." Johnston says the key question is how quickly can these animals adapt by shifting latitudinally or moving further north when it's time to give birth. "We don't yet understand what cues the animals actually use to find breeding locations," he says. Johnston describes a fascinating reproductive strategy that evolved in pinnipeds, including the harp, harbour, hooded and grey seals, as well as in a number of other mammals including rodents and bears, that results in the pregnant females giving birth at the same time each year. In the case of harp seals, after the egg is fertilized the embryo goes into a dormant stage and floats freely in the mother's uterus for about three and a half months before it implants in the wall of the uterus, where it will begin to develop. This delayed implantation — called "embryonic diapause" in scientific lingo — ensures that the gestation period will coincide with when ice will be available. Johnston adds that the reproductive cycles of harp seals are governed partially by photoperiod, or length of the day, and, as a result, "if the ice changes latitudinally, but the time of day doesn't, the animals expect the ice to be at a certain place at a certain time and they will continue to show up ready to give birth in the same place every year," ice or no ice.

It's highly questionable whether the DFO, in its current configuration, would be prepared to make precautionary management decisions with loss of sea ice in mind. As we have seen, Hammill's warnings about the loss of sea ice and his specific recommendation that the 2011 harp seal TAC be reduced by 100,000 fell on deaf ears.[92] Despite advice from one of its own highly respected scientists, DFO fisheries managers in concert with industry recommended the higher quota instead — advice that Minister Keith Ashfield, armed with what many argue is an undue supply of discretionary power, decided to accept.*

Despite incidents like this, Hammill is still confident that as long as the management plan is followed, the effects of the climate and the hunt will be accounted for. He argues that focusing on the hunt is a waste of time and that we should be focusing instead on climate change: "If we concentrate on that, the seals will help themselves," he says. There is no question that reducing greenhouse gas emissions now is needed if there's going to be any hope of stopping further climatic upheaval, but Canada is now one of the world's leading climate change deniers and continues to promote greenhouse gas production.

Hammill also contends that "scarce monies" should be allocated "towards things like blue whales, or belugas — animals that really need help." But David Johnston believes it's time to take a different approach. "Our ultimate failure when it comes to natural resource management is that we literally don't do anything until we've depleted them. If we could spend our money listing and protecting species that are vulnerable as opposed to spending all of it on the conservation train wrecks, we could do a lot more."

---

* In 2012, the Royal Society of Canada released a 316-page report on marine biodiversity in light of the challenges posed by climate change, fisheries, and aquaculture. The panel of ten experts, chaired by Dalhousie University's Jeff Hutchings, recommended that the government of Canada reduce the discretionary power in fisheries management decisions exercised by the Minister of Fisheries and Oceans. The report described the power afforded to Canadian fisheries ministers as "czar-like" and stated that their "powers to approve, deny, or otherwise change proposals affecting activities coming under their aegis" have impeded Canada's progress in meeting obligations to sustain marine biodiversity. See Hutchings et al., 2012.

Chapter 7

Pandora's Box

I think real science has to be a spiritual endeavour because real science is [about] understanding deep patterns, understanding lasting process, and understanding how things hang together. Spirituality is the same thing. It is about understanding our place in the universe. It is about connecting to the rest of life and that connection creates, in its very existence, a humility of you being just a small part of a very, very large limitless piece. And, while creating humility in you it also creates responsibility, that what you do has impact on a lot, on the whole fabric, on the whole web of life.

— Vandana Shiva, Physicist and Environmental Justice Advocate

Once [the ocean] is bust, we don't know how to bring it back, other than leave it alone… If it recovers on its own, it will do so quicker and more completely in an ecosystem that has a lot of species in it… We can't engineer a recovery.

— Boris Worm, *Hansard*, January 23, 2007

When viewed from a satellite, phytoplankton blooms look like turquoise rivers of smoke, swirling in ethereal and circuitous patterns beneath vast areas of ocean. Close up, this greenery is composed of microscopic algae: the first, and most important link in the ocean food web and the foundation of all life in the sea. In 2010 when a study published in *Nature* reported that this tiny plant life was in peril, it justifiably raised some alarm. Dalhousie University researchers Daniel Boyce, Marlon Lewis and Boris Worm reported that phytoplankton had declined substantially in the last century, by as much as 40 percent since 1950 alone. The findings, based in part on satellite images of these blooms, indicate that the entire global ocean is slowing down and producing less phytoplankton. One likely factor is a warming ocean surface. According to the authors, when this happens there is more ocean layering or stratification, which creates barriers to mixing, making it harder for nutrients in the deep waters to move up to the sunlit surface, where plankton need them to grow.[93]

Around the same time these disquieting findings appeared, another study was published suggesting that marine mammals may play a role in mitigating climate change. The 2010 study by Joe Roman and James McCarthy describes the "whale pump": the biological pump created when air-breathing predators feed at depth and rise to the surface to breathe, creating an upward movement of water — and nutrients — to the surface. The study, which looked specifically at the Gulf of Maine ecosystem, found evidence that whales, seals, and sea birds play an important role in cycling nutrients — the very ones needed by phytoplankton to grow. These findings came as no surprise to Debbie MacKenzie. She's been arguing this very point from the moment she spearheaded the Grey Seal Conservation Society in 2004. She says the decline in ocean productivity is reason for alarm, but she says this is even more reason for having an abundance of air-breathing, deep diving, marine mammals around. She says scientists now know how everything benefits from phytoplankton, but not the other way around. "The question should be 'how many things are a benefit *to* phytoplankton.'" A growing body of science is now describing how the swimming, diving and surfacing behaviours of marine mammals, including grey seals, helps to mix ocean water and transport significant amounts of nutrients from the deeper waters to the surface. "This stimulates the growth of plankton, the uptake of atmospheric carbon dioxide by the ocean, and the production of food and oxygen for many consumers including the grey seal's own prey fish," says MacKenzie.

Grey seals have been known to dive to four hundred metres and remain under water for as long as twenty-three minutes. But most adult diving is shallower than 120 metres and less than eight minutes. When they dive, they don't hold in their breath, like we do, they exhale the air from their lungs, which reduces buoyancy and allows the lungs to collapse, avoiding problems like compression as the underwater pressure increases. Roman and McCarthy's 2010 study found that pinnipeds that breed on shore and seaside ledges are a source of nutrients in coastal waters.

In the Gulf of Maine, where the study was conducted, nitrogen is generally considered to be the limiting nutrient for plankton growth: the study found that whales and seals may be responsible for releasing 23,000 metric tonnes of nitrogen every year from the deep layers to the surface waters — more than that provided by all rivers flowing into the Gulf of Maine combined. Roman and McCarthy's study also makes the following compelling point: the full recovery of marine mammal populations can help to counter the effects of climate change and the related decline in nutrients available for phytoplankton growth. It goes further and concludes that an unintended effect of bounty programs and culls could be reduced availability of nitrogen and therefore less overall production of the tiniest plants, the foundation of all life, in the oceans.

Grey seals play an intrinsically valuable role in the marine ecosystems they inhabit; part of this value involves their relationships with other species.

As an apex, or top, predator, grey seals have evolved along with their prey for millions of years in a process of "co-evolution," where each species has adapted to each other's adaptations. For instance, grey seals have influenced the evolution of cod in every way possible: how they behave, how they've adapted to ensure they reproduce successfully, even influencing their shapes and physical characteristics. Relationships like these are what provide stability and resilience in complex ecosystems and make a rich biodiversity possible in the first place. In other words, top predators, like grey seals, may even be helping to hold the marine food web together.

In 2006, University of Guelph biologist Neil Rooney and his colleagues found just that. They reported in the journal *Nature* that top predators have a very valuable role in the marine ecosystem and may even be the key to long-term ecosystem stability. They do this by linking or "coupling" the two energy channels in the marine ecosystem and in doing so prevent boom and bust dynamics. Rooney explains: There are two distinct energy channels — or food chains — in the ocean. One starts with the phytoplankton, where, one trophic level at a time, the energy is transferred to the top predator. The other, much slower, energy channel starts with the detritus — the dead organic material that sinks down to the bottom — which gets taken up first by the benthic invertebrates living in the sediment but eventually also makes its way to the top predators.

Rooney says top predators, like sharks, seals, and tuna, go back and forth between eating animals that derive most of their energy from the detritus, like crustaceans, to animals that derive most of their energy from the phytoplankton, like herring and other forage fish. "This feeding behaviour generates asynchrony of production in the energy channels so that when one is waxing, the other is waning, resulting in less variability in food web dynamics." He says that grey seals help keep things in check: removing them could destabilize marine food webs.

The value in maintaining food web stability points directly to some of the work GPI (Genuine Progress Index) Atlantic has been doing. The Nova Scotia-based organization has been tracking environmental health and quality indicators for the province since 1997. In 1999 and again a decade later it compiled data and trends for a number of indicators aimed at measuring the health of Nova Scotia's fisheries and marine environment. This fisheries work was led by Tony Charles, a professor of Management Science and Environmental Studies at St. Mary's University in Halifax, who specializes in the interdisciplinary analysis of fisheries. He was also a founding member of the Fisheries Resource Conservation Council (FRCC) and was on the council for five years. On the ecological front, Charles looked at data regarding the health of commercial fish stocks, of non-fished species, and the state of the marine food webs. His study found that the ocean was being emptied of fish, particularly large predators, and that over time the structure and function of the marine food web had been altered. Industrial fishing, the report concluded, has left a much less diverse ecosystem in its wake and is now dependent on species lower down in the food web — notably lobster and shellfish. All this points to a less resilient system: studies now show that if we undermine resilience to such an extent, even the slightest disturbance could result in collapse.

Charles says the idea of resilience, whether it be human or ecological, is the capability of a system to bounce back from shocks. "If we talk about the human body — we get sick now and then and our body, if we are healthy enough, bounces back from the sickness," he explains. "If ecosystems are healthy, they'll bounce back from shocks too. A healthy ecosystem is one that has biodiversity — an abundance of many different species of different sizes, all playing different roles in the food chain."

Maintaining resilience and a healthy marine ecosystem isn't just good for the fish. It also provides a number of benefits to society — or what are called "ecosystem services." These include healthy seafood, clean water, and protection from natural disasters and storms. Oceans also absorb carbon and produce half of the oxygen we breathe. We also experience physical, psychological, and even spiritual rejuvenation from interacting in some way with the ocean.* Trying to communicate the value of these free and irreplaceable services in an attempt to raise their profile in the policy arena has been the goal of a growing number of organizations, including Nova Scotia's GPI Atlantic. "The assumption for centuries was that these basic services go on indefinitely, but now we're seeing that these can be disrupted as a result of human activity," says Charles. "If we measure things the way we have been doing, then we miss out on most of these values," he says.

One example of how the conventional thinking has gotten us into serious trouble is climate change, says Charles. "We can dump more carbon into the atmosphere and the way we measure things now, this is a good thing," he explains. "That means more industrial activity, more use of electricity, more production of *stuff* — these are all good for the economy." At the same time,

---

*   There are four broad categories of ecosystem services for both marine and terrestrial ecosystems: perhaps the one we are most cognizant of is nature's "provisioning" function, which includes all the goods we extract or use — nature's bounty — which includes food, water, minerals and energy. Ecosystems also have "regulating" functions such as water purification, pest control, carbon sequestration, climate regulation, crop pollination and flood control. There are the "supporting" or "habitat" services, such as seed dispersal and nutrient cycling, and there are the "cultural" benefits we derive from the natural world, including recreational, aesthetic and spiritual sustenance, as well as scientific discovery.

many of the human and ecological costs associated with these activities such as human illness, environmental degradation, pollution and biodiversity loss, to name just a few, are externalized, which means the costs are off-loaded onto the shoulders of taxpayers or to future generations.[94] Charles says unbridled growth is what's causing climate change, ocean acidification and a decline in ecosystem services, which are fundamental to our lives. "One day we'll say 'that was quite the trade off.'"

Studies are already finding that the loss of biodiversity is taking a toll on ecosystem services — impairing the ocean's ability to provide everything we now take completely for granted: food, water quality, and resilience. But there is good news. Scientists say the trends are reversible. But this will require no less than a shift in thinking. Thus far, the economic performance of Nova Scotia's fishery has been based exclusively on the annual revenue obtained from catching and selling fish. It doesn't account for the intrinsic value of fish and all the other creatures remaining in the ocean or for the value of the essential services the marine ecosystem provides, or register any damage incurred on the natural system that maintains the fishery. In other words, a shift in thinking would require that all the elements of the marine ecosystem that actually keep the fishery functioning — the creatures in the sea, the quality of the water, the complexity of the seafloor habitat — have to be recognized as having real value. The same holds true for grey seals. In our current system they are only considered valuable when they can be killed and exchanged for money, and even then the monetary value placed on one only reflects what it can fetch in the marketplace. But as we have seen, they are much more valuable than the market dictates.

Where the Cull Numbers Come From

In the spring of 2012, Jeff Hutchings, testified before the Standing Senate Committee on Fisheries and Oceans. The Committee had been listening to testimony from scientists, environmental groups and fishing interests since the previous fall regarding the "management" of grey seals. It will be recalled that the Fisheries Resource Conservation Council (FRCC) had recommended killing more than 140,000 grey seals in the Gulf of St. Lawrence — 73,000 in year one and 70,000 more within the next four — and the Senate Committee was now charged with coming up with its own recommendation for the fisheries minister on what should be done.

During the meeting, New Brunswick Senator Rose-May Poirier asked Hutchings how many pounds of fish a grey seal eats in a day. "We are hearing a lot from the people out there, and they are putting two and two together," she said. "We had plenty [of fish] and all of a sudden one species is going up and the other species is going down." Hutchings cautioned the Senator: "The perception of the fishermen and many others is, indeed, that if one removes grey seals, cod will come back," he said. "But because there are multiple species interacting in the ecosystem, there is scientific uncertainty as to precisely what the response of cod would be." Hutchings added that the uncertainty lies in the fact that so much depends on the assumptions and "we are really not in a position where we can say that this set of assumptions is much better than another set of assumptions."

Morley Knight also testified before the Committee. As director general of resource management for the DFO, a big part of Knight's job was to consult with the fishing and sealing industry. Once the FRCC made its recommendation, he had been busy meeting with industry representatives to work out what a cull in the Gulf of St. Lawrence might look like. There are three ways it could happen, he explained to the Committee. It could be set up as a bounty program — much like the one in the 1980s when the DFO paid licensed fishermen to kill grey seals and provide their lower jawbone as proof. This kind of cull could be done during the course of normal fishing activity, Knight said. But fishermen were not enthusiastic about this idea, he conceded, because when grey seals are shot in open water they tend to sink and retrieving the jawbone is impractical. The second possibility is the seals could be targeted in areas where they gather: on land or on ice when they're giving birth or whelping. A DFO observer would be present to count the number of animals killed — and tally the amount sealers would be paid. The third option would be a combination of the first two.

But in the absence of a market, there are no real financial incentives for fishers or sealers to kill grey seals. According to Knight, the fishing industry recommended that sealers get a minimum of $100 per jawbone, but DFO was looking into the matter. It hired Gardner Pinfold, a consulting firm based in Nova Scotia, to provide expert opinion on how much a sealer should be paid, taking into consideration the cost to the sealer.[95] Knight told the Committee that if a cull were to go ahead, various levels of government as well as the fishing industry would have to pony up the funds.

Six months after hearing from Hutchings, Knight and others, the Senate Committee issued a report recommending the killing of 70,000 grey seals over four years, starting in 2013 — half of what the FRCC recommended. Senator Fabian Manning, chair of the Committee, told a news conference the proposed cull was an "experiment" and that while he admitted there was "no solid research anywhere" to support the decision, he suggested data could be collected during the four-year slaughter.

Reaction was swift. Rebecca Aldworth, head of Humane Society International, called the recommendation "unethical" and said it had "everything to do with handouts to the commercial sealing industry," which by all accounts was in its death throes, and "nothing to do with the protection of fish stocks." She also warned that a cull might not stop with the southern

Gulf population. The Senate report recommends action should be taken on Sable Island as well.

Later during an interview, Hutchings said there was no scientific evidence a cull would work. He explained that the reason the cod stocks are all doing poorly is because of overfishing, which depleted the populations to record lows. "When you do that to any animal population you're in a zone where it's really hard to predict how they're going to respond," he said. "We humans have pushed the cod populations into these areas where predictive capabilities kind of fall apart." He added that it's far too simplistic to say that if you removed the seals the cod would automatically bounce back.

While these cull numbers were widely reported in the media, little attention was paid to where they came from or how they were derived. Remarkably, both the FRCC and the Senate Committee cull numbers come from key DFO documents: ones that never actually recommended a cull in the first place.

It will be recalled that in the winter of 2008, DFO hired sealers to kill grey seals that were foraging near St. Paul's Island, northeast of Cape Breton Island — near the cod overwintering area. They were trying to figure out whether the grey seals were responsible for the high natural mortality of the southern Gulf cod. When the gut contents of the ninety seals were analyzed, scientists were able to find and reliably measure thirty-three large cod in eight stomachs and five intestines of a total of thirteen grey seals. There were more otoliths of cod found, but they were too eroded or partially digested to tell the age and size of the cod eaten. From these thirteen seals, scientists concluded that 58 percent of cod consumed by the seals were thirty-five centimetres or longer, which would be about the size of an adult cod.

When they looked at the overall diet, they found that only a few of the male seals in the sample were the cod-feeders while this was not the case for females, some of which had eaten zero cod. When it was averaged out, the males in the sample had 25 percent cod in their diet and females had closer to 10 percent. These two pieces of information — the "size composition" from the thirteen seals and the "consumption estimates" from the ninety seals — were then taken to represent what scientists referred to as the "aggregated diet," which was then applied to tens of thousands of seals that feed in the southern Gulf.[96]

Critics of the study say it's not at all representative of the way the entire population of grey seals feeds. Sara Iverson has studied the diets of grey seals on Sable Island for nineteen years using the fatty acid analysis technique. As we have seen, this technique enables her to calculate both the mixture and amount of prey the seal has eaten over several months. She's found that cod are not a staple food for grey seals. She says that while there may be some individual seals that target cod aggregations, this doesn't compare to the general population, which she says has been sampled very widely across the Scotian Shelf.

Bowen says the information about a few male seals eating large cod around St. Paul's Island is "new" information but he says it doesn't really mean anything. He provides the following analogy to illustrate his point: "It's like trying to estimate the diet of Haligonians by going to McDonalds. You'll find that some people eat hamburgers but I don't know what you do with that number," he says. You can't then take that number and apply it to everyone that lives in Halifax. Bowen says that in the case of grey seals, in order for the information to be meaningful — to be able to estimate the mortality of cod — you need to know how many seals are eating the St. Paul's diet and for how long. Bowen says scientists have the answers to neither of these crucial questions.

DFO scientists also tried to estimate what the diet of grey seals might look like at other times of the year when the cod are dispersed and they called this the "dispersed diet." They also had to come up with what the overlap might be between cod and seals in other parts of the Gulf at other times of year and then had to decide which of the two diets would apply. There were more data gaps than there were actual data.

This is where, to put it mildly, the science gets murky. The diet data were then plugged into mathematical models along with a myriad of assumptions — many of them unverifiable — about the way grey seals and cod interact, and different assumptions led to very different conclusions. For instance, one of the models showed that even if all the grey seals were slaughtered it would still not bring back the southern Gulf cod. The results of another model — the source of the Senate Committee recommendation[*] — showed that killing 70 percent of the 104,000 grey seals foraging in the southern Gulf could reverse the cod decline.

Doug Swain, one of the DFO scientists who worked on the cull "scenarios," says they should be viewed as "what if" scenarios and were never meant to be interpreted as a recommendation for a cull. He says there are too many data gaps, particularly about grey seal diets, and so "it is not possible to determine the seal reductions that would be required to allow cod recovery." He points to two key DFO documents — one of which he co-authored — that came to the same conclusion.[97]

However, since the FRCC recommendation for a cull had been made, and while the Senate Committee was hearing testimony and deliberating about what to do, DFO scientists were crunching numbers from two more years of

---

[*]   The FRCC estimate is roughly double this amount because it included killing all the pups born each year in the Gulf for four years, something discussed at DFO workshops, but that both DFO and the Senate Committee were vague about in writing.

St. Paul's data that indicate fewer seals might need to be killed to achieve the same hypothetical effect. According to Mike Hammill, the new data suggest that just a few of the males are the big cod-feeders and that, if they could be targeted, fewer animals — possibly as much as 50 percent fewer — would need to be killed to get the same "beneficial effect."

But according to David Lavigne, there's just no evidence a cull of any size would result in a "beneficial effect" on cod. He points to an important glitch in the DFO's rationale, an inconsistency raised by DFO scientists themselves.[98] If grey seals are responsible for the high natural mortality of cod, then why would cod stocks in the vicinity of Sable Island recently be showing signs of recovery? After all, this is where the bulk of grey seals live and continue to increase in numbers. Lavigne says scientists cannot explain why natural mortality of cod appears similar in the southern Gulf and on the eastern Scotian Shelf despite a four-fold difference in the numbers of grey seals in the two areas. Lavigne poses the following question: "If adult cod mortality is not directly related to the number of grey seals, then why would a reduction in the number of the grey seals be expected to reduce adult cod mortality?"

The EAC has never been against the commercial seal hunt, but it says a cull is different. Susanna Fuller says the EAC is not an animal rights organization and as far as marine conservation issues go, seal hunting isn't one of them. She says seal hunting is not ecologically unsustainable. "It's a human activity issue, and from that perspective I think our ecosystem is much more at risk from bottom trawling," she says. But Fuller is challenging the cull recommendation. "A cull is trying to make up for poor management of human impacts on the ecosystem." Fuller explains that while we can never manage a marine ecosystem, we are supposed to be managing the effects of human activity on the ecosystem, and we're not doing a very good job of that. Culling the seals — to address the seal worm problem on the Scotian Shelf or the cod mortality problem in the Gulf — diverts attention away from issues the government doesn't want to deal with, like bycatch. In other words, the seals have become scapegoats for the government's mismanagement of the fisheries. "Efforts to improve fisheries productivity should first look at the human impacts rather than seek other explanations that would not require us to change fishing practices," she says.

Fuller's comments about first looking at human impacts are similar to ideas expressed in a 2012 report, written by Hutchings and others, from the Royal Society of Canada on marine biodiversity in light of the challenges posed by climate change, fisheries and aquaculture. The report concluded that Canada is failing its oceans. When it comes to fisheries, the panel looked at a number of issues affecting biodiversity: including the long-term and sometimes irreversible damage of trawling and dredging on fragile and vulnerable seafloor habitats and the species that depend on them; the effects of fishing on food web structure; and the decimation of a number of commercial and non-commercial fish species due to overfishing. The report listed the marine fish populations on the Atlantic coast that have declined by more than 80 percent since the 1960s and 1970s and for which overfishing has been identified as the cause of the decline: Atlantic cod, American plaice, northern wolfish, spotted wolfish, winter skate, roundnose grenadier, porbeagle (shark), deepwater redfish, Acadian redfish and white shark.

The panel of ten experts, chaired by Hutchings, recommended that Canada should enact "prescriptive legislation" with stated objectives to prevent overfishing and rebuild depleted fish stocks. But Hutchings says the federal government has shown no real commitment to developing a recovery plan for cod. He says it's remarkable that nearly two decades after the collapse, fundamental change in fishery management has not taken place. DFO still has no recovery targets, no timelines and no harvest control rules. According to Hutchings, going ahead with any form of seal cull or sterilization plan in the absence of a comprehensive recovery strategy would simply be "irresponsible."

The panel recommended that, as a first step, all endangered or threatened marine species should be legally listed under the *Species at Risk Act* (SARA). Even though a legal listing of a species is not required for governments to initiate a recovery strategy, it does automatically result in one. Even though currently four stocks of Atlantic cod and one of winter skate have been identified by the Committee on the Status of Endangered Wildlife in Canada (COSEWIC) as "endangered," these species have not been officially listed. Hutchings, who chaired COSEWIC from 2006 to 2010, says this is because of what are called "socio-economic" consequences, which DFO concluded to be excessive.

Among the reasons given by the DFO not to list cod was that it could "extinguish any hope" that the cod fishery might return, increasing the out-migration from rural communities. It also argued that listing cod would prohibit selling it and while there are still some cod fisheries open, this would result in the loss of jobs. Listing would also affect other groundfish fisheries, namely yellowtail flounder, skate and redfish, in which cod is often caught incidentally as a bycatch.[99] The decision not to list cod ultimately came from the federal cabinet, but that decision was based on the recommendation from the Minister of Environment, who was following the marching orders of the Minister of Fisheries and Oceans.

"DFO has sent a clear signal that any species perceived to be of economic importance will not be listed under SARA," Hutchings says. He questions how serious DFO is about species at risk issues since, he says, it has not listed any threatened or endangered marine fish except for two non-commercial marine species — white shark on the east coast and basking shark on the west. In other words, listing cod would mean being legally required to protect it, and this would mean having to change the way we fish.

Hutchings says a cull of grey seals is not defensible from a "fisheries improvement" perspective.

> From a personal perspective, and for ethical reasons, the deliberate killing of one native species for the sole purpose of possibly increasing the economic gain obtained from harvesting another native species is something that I cannot condone. From a professional perspective, the likelihood that a seal cull will lead to measurable and substantive increases in the abundance of cod is not known. Given such uncertainty, the "potential" benefits of a cull, from a fisheries-improvement perspective, would seem to be outweighed by "known" costs — such as national and international outrage — and by potential, albeit unknown costs — such as rendering the recovering prospects for cod, and other species, potentially worse.

The only way a cull could be justifiable for Hutchings is from "a species-at-risk perspective," in an attempt to save cod, winter skate, and white hake from disappearing from the southern Gulf. But even then, he says, the outcome is highly uncertain. He also points out that culls are never proposed in an attempt to save fish, but rather to save fisheries.

The Law of Unintended Consequences
At the time the Senate Committee made its recommendation, it will be recalled that the chair of the Committee, Fabian Manning, referred to the cull as an "experiment" that would test whether the grey seals are responsible for the cod non-recovery. A number of scientists balked at this claim, including Hutchings, who told the media a cull "violates all of the characteristics of an appropriately designed experiment." In order for it to be an experiment there would need to be a group that remains unaltered, a control group, which allows for comparison. He says we can't do this in the ocean. "All we can do is affect the abundance of grey seals and we're not going to be able to control anything else."[100] In other words, if the cod population goes up after a cull, it doesn't necessarily mean the seals were responsible for their failure to recover.

The general consensus among scientists is that tinkering with the marine ecosystem in an attempt to solve some problem could unleash greater havoc and result in any number of unintended consequences. Hutchings, for instance, says there's just no way to predict a cull would result in a desired outcome. "I don't think any scientist with any integrity would want to make that kind of forecast," he says. In a complex multi-species ecosystem any number of things could happen. "If you remove grey seals, then other things that grey seals consume, like herring and mackerel might increase and they consume cod eggs, and young cod, and so you might not actually make a difference at all," he says. "You remove one predator [of cod] but you might increase the abundance of two others."

In fact, DFO's own review of the scientific literature worldwide concluded that there was little evidence that culls of marine mammals actually work and that there was every chance they could backfire. It found that culls "often" had "non-intuitive and unintended consequences for both target and other predator and prey species." In the 2011 review, DFO's Bowen and Dalhousie University zoologist Damian Lidgard looked at no less than thirty examples worldwide of marine mammal culls ostensibly to protect fisheries and found that either the result was unknown, there was no noticeable response by the prey species, or the prey species was even worse off after the cull. For instance, here in Nova Scotia between 1927 and 1976, harbour seals were culled in a bounty program and the population was substantially reduced. Grey seals were also the target of culls in the Gulf of St. Lawrence between 1978 and 1990 and elsewhere along the east coast, except for Sable Island, between 1967 and 1983. Culls of grey and harbour seals have already taken place here in the name of cod, salmon, mackerel, herring, lobster and fishing gear. The results of every single one is unknown.

"I am not in support of the recent call for a cull on grey seals," says Lidgard, one of the authors of the study and a researcher with the Ocean Tracking Network (OTN) — a project that tags marine animals, including grey seals and cod, with electronic transmitters to document their movements, migrations and survival.* Lidgard is also an accomplished wildlife photographer and recently published the book *Sable Island*, featuring photos of some of its magnificent fauna including the island's famous wild horses and, of course, the seals. He's worked on both sides of the Atlantic studying grey seals and has worked in collaboration with other scientists on the issue of grey seal predation on cod. "It's not known what the outcome would be if grey seals were culled," he says. Lidgard says changing the abundance of grey seals could result in negative impacts on cod.

In their study, Bowen and Lidgard describe one situation where a marine mammal cull had unintended consequences. In British Columbia, the fishing industry complained that the Steller sea lions were eating too many salmon.

---

* According to the OTN web site, acoustic receivers, about the size of a food processor, are arranged in strategic locations (in fourteen ocean regions of the world) along the seafloor at eight hundred metre intervals. When a tagged marine animal passes within half a kilometer of the receiver, it picks up a coded acoustic signal that identifies the animal. Receivers can also relay data to shore via satellite.

Between 1923 and 1939, one of the large sea lion rookeries off Rivers Inlet was completely eradicated and the sea lions were rendered locally extinct in an attempt to protect the Rivers Inlet sockeye salmon. At the time, there was no noticeable change in sockeye salmon catches and since then, even in the absence of Steller sea lions, the stock has collapsed.

Bowen and Lidgard highlight another so-called cull, one that bears some resemblance to the hunt of grey seals in Nova Scotia. Cape fur seals gather in the tens of thousands in gregarious and crowded colonies on Namibia's desert coast. Since 1993, during a period of declining fish stocks, the seals have been targeted in a commercial hunt for their fur. The government has justified the cull, claiming the fur seals eat the equivalent of a third of what's landed by the fishing industry.[101]

Critics consider the hunt of Cape fur seals to be one of the cruelest hunts of marine mammals in the world. According to a 2010 study by Stephen Kirkman, from the University of Cape Town in South Africa and IFAW's David Lavigne, the hunt is inherently cruel because of how it's conducted: animals are herded and rounded up inland, away from the water and the weaned pups are clubbed with crude wooden bats and skinned in the presence of other animals, including females with nursing pups. The authors note that this resembles what takes place during the hunt of grey seals on Hay Island — one of Nova Scotia's "protected" wilderness areas.

According to Bowen and Lidgard, the number of Cape fur seals culled during the breeding season has increased from 50,000 in 1993 to 85,000 in 2009, and since 2006 an additional 6,000 adult males have been culled. Despite two decades of fur seal slaughters, the authors report there has been no Namibian government evaluation of the impact of the seal cull on fish stock productivity.

Iceland also allows culling of grey seals: according to fishing industry representatives here, including Denny Morrow, theirs is a shining example of how culls can work to benefit fisheries. "They do a cull and they don't want any anti-sealing groups there, so if you're an anti-sealer you won't get a hotel room. It's just too important to them," Morrow says. "They pay a bounty and they bring jaw bones in. Some of the carcasses are used in fur farms — they grind them up and use a maximum percent that they can put in. They believe in this." He says the proof that the culls are working is that in 2012 fishers had a quota of 160,000 tonnes of cod. "I think that's confirmation to those countries [with a cull] to continue what they're doing," he says.

But according to Bowen and Lidgard, the effects of culling in Iceland are nowhere near this definitive. They say grey seals and harbour seals have been hunted in Iceland for centuries and that shooting seals is permitted everywhere except on Iceland's west coast. Since 1982 there has been a bounty program, as Morrow describes, to address conflicts with fisheries. It is thought that the seals compete with cod and show a preference for cod, but Bowen and Lidgard noted there was no evidence provided by Icelandic scientists to support either of these claims. Furthermore, there's been no formal evaluation of the effect of culling seals on cod, and over a twenty-year period of culling (1982 to 2002), cod spawning stock biomass — the population capable of reproducing — fluctuated but no trend was apparent. In fact, the average recruitment, or the number of new fish that enter the population, declined slightly. In other words, there was "no obvious [cod] population response to seal culls."[102]

But Morrow's point still begs the question, "why are Icelandic cod doing so much better than our cod?" According to the International Council for the Exploration of the Sea (ICES), since 2000 there have been reductions in cod quota. Perhaps as a result of this lessening of fishing, in 2012 the spawning stock biomass (SSB) was higher than had been observed over the last four decades.[103] Another important difference is that unlike the stocks here, which suffered a prolonged decline followed by a collapse from overfishing, Icelandic cod stocks never actually collapsed.

Important Ecological Role

It's a common misperception that a predator can only affect its prey in a negative way — essentially by eating it. As we have seen, when viewed within the context of trophic systems, or food webs, predators can have an overall positive impact on their prey. This was the finding of a 2006 study that looked at the role of marine mammals in the trophic system of the northern Gulf of St. Lawrence. This study found that marine mammals benefit, more than they hinder, small bottom-feeders such as young cod.[104]

Studies like this one, showing the beneficial effect of predators as well as their important ecological role, appear again and again in the scientific literature. It has even recently been shown — perhaps counterintuitively — that marine mammals may actually benefit commercial fisheries. "In some circumstances, by feeding on other species that could be competing with fisheries, marine mammals and other high-level predators may, in fact, actually be increasing fisheries catches."[105]

This remarkable finding was corroborated in a 2012 study by Lyne Morissette, Villy Christensen and Daniel Pauly, which looked at seven marine ecosystems worldwide, including the Gulf of St. Lawrence, and addressed the perception that the fishing industry is in direct competition with marine mammal populations for commercial fish stocks. Using ecosystem models, the authors simulated the extirpation of marine mammal populations to see how this would affect the structure of the food web in each of the ecosystems studied. That is, would large-scale culling result in an increase in commercially targeted fish and benefit the fisheries? The authors found that when all the seals, whales, dolphins, and porpoises were removed from the Gulf ecosystem, the ecosystem structure changed but when it came to commercially important species such as adult cod, capelin and small plankton-eating fish, the increase was limited: "Without marine mammals, most of the target species showed no significant change, or decreased slightly," the report concluded.[106] In other words, ecosystem modelling shows that a cull would definitely not lead to the recovery of the cod, nor would it benefit the commercial fishery.

Sidney Holt is arguably one of the most influential marine biologists of the twentieth century. In 1957 he co-authored (with R.J.H. Beverton) the book *On the Dynamics of Exploited Fish Populations*, which has been described as "the bible of fisheries science" and is possibly the most widely cited fisheries book ever published. For twenty-five years, Holt worked in senior positions with the United Nations, mainly as director of the Fisheries Resource and Operations Division of the Food and Agriculture Organization (FAO). Since 1960, he's been devoted to the conservation of whales and has served on the scientific committee of the International Whaling Commission as well as on the national delegations of Italy and the Republic of Seychelles and as scientific adviser to the delegations of France and Chile.

Holt was a keynote speaker at a 2004 symposium put on by the Mediterranean Science Commission (CIESM) on the role of whales, dolphins and porpoises in marine ecosystems. At the time, the argument that whales eat fish, and commercial ones at that, was being used to persuade the world that the moratorium on commercial whaling — which has been in effect since 1982 — should be lifted or modified. Holt pointed out that this claim was being supported by various documents, not unlike ones we're seeing today regarding grey seals and cod, comparing the amounts of marine living resources consumed by whales and other cetaceans, with the scale of human catches. He described the documents and ensuing arguments as "propaganda" and "not deserving the title of 'science.'" Nevertheless, he noted, they were "persuasive" to some politicians, fishers, journalists and the lay public.[107]

He told me about a classic case illustrating the self-serving nature of diet studies in which Japanese scientists — working for the whaling industry — had calculated how much minke whales eat, from metabolic-rate calculations in which it was assumed that more than half the crustacean food — the chitin carapace, legs, and head — was indigestible. But later Norwegian scientists found that the front "chamber" of a minke whale's stomach is actually full of specialized chitin-digesting microbes, much the way a cow's fore-stomach is full of cellulose-digesting microbes. So the whales were actually consuming less than half of what the Japanese scientists had calculated.

Holt says, "Over-fishing is now a recognized global phenomenon, with some countries having huge stakes in large industrial fleets. There is a rearguard that is reluctant to accept that fishing is the prime cause of the collapse of fish resources. So, scapegoats are sought."[108]

When Holt, who now resides in Italy, was asked about his opinion on the recent move by the European Parliament to approve a plan to "manage" its seal population by culling, the same parliament that in 2009 voted to ban imports of commercial seal products from Canada,[109] he replied in no uncertain terms. "There are no circumstances in which it is justified to kill predators, mammal or not, to 'save' fisheries. Both for moral reasons and because I know of no single research study in which such action is reasonably scientifically justified."

Chapter 8

Boomed and Busted

> Our economic models are projections and arrows when they should be circles. To define perpetual growth on a finite planet as the sole measure of economic well-being is to engage in a form of slow collective suicide. To deny or exclude from the calculus of governance and economy the costs of violating the biological support systems of life is the logic of delusion.
>
> — Wade Davis, *The Wayfinders*, 2009

> We can't have a relationship with animals that's humane under capitalism.
>
> — Dean Bavington, Memorial University, Newfoundland

For at least a couple of centuries, seals of all kinds were seen as a source of profits, and this view, for the most part, overshadowed the other prevalent view of seals — as pests. "Today, they move from one to the other and so we treat them worse — we rage against the animal and this rage expresses itself in very negative behaviour," said the late Jon Lien. Lien was a highly respected professor at Memorial University of Newfoundland and became known as the "whale man of Newfoundland and Labrador." In the 1970s, when humpback whales were colliding with and becoming entangled in the fishing gear of inshore fishers, Lien received a call one day about a whale that had been entangled for several months and was starving. He managed to release the whale and from that point on, he was often called upon by fishers to liberate trapped whales. He became interested in human–marine mammal conflict and went on to found the Whale Research Group, but also studied the impact of incidental live captures of marine mammals in fishing gear for the DFO.

In a radio interview that aired in April 2000 in Newfoundland, Lien talked about how fishers who don't depend on the seal as a resource anymore, see them solely as a pest or nuisance and as a threat to profits. He said that politicians are taking advantage of that sentiment, making it a highly charged emotional issue. "[They] have moved from this sort of mythical monster to a commodity where we hunted them ruthlessly," he said. Working out a new relationship with these animals is going to be a very difficult task, he explained — one made even more difficult now because they've "come to symbolize everything that's right and wrong with the ocean."[110]

If you look at a graph showing the last five hundred years of cod landings, it's easy to see how things went wrong. It's also easy to see why 1968 was a defining moment. In that year, the line peaks, and towers ominously over the previous four and a half centuries. Then it drops right off. That's because in that year, more than one million tonnes of cod from the stocks off Newfoundland were reported landed, including more than 800,000 tonnes from the now mythic northern stock alone — nearly quadruple the average annual catch that had been sustained for at least the century before. In his book *Cod: The Ecological History of the North Atlantic Fisheries,* George Rose says the northern stock never recovered from this "onslaught." He described what it would have looked like: "The Grand Banks were lit up at night by cities of hundreds of trawlers and their mother ships — huge floating factories that could carry thousands of tonnes of fish." Rose says that in 1968, the foreign catches were six times higher than the total Newfoundland fishery and that, in roughly one decade — from 1960 to 1972 — four to five billion fish, more than fourteen million tonnes, were caught, most by foreign fleets. The effects on the traditional inshore fishery were felt almost immediately: "The trawlers were fishing the same fish stocks that had supported coastal fisheries for centuries," he wrote, and the inshore fishers were having trouble finding fish.[111]

The strip mining of cod and other ocean life was, according to Rose, also harming the smaller and lesser known stocks and this was already being noticed as early as the 1960s. "Relatively small stocks in the Gulf of St. Lawrence and on the Scotian Shelf were first to suffer," he wrote. By this time, he says, Canadian scientists were already describing what they saw as the symptoms of overfishing: cod and haddock populations had been so severely reduced that they were no longer able to sustain themselves through reproduction.[112] Nature was being pushed beyond its limits and the end of the overfishing was nowhere in sight.

The cod landings of 1968, now referred to as the "killer spike," would prove to have profound and, some argue, permanent, ecological consequences. But it was also an example of how the traditional knowledge of inshore fishermen had been devalued and ignored. Their finely tuned and sophisticated understanding of fish and their natural cycles as well as an acceptance of the limitations and uncertainty in the natural world were not deemed important. The "killer spike" also raises important questions about unrestrained greed and how our relationship with nature and each other has been determined by a particular economic system — one that is in dire need of reform.

Dean Bavington says it's now understood there were permanent effects from the killer spike. "It turns out that what you need for a population that can continue to reproduce itself is a lot of large, old female fish."[113] The record catches of 1968, when all the old fish were landed, represented the removal of this accumulated reproductive potential. Bavington says the inshore fishermen understood the importance of "mother fish" — the fish you weren't supposed to catch — but their knowledge and understanding was often disparaged as "anecdotal" stories and not "real" knowledge. He explains that protecting the larger females was crucial because they not only produce more eggs — between five and eleven million eggs compared to fewer than one million for small females — but also because they produce larger and possibly more viable eggs, which therefore increase the chance of survival of those eggs. Since the odds are that only one in a million cod eggs will reach adulthood, fewer old spawners mean fewer eggs, which mean fewer cod.

In 1962, the biomass of cod off Newfoundland and Labrador capable of reproducing was estimated to be 1.6 million tonnes. By 1992, the stocks had been all but wiped out, reduced to a mere 22,000 tonnes. In other words, nearly 99 percent of the cod off Newfoundland and Labrador had disappeared in just three decades.[114] First, the old fish were caught by off-shore draggers when they were highly aggregated, and spawning; then, as the populations collapsed, more younger fish were landed, so that in the last years of the fishery, "almost ninety percent of the reported landings were immature fish."[115] According to the late Ransom Myers, a fisheries biologist with the DFO in the 1980s and 1990s, "No one understood how fast the decline happened at the end — it was only a couple of years. The quotas had been too high. They refused to slow down because they had seen lots of little fish coming in — a good year class. The little fish were caught and discarded and there was no future."[116]

Bavington traces the causes of the collapse back to the nineteenth century. He says that by the 1930s, two shifts were well underway that would seal the cod's fate. One had to do with science and the other with economics. In the century between 1850 and 1950, a transformation occurred within the fishery: it changed from a mercantile system, where people would catch fish for personal use and sell the surplus to the local merchant, or exchange fish for other products, to an industrial capitalist economy, where privately owned, profit-driven factories emerged employing wage labour. Bavington says the pressure to catch more fish to generate bigger profits, coupled with the demand for fish landings that were steady and predictable, led to a "turning point" and the rise of what he calls "scientific management."

The idea of codfish as an aggregated population to be "managed" was a mathematical approach that had been developing since the early 1900s. It replaced the view of codfish as individual fish with unique life histories. In a "quantitative flip," the fish suddenly became more abstract. They were now seen as populations or what Bavington calls "swimming inventory" — inventory to meet the demand of merchants and bankers who were investors in what had now become a fishing industry. To them, the normal and natural fluctuations in landings — the ebb and flow of codfish themselves, which had been an accepted fact by the inshore fishermen — were now seen as a problem because it created economic uncertainty, with no firm guarantees of predictable returns on invested capital.

Bavington explains that this new science would solve this problem. Scientists would take the characteristics of the fish population — its fertility, natural mortality, and so forth. They would then factor in the carrying capacity of the environment and work out the surplus amount, or what is called the "maximum sustainable yield" (MSY) that could be taken from the population year after year and still have the population bounce back. This notion was naturally appealing to investors in the fishery but it was not necessarily good for the fish. Consequently, the belief in a maximum sustainable yield did not go unchallenged.

In 1977, when Canada was creating the two-hundred-nautical-mile exclusive economic zone and MSY was being enshrined in national policy documents and incorporated in international treaties, Peter Larkin, a prominent fisheries biologist, came out strongly against it. In a now famous paper titled "Epitaph for the Concept of Maximum Sustainable Yield," the U.B.C. professor referred to MSY as a "doctrine," and likened it to a "religious movement" based on faith rather than facts. Essentially, he argued that using MSY as a management tool was very risky because it ignored the fact that fish populations undergo natural fluctuations in abundance and will eventually be depleted if fixed amounts are fished continuously year after year. MSY also ignored the complexity of marine food webs and inter-species interactions and therefore, its use could never achieve maximum sustainable yields for all species at the same time.[117] "It is a pity," he wrote, "that now, just when the concept of maximum sustainable yield … is on the verge of worldwide application, it must be abandoned. But that's the way it goes with the things we believe."[118]*

But MSY was not abandoned. Rather, it became the "holy grail" of fisheries management.[119] "Right when the natural scientists were rejecting it," Bavington explains, "it was being embraced by lawyers and self-styled social scientists — economists — to come up with a model that allows for profitable investment in fisheries." Today, fisheries models do incorporate some

---

* Larkin's famous epitaph for MSY appeared in a prominent fisheries journal in 1977. It read: "Here lies the concept, MSY. It advocated yields too high, and didn't spell out how to slice the pie. We bury it with best of wishes. Especially on behalf of fishes. We don't know yet what will take its place. But hope it's good for the human race."

"buffer," so that, instead of fishing at MSY, they may set the quota slightly lower to allow for some measurement error and fluctuations in the underlying variables. But, he says, "the basic assumption that fish can be understood as single species stocks producing a surplus has remained constant."

As the economic shift to industrial capitalism was occurring within the fishery, new fishing technologies were introduced, each one more "productive" — capable of catching more fish in less time — and more profitable than the last. The new technologies also meant that the amount of money needed to buy the new equipment and participate in the fishery increased, which also put pressure on fishers to catch more fish.

On the early schooners, cod were caught one at a time with hand-lines right off the deck, but by 1850, this method was largely replaced by hand-lining from small seaworthy boats called dories that were launched from schooners. Hand-lining was soon replaced by long-lining, or "tub-trawling," from dories. This technique involved fishers rowing out in dories where they'd set hundreds, if not thousands, of baited hooks. This resulted in more fish being caught by each fisher; as well, it covered more ocean ground. But this wasn't to last long. In the book *Shifting Baselines: The Past and the Future of Ocean Fisheries*, Jeffery Bolster and his colleagues studied fishing journals and logbooks from New England fleets dating back to the 1850s in the age of sail and found that the ecological impetus behind the transition to a larger "hook footprint" was based on the fact that fishers were already aware of the fact that annual catches were declining. "The declines continued and, by 1856, the average catch per vessel had dropped by 7,000 fish in just four years. The seven men fishing from an average schooner in 1855 caught what five men had expected to catch in 1852."[120]

In the early 1900s, the schooner fleets and their flotillas of dories were replaced by steam trawlers equipped with conical shaped nets that were dragged along the ocean floor and held open with iron-shod "doors." By the 1950s, floating fish factories, four times the size of the steam trawlers, appeared on the scene. With trawl nets the size of football fields and sonar to detect and track schools of fish, these fish factories were capable of locating and killing cod at unprecedented and eventually catastrophic rates.

Bavington says each time new and potentially destructive technologies were introduced, inshore fishers actively resisted them. "As early as the 1850s fishermen were articulating an argument about fishing, that new technologies changed the person fishing as much as the fish," he says, expressing an insight whose prescience would prove to be uncanny.

More than a century later, fishing was indeed found to have profound effects on fish, and not just in terms of their abundance. Intense trawling of bigger adults favoured the evolution of early-maturing cod. That is, in a remarkable feat of self-preservation, the cod's genetic makeup changed:

they began maturing at a younger age to ensure that they lived long enough to reproduce. Scientists have also recently documented that, over several decades, this size selection has led to significant declines in size to the point that the average weight of cod (at a particular age) is up to 60 percent less than what it was in the early 1970s. These scientists say that the now smaller predators are also in poorer condition and speculate they may be "less effective hunters."[121]

While it is astonishing that a particular fishing technology practised for a relatively short period of time could change the evolution of fish, it may not have come as much of a surprise to the inshore fishers Bavington talks about. He says they used to talk about fish "as if they were living things that respond to the things we do," and he thinks that this perspective has been lost, for the most part. "There are still fishermen that come out and say we should go back to the hook and line," he says, arguably a more sustainable technology where the fisher plays a more passive role, attracting the fish by naturally or artificially baiting hooks fixed to the end of lines.

In fact, hook and line fishing dominated the history of commercial cod fishing on Canada's east coast — particularly on the inshore and offshore banks of Newfoundland. Bavington says hook and line fishing was practised over a relatively short period of the year when cod were migrating to follow their prey. "They would follow the capelin in from the offshore banks where they spawned," he says, "and fishermen would catch fish that were going after the capelin. They would catch capelin, cut them up for bait, and put them down on a hook, and when cod were hungry they'd go for the baited hook."[122]

But history suggests that these simple technologies weren't as benign as we'd like to believe. Bolster and his colleagues showed, contrary to what is conventionally believed, that New England sailing fleets using simple hooks, lines and handmade nets were able to deplete the abundant fish stocks by the middle of the nineteenth century. Today we blame the collapse of fish stocks on overfishing that took place within the last seventy years, but their study shows that, while destructive human-induced impacts on the oceans may have accelerated in this time period, the roots of the destruction may go much deeper.

I ask Bavington, "Do you think industrial capitalism just quickened the process of destruction, or is there something more?" He answers that the hook and line definitely did cause local depletions. In a bay, for instance, if you have too many hooks and lines, you take too many fish. But he says, in the past, in a subsistence-based system, the fishermen would have switched to something else. "If there's no cod in the bay they wouldn't fish for cod for a few years but would fish for salmon, or some other species," he says. Today we respond to the decline in stocks by "scaling up the fishery as opposed to adapting to it." Once you have an industrial capitalist system, any recognition of natural limits disappears and effort just gets ramped up. "There seems to be no way out," he says.

Fishers Are Feeling Squeezed

As we have seen, scapegoating seals — the practice of assigning blame that is not based on facts — does provide a powerful distraction from a number of public policy issues we should really be rallying over. But it is also motivated by another very powerful reality. According to David Lavigne, contemporary calls for culls — like the current one for grey seals — come when the vast majority of the world's fisheries are either fully exploited, overexploited or depleted. He says there is a relationship between the availability of fish stocks and the prevailing attitude among fishers toward seals, and that scapegoating is a response to both scarcity and a perceived threat to profits.[123] Given the state of the fisheries today, the uncertainty that prevails and the way that fishers are feeling squeezed — topics we'll discuss in the following pages — it is easy to see where this tendency to scapegoat seals is coming from.

The Food and Agriculture Organization (FAO) first began assessing fisheries on a global scale in 1974. At that time, 10 percent of fish stocks were considered "overexploited," or producing "yields" that were lower than their biological or ecological potential. But over six decades, the reported global landings of marine fish have skyrocketed from seventeen million tonnes in 1950 to more than eighty million tonnes. Today, nearly one-third of all fish stocks fall into the "overexploited" category. An additional 57 percent of stocks worldwide are now considered to be "fully exploited," which means they have no more room for expansion and are on the verge of decline. Only 13 percent are categorized as "non-fully exploited."[124] Here, in the northwest Atlantic, FAO reports that only 6 percent of fish stocks are "non-fully exploited," 17 percent are "overexploited" and 77 percent are "fully exploited," with no where to go but down.

As dramatic as these official numbers may sound, Daniel Pauly says the reality is much worse. He says that at the onset of the twenty-first century, world fish landings were actually in the order of 120 to 140 million, much higher than the eighty million reported by the FAO, which do not account for illegal, unreported, or undocumented catches (IUU). Pauly says IUU catches include fish that have been dumped by shrimp trawlers, which is usually 90 percent of their actual catch, the catch of fleets operating under flags of convenience, and the individual small catches of "millions of artisanal fishers (including women and children) in developing countries which turns out to be very high in the aggregate, but still goes unreported by national governments and international agencies."[125]

Pauly also says that up until the 1980s, the catches of the world were increasing, but since then they have been declining, by about 700,000 tonnes per year. "Catches are declining in spite of a tremendous increase of fishing effort," which he says is an indication of depleted stocks. He also says that not only have the fisheries expanded technologically, they've expanded geographically. Up until the 1950s, industrial fishing was largely contained around industrial countries but depletions of these fish stocks meant industrial fishing had to go elsewhere, into unexploited regions. First, this meant the offshore, then it moved southwards. Pauly explains that between 1950 and 1980, the fishery expanded at a rate of one million square kilometres per year, and in the 1980s, it accelerated to three or four million square kilometres per year — a size roughly equivalent to the Amazon rainforest. "Then [the expansion] flattens out because there is nowhere else to go ... and that's the reason why catches globally are declining," he says. "It's like a Ponzi scheme: when you have gotten all the capital from your friends and their friends, the whole thing implodes."[126]

Pauly says people expect this implosion to be "dramatic," similar to what happened when the cod collapsed and the fishery was shut down. But he says this isn't likely the way it will happen. "Rather, what happens is that this skipper or this fisher cannot operate and quits and this area is not fished anymore because it's not worth going there," he says. "This little decision, repeated millions of times, produces a declining catch without anybody really noticing."[127]

Another disturbing trend Pauly revealed more than a decade ago was one he called "taxonomic expansion," more commonly known as "fishing down the food web." He says that if you analyze the catches of the world, the data reveal that we are now capturing and marketing "previously spurned species of increasingly smaller fish and invertebrates to replace a diminishing supply of traditionally targeted larger fish species."[128] In other words, we used to catch big fish, higher up in the food web, such as cod, and now we're catching smaller fish and invertebrates, lower down this web, such as lobster and shrimp.

According to Tony Charles, fishing down the food web poses two formidable problems. One is that it threatens the very functioning of ecological food webs and the overall resilience of the system to shocks. But perhaps less obvious is the threat it poses to human community resilience. He says when the cod and other groundfish collapsed, many fishers in Nova Scotia who remained in the fishery adapted to the crisis by entering the growing lobster fishery. In Newfoundland and Labrador the fishers who remained turned to shrimp and crab. Much of the increase in these species, as previously discussed, has been linked to the decrease in predation by predator fish, such as cod. But with fisheries now dependent on these species at the bottom of the marine food web, "there is less room to manoeuvre," says Charles.

This is certainly what DFO data seem to indicate. In 2010, the value of commercial landings of lobster, crab and shrimp in the Atlantic region was more than $1.1 billion — representing more than 73 percent of the value of all fisheries landings in that year.[129] If anything were to go wrong with these fisheries, Charles says, it would not be possible to "fish down" any further: with few remaining options, such a failure would cause "even greater socio-economic devastation than the collapse of the cod."[130] Given how climate change is predicted to play out in the oceans, the future of fishing is very uncertain, to say the least.

In early 2012, the potentially disruptive effects of climate change on the lobster fishery were very much on the minds of fishers and scientists who gathered for their annual conference in Truro, Nova Scotia. Liette Vasseur, a professor at Brock University who is an expert on the marine effects of climate change, was a keynote speaker at the nineteenth annual conference of the Fishermen and Scientists Research Society — a group that was created in Atlantic Canada after the cod collapse to collect and share information about fish stocks. Vasseur told the conference that climate change was "the elephant in the room," that, while lobsters might initially experience some gains from a warming sea surface — resulting in faster growth and a larger number of larvae surviving to the post-larval stage — she warned the gains would likely be short-lived and that, at some point, the populations may crash. She said the increase in temperatures coupled with acidification will put pressure on the species, which could also lead to a higher incidence of disease. "At some point there is a threshold in terms of temperature and pH," she says. "It's really the tipping point, and if by then you haven't already done something, I think it's already too late."

In fact, the future for any larvae-producing sea creature — fish and shrimp included — is precarious. These were among the findings of an international research project led by now-retired DFO shrimp expert, Peter Koeller.[131] Warmer oceans could result in the disruption of a once perfectly synchronous event: the hatching of larvae timed to the availability of food. Rising ocean temperatures could cause a "mismatch" in this timing, say scientists, so that shrimp eggs, for instance, which are very sensitive to bottom water temperature, could hatch earlier, before the spring bloom, when food is scarce.

The depletion of global fish stocks and fishing down the food web, as well as climate change, all just mean that everything we thought we could count on is shifting and tentative. Fishers, particularly the small inshore ones, are being squeezed, not just by these ecological realities, but by economic ones.

Marc Allain is a research associate with the Canadian Fisheries Research Network at the University of New Brunswick. The Network brings academics, government scientists and industry representatives together to look at issues of relevance to the fishing industry. Allain says the "race for fish" — the competition between fleets that eventually led to the collapse of the ground-fish — resulted in overcapitalization, a situation in which fishers struggled to achieve unrealistic returns on their investment. In 1992, when then federal fisheries minister John Crosbie announced the moratorium for the northern stock, he also said that too many boats and too many people were chasing too few fish. In other words, a move to "rationalize" the fishery and reduce capacity was imminent. Allain says that in order to deal with this overcapacity, the government eliminated some of it by using market mechanisms and what are called Individual Transferable Quotas (ITQs). "You give everyone a share and then you let them trade so the most efficient operator will buy out the others," he explains.

ITQs, introduced in the smaller vessel (under 45-foot) groundfish fleets in the 1990s, gave licence holders a guaranteed percentage of the total allowable catch based on their "catch history" over a six-year period. Owning it gave them the freedom to sell it, or lease it, and thereby transfer it to the highest bidder. Prior to this there was a collective quota for entire fleets. Those in support of the new scheme say it eliminates the competitive "race for fish," because fishers own a guaranteed share of the "resource." But critics of ITQs say they result in corporate concentration and benefit those who overfished in the first place. "In Nova Scotia it became very prejudicial to longliners, handliners, and gill netters," says Allain. "[The government] took the last years of catch history and rewarded those who created the overfishing problem." Not only that, it was only the licence holders who were recognized and essentially gifted the fish, while crew-members who also helped amass the catch histories lost out.

Ronnie Wolkins knows about this first hand. It will be recalled that he heads up the South West Fishermen's Rights Association based in Clark's Harbour and fishes using hook and line. He tells me the story of when he was a crew member aboard a forty-two foot fishing boat that ran into some trouble. On its way back to Cape Sable Island from George's Bank and carrying 36,000 pounds of fish, the boat hit a strong wind from the northeast and started taking on water. "We started bailing and used cotton gloves and screw drivers to chink the cracks in the deck," he says. Even though all those aboard the boat were fishers, none of them actually owned the licence to fish; based on the new rules, when it came time to allocate percentages of quota, Wolkins says that, even though the men risked their lives for those fish, "not one man aboard that boat got a catch history from that trip."

Judith Maxwell runs the Scotia Fundy Inshore Fishermen's Association, which also represents inshore fishermen. Her group differs from Wolkins' because it adopted what she calls an "informal" ITQ system. "Every fishing licence has a catch history attached to it," she explains, "and fishermen can choose whether they go into the informal ITQ system or the competitive fishery." She says the majority of inshore fishers in southwest Nova Scotia are part of this informal ITQ system, but, if they choose to go into the competitive fishery, they would join an association like Wolkins' group, where they combine all their catch histories and pool the fish. This total amount is then distributed among the fishers and allocated on a weekly basis.

Maxwell says that because the DFO cut the fishing quotas so much, the percentages allocated to the licence holders translates into a lot less fish; for some, it's not enough to operate economically. In 1998, demonstrations erupted largely as a result of the fall-out from DFOs catch history allocations in the fixed-gear groundfishery. In February of that year, Wolkins was among those who occupied a DFO office in Barrington Passage. By March the fishermens' anger and discontent had spread to the point where ten DFO offices around the province were occupied. Three months later, Scott Nickerson and three other fishers from southwest Nova Scotia made the news when they chained themselves to the flagpole on the lawn of the Nova Scotia legislature and pitched a tent with the words "we need fish" on the side. Called "The Flagpole Four," they argued that the push toward ITQs was an attempt to squeeze out the little guy. They said the DFO didn't give them enough quota to feed their families. Later the same year, Nickerson made the news again when he committed suicide by shooting himself in the chest with a rifle.

Maxwell says that, because of the shortage of fish, out of the 250 members in her group, only fifty actively fish, while the remaining two hundred lease their quota to other fishermen. That way, fishers can accumulate quota, making it more worthwhile to go fishing. She says another way to transfer the quota is to sell a fishing licence. "I know a lot of fishermen who are now in their sixties and they know they're never going to go fishing again so they sell their licence. The guy purchasing it doesn't get the licence number — that disappears for life — but he gets all the benefits," she says. "That includes the quota." Maxwell says this is largely how the fleet got downsized. She says that in the mid-1990s there were about 750 fishing licences in Shelburne County alone; today there are only 560. DFO data show a similar trend: In 1996 there were 15,245 licence holders in Nova Scotia; by 2009 there were 5,898. In Atlantic Canada overall the number of licence holders plummeted from 49,957 to 17,751 in the same time period.

Critics of the system say those with greater access to capital can accumulate quota, whether it's by leasing it or buying out fishing licences, which results in corporate concentration. Details about how the "informal" ITQ system has specifically led to this concentration in Atlantic Canada is largely unknown, mainly because the information is not publicly available.

However, according to Maxwell, there is an "ongoing battle" over keeping the inshore fishery alive. Right now, there are DFO restrictions in place that do not allow quota to be mixed between fleets. For instance, a dragger, which is part of the mobile-gear sector, could buy out the licence of an inshore fisher in the fixed-gear sector, but he would not be allowed to add the quota attached to that licence to his own. He would have to either lease the quota back to an inshore fisher or fish it himself by acquiring a fixed-gear boat. This is called "fleet separation": Maxwell says that, if DFO were to ever do away with this restriction, the fishery would concentrate into the hands of a few extremely quickly. "Our fear is mixing of the histories between the two different fleets because then as the stocks keep depleting and mobile gear needs to access the fishing grounds twelve months of the year to keep their enterprise going, if they could buy fixed gear quota and add it to theirs, then our stock and resource would slowly disappear," Maxwell explains. From a community perspective this would mean that fishing communities would lose access to fish.

There are already indications that concentration is happening, as draggers buy out fishing licences from the fixed gear sector and lease the quota back to the inshore. In 2004, DFO surveyed small boat (less than 45 feet) inshore fishers in the Maritimes about their operating and maintenance expenses and found that on average the fleet paid more than $7,000 a year to lease quota, which amounted to roughly 7 percent of all expenses. While this isn't good, it's still nowhere near as bad as it could be.

Like Maxwell, Marc Allain is worried the DFO might abandon restrictions that are currently protecting the inshore fishery in Atlantic Canada, and bring in policies like it did in the west that allow non-fishers to own quota and lease it back to the fishers. When ITQs were first introduced in the Pacific fisheries, the original quotas were allocated or "gifted" to vessel owners based on catch histories: this process was similar to the one used in Atlantic Canada. However, in the west, there is no restriction on who could own quota; as a result, outside investors can own quota and lease it back to fishers. In a 2012 paper on the effects of the quota scheme in the Pacific fisheries, Marc Allain wrote, "In the space of a few short years, access to the most lucrative species has gotten concentrated in the hands of 'investors.'"[132] Since the new quota scheme was introduced out west, leasing fees have skyrocketed: in some cases the leasing cost was as high as 75 percent of the landed value of the fish. To illustrate the problem, Allain provides the cost breakdown for one representative small-boat fishing trip that went out in the spring of 2011. On this particular trip the fishers landed 22,000 pounds of fish including sablefish, halibut, rockfish and lingcod, valued at $64,000. From this revenue, the fisher who owned and operated the vessel paid $9,000 to his crew and $6,000 to vessel expenses, while the lion's share — $42,000 or 66 percent of the landed value — went to lease quotas. This left only $7,000 for the boat share, which is essentially the boat owner's income.

Here in Atlantic Canada restrictions like "fleet separation" and "owner-operator" rules are still in place, which means the owner needs to operate the boat, and fishers or processors are still the only ones allowed to own fish quota. "But we're always fearful that some back door will open up," says Maxwell. "If that happens, it could end up that lawyers, drug-store owners and Walmart, could end up owning the quota."

The way Wolkins sees it, things have gotten worse for inshore fishers since the protest years. Wolkins says fishers are leaving and heading west, because there just aren't any fish. "I went to Brown's [Bank] when it opened for hook and line and I went to fish for halibut on the inside edge and I didn't see a single boat. None. That kind of surprised me. When I set my gear I realized why there weren't any boats, there wasn't anything there anyway."

I ask Wolkins about the grey seals. "They're some smart," he says. "They will eat the halibut right off the hook. When we were young, we never caught a seal on a hook. I think something's happening to their food source and so they're looking for something else." Wolkins supports the idea of a cull. He says the seals are costing him a lot of money. But, he says, that wouldn't bother him so much if there were enough fish out there for him to catch.

Fish Full of Dollars

Harry Thurston has witnessed some of these changes in the fishery over the years. He's an award-winning journalist, naturalist, poet and the author of the book *The Atlantic Coast: A Natural History*. Thurston grew up on a farm in Yarmouth, Nova Scotia and has lived a good portion of his life on the tidal Tidnish River that flows into the Northumberland Strait of the Gulf of St. Lawrence. He says his education as an environmentalist came in the late 1960s when he was eighteen years old and working as a fisheries technician at a DFO lab in Yarmouth. His job was to analyze the reusable protein from herring meal offal.

> At that time there was a fleet of sixty seiners going out of Yarmouth harbour every night and they were supplying eight or ten herring meal plants in southwest Nova Scotia, and every day I would get a sample — a green, putrid sample — the offal, the guts, parts that weren't getting ground into herring meal. I started in May and by the first of August I wasn't getting any samples, because they had so overexploited the herring that they weren't catching any more. So here I was, working on a DFO-sponsored research project to try to recover protein from the offal when they were out completely decimating the resource. I very early learned there was a kind of inverted logic to how we were managing the resource. I mean, the irony couldn't be any more stark.

Thurston's story makes me wonder if anything has changed. Can we now safely say we've learned our lesson and are showing some restraint in the way we fish? According to what Denny Morrow tells me, this is not the case. The former head of the Nova Scotia Fish Packer's Association is now semi-retired and runs a consulting business, working to maintain the moratorium on oil and gas drilling on George's Bank. When we met, it was mid-November, just before the opening of the lobster fishing season in southwest Nova Scotia — the most lucrative fishery in the province and one that really only started to boom after the groundfish went bust. Morrow explains that even though there are no quotas for lobster, there is still a race for them. "We have a trap fishery that's catch all you can, but you fish twenty-four hours a day," he says. "They'll be starting next week and up until New Year's time, close to twenty million pounds of lobster will be caught. That's in just one month." He says this quantity overwhelms the fresh lobster market and drives down the price so that lobster fishers are not breaking even. "The quality isn't even that good at this time of year," he says. As a result, a lot of it ends up getting processed. "So here's a non-quota fishery that's competitive and it's unbelievable — to the point where people are shooting themselves in the pocket book and they all know it. The industry that ships them knows it, the government knows it, but we can't do anything about it."

Morrow says it's the competition that has created this situation. "The gun goes off and the boats go out," he says. He explains the thoughts that run through the head of a lobster fisher: "I have to do everything I can to be more efficient and catch them as fast as possible. If I don't, [the lobsters] are going to be gone." Morrow says the competition is driving investment in bigger boats that are able to carry all the traps and maybe even have a well of seawater to keep the lobsters in. This way fishers can just keep pulling traps, he says. "I don't know if you know what lobster boats used to look like. They used to be about eighteen feet wide, now they're twenty-six feet wide," he says. "If I fish with a small boat, I'm going to be left behind."

According to Thurston, there's an imbalance in the way our society compensates for work, particularly in primary producing industries, such as fishing and farming. He says that in these industries there is a drive to produce more with fewer people:

> If you go to Yarmouth, which is my home town, and see what they call a Cape Island boat today — you could take a traditional Cape Island boat and put it in the stern of this [modern] boat. I mean they're getting to be very big boats, which cost a half a million dollars. When you've got that kind of capitalization and a family to feed, you have to go out and catch a lot of fish. That changes your relationship with the natural world.

Thurston says the non-recovery of the cod and the recent call for a grey seal cull is "a good object lesson in how we have mismanaged resources in the past." But it's also a lesson in how our relationship with nature has gone askew. "Now we have to go further and try to understand, frankly, what is happening out there," he says. While some would have us believe that seals have caused all these problems, the real culprit is much more difficult to define, and to contain.

Technological innovation, driven by the powerful forces of industrial capitalism, has increased productivity and profits (for an elite few) but at the same time, it has put increased stress on marine ecosystems and has displaced fisheries workers. This reality has been particularly hard on small communities dependent on extracting goods from nature. Evidence suggests that the long-term stability of these communities may be at odds — in contradiction even — with the stability of the fishing industry itself. In other words, if the fishing industry can no longer grow by extracting more marine life from the oceans, the only way for it to increase productivity is to reduce employment, and this is how small communities wither and die.[133]

This is a subject Morrow is passionate about. He strongly supports a cull of grey seals: the way he sees it, a show of support for culling is also a show of support for fisheries and for viable coastal communities. However, he feels that it is too late to do anything in Atlantic Canada. "It would be too costly to reduce our herds to a size that would allow cod stocks to rebuild," he says. "At some point, nature will step in and disease will hit these seal herds and reduce the numbers." Morrow is convinced that, if the federal government decides against a cull, their decision would be based on the wish to have less fish and fewer fishers and fish plant workers: "Fewer fishermen means less opposition to off-shore oil and gas development," something he says the government is pushing for now because of the lucrative royalties that come with it. He explains,

> In the event of a catastrophe like the Deep Water Horizon, there will be greatly reduced damage claims by fishermen. Off-shore oil and gas projects don't seem to produce a lot of jobs in coastal communities. They don't even produce cheaper heating. The result for our coastal communities will be a continued export of our young people and a sad future for many communities.

Reimagining Our Relationship with Nature

A startling 2006 study led by Boris Worm found that the loss of species diversity in the ocean was accelerating and that, if this trend continued, there would be a global collapse of all species currently fished by the year 2048. According to the authors, one antidote to this almost inconceivable trend is to create marine protected areas where marine life is allowed to exist without human intrusion. The authors examined forty-four marine protected areas and four large-scale fisheries closures worldwide — all were effectively large-scale experiments — to see whether there was any effect on biodiversity and ecosystem services, which includes the provision of seafood. They found that reserves and fisheries closures were associated with increased "species richness" and that there were large increases in fisheries productivity nearby.[134]

Despite these tangible improvements, only slightly more than 1 percent of the world's oceans are protected in this way. This is not surprising given that the benefits provided by the natural world — the ecosystem services we discussed earlier — as well as the intrinsic or inherent value of the natural world regardless of its utility to humans, are largely ignored in our current economic system. But at the same time, this lack of recognition is astonishing because these are services without which we, as a species, simply cannot live.

American essayist and author Curtis White argues that, for the most part, the environmental movement has contributed to the problems the world faces today because, rather than dealing with the deeper, root cause of the problems, it has isolated problems from their true context and gone after the smaller, more manageable issues: the point sources and the obvious offenders. "Confront the bulldozers. Confront the chainsaws. Confront Monsanto. Fight the power," he writes. White argues we need to go much further: "Something in the very fabric of our daily life is deeply anti-nature as well as anti-human."[135]

I have argued that the scapegoating of the grey seal is a result of the current crisis, which is the failure of cod to recover. But I am also arguing that the failure of cod to recover is a symptom of a much larger, much deeper, problem. In his book *The Wayfinders: Why Ancient Wisdom Matters in the Modern World*, Wade Davis traces the deeper issue back to the time when humans began to reduce the world to "a mechanism." In this new worldview, nature became "an obstacle to overcome, a resource to be exploited," and "has in good measure determined the manner in which our cultural tradition has blindly interacted with the living planet."[136] In describing this ancient worldview, Thurston examined the way that Indigenous people, who historically depended on wild animals and plants for survival, brokered a "moral deal," whereby "survival for both animal and human depended upon a reciprocal relationship." He writes: "Animals offered themselves to the hunter, and without this gift of self-sacrifice, the hunter could not be successful. In return, the hunter had to treat all animals with respect or perish."[137]

We have come a long way from this sacred relationship and this holistic worldview. The perspective Davis describes, imbued with meaning and symbolism, has been transformed, as we have seen, into one that views the world in terms of commodities and resources. Value is applied very selectively — to products that can be extracted and sold — with no recognition of the health of what is left behind or the value of the services it would have provided indefinitely, if left alone. If only a fraction of this value were acknowledged, we would be making valiant efforts not to recklessly destroy the living world or the complex structures that support it. We would also make many of the changes that prominent fisheries scientists call for today: the creation of vast marine protected areas, an end to using destructive fishing gear, a reduction in commercial fishing effort, and (straight from Daniel Pauly's wish list) the outright "abolition of capacity-enhancing subsidies," such as tax-free fuel and loan guarantees for boat purchases.[138]

The worldview that has promoted the liquidation of the natural world — on the land and in the sea — has also encouraged the exploitation and displacement of people. In other words, the forces that place the small inshore fishers at the brink of their own financial collapse are precisely the same forces that destroyed the cod and may now threaten the future of the shellfish fisheries that replaced it: an economic system rooted in the delusion that its own growth is limitless and possible despite its dependence on a finite planet.

This long-standing drive to manage and control nature needs to be replaced with a commitment to live within the limits of the ecosystems of which we are a part. Such a commitment could be informed by the ancient wisdom that Davis and Thurston so eloquently describe. Dean Bavington suggests a return to a way of fishing that is not only sustainable for the fish but also preserves the integrity of the fisher. Is it possible to work out a new relationship with nature, and as Jon Lien recommended, with the species that share this planet? It seems that the answer to such a question would have to be: not without a great deal of difficulty.

The solution will have to involve reinventing the economic system so that it serves humanity and the planet, and places value on what actually matters to most of us: vital community life, healthy and happy human populations ,and the health, beauty and integrity of the natural world. Governments and public servants must be called upon to act on behalf of the public interest — which includes being responsible stewards of the natural world — not as facilitators for corporate and other vested interests.

In his book, *I See Satan Fall Like Lightning*, Rene Girard explains that the practice of scapegoating satisfies "the appetite for violence that awakens in people when anger seizes them and when the true object of their anger is untouchable."[139] As we have seen, fishers, fishing communities and the general public have good reason to be angry — for the collapse of the cod and the resulting ecological, cultural and social upheaval and for the cod not coming back — but it is becoming more and more difficult to find political avenues to express this anger.

Historically, communities often practised scapegoat rituals when there was a crisis or state of emergency: the idea was that removing the scapegoat would purify or cleanse the community of the evil responsible for the crisis. Killing thousands of grey seals could never cleanse us of what ails us. It would only perpetuate the greed and hubris that brought us to this present juncture. It would also represent our wholesale denial of the complexity and uncertainty that characterizes the marine ecosystem. We have the capacity to understand the consequences of our past mistakes and enough knowledge to foresee where they may lead, but the question is do we have enough collective wisdom and imagination to see our way out of it? In this way, all of us — the cod and the seals included — are in the exact same boat. Keeping it afloat depends a lot on what we do next.

Epilogue

In the process of researching this book, I naturally sought out the expertise of a number of DFO scientists. I had heard news reports about how they were not allowed to speak to the media without permission and that obtaining permission was getting more and more difficult, but I wasn't fully aware of how serious a problem it had become. So in February and March 2012 I began what would become a very long and drawn-out process.

By mid-April, after having heard nothing about the status of a number of my requests, I received a telephone call from Melanie Carkner, media relations advisor at national headquarters in Ottawa, who asked me to "consolidate" all my requests into one email. She also wanted me to explain what I was doing, what the information would be used for and by what date I needed it. I complied with her request, explaining in my email that I was working on a book with a broad focus on the grey seals and the cod. I also explained that while the deadline for my manuscript was December — eight months later — I needed the information for the research I was doing at that time. I also mentioned that the information could be used in news or magazine articles.

Five months later I was still waiting for my requests to be dealt with. In frustration, and with a certain amount of curiosity, I decided to file an Access to Information (ATIP) request. I asked to see all the internal DFO emails pertaining to my requests to interview the DFO scientists. In October — following my ATIP request — Carkner called asking me (again) to send her an email consolidating all my requests. She said she wanted to provide "closure" on my file. By late November I had received word from the ATIP Information Commissioner that my request was completed. Once I paid for the photocopying they would send me the file of emails totalling an astonishing 320 pages.

Even though I had heard nothing from DFO Communications, it didn't mean that within the busy network of communications officers, advisors, directors and managers, quite a lot hadn't transpired.

Poring over the two-inch high stack of emails, I discovered that no less than eighteen communications employees in the DFO's Maritime, Gulf, and Quebec regions, as well as in its Ottawa headquarters, were involved in some way with my requests for information and interviews. This partly explains the sizable file: with so many people involved, many of the pages were repeats of the same emails, just in different inboxes. But within this quagmire of repetition, there were also a few telling correspondences.

One of the interviews that I requested back in February 2012 was with Alida Bundy, a scientist at the Bedford Institute of Oceanography who does ecosystem modelling, a subject I wanted to explore in the book. That interview, surprisingly, was granted to me shortly after it was requested and in the ATIP files I discovered why. DFO communications felt that an interview with Bundy would be "a good opportunity to increase the visibility for Fisheries and Oceans Science and to highlight the evolving field of ecosystem research and modelling." They also noted there was a "small risk" that an interview with Bundy would be used to "promote the cause of the anti-sealing groups," but that overall the benefits outweighed the risks and that an interview would put DFO in a positive light. Emails further indicate that Bundy was provided with "media lines" drafted by communications people: a list of key messages to which she was instructed to adhere. She was also told to focus on the ecosystem modelling and not to comment on the recent seal-cod interaction study by Robert O'Boyle and Michael Sinclair — a study discussed in some detail in the book — and that if I did inquire about it she was to direct me to the study authors. That Bundy did nevertheless comment on the O'Boyle and Sinclair study during our interview, which was attended by communications manager Carl Myers, indicates that either she never received these aforementioned instructions or she decided to ignore them. The emails also indicated that, before being sent to Bundy, the "media lines" underwent an approval process and were ultimately "signed off" by Faith Scattolon, the Regional Director General of Fisheries and Oceans Canada, as well as Siddika Mithani, an assistant seputy minister, who was formerly with Health Canada. Mithani's official views about the proposed cull of grey seals are no mystery. When she testified at the Senate Committee hearings on the management of grey seals in October 2011, she told the Committee that in her view the science behind the proposal to cull 70,000 grey seals in the southern Gulf of St. Lawrence was "very sound."

In February of 2012 I also requested an interview with Don Bowen — who directs the Sable Island population survey. I was asked to provide the communications department with a list of questions for Bowen. The ATIP file indicated that Bowen did answer a list of questions, but they weren't exactly mine. The questions he received had been revised by DFO communications to the extent that one of my questions was eliminated altogether. One communications advisor identified the question, in which I asked Bowen if he was in support of culling seals, as a "red flag" issue. Bowen sent the communications department his answers sometime in May, but they were never forwarded to me. The reasons why an in-person interview was finally granted, nearly ten months after my initial request and with a draft manuscript nearly completed, remain somewhat of a mystery.

At the same time that DFO Communications informed me that I would finally be able to interview Bowen, they "respectfully denied" my request to interview Wayne Fairchild — a scientist with expertise in aquatic ecotoxicology — the study of the biological effects of toxic chemicals, including pesticides, in fish and other aquatic organisms. I heard about Fairchild when I attended the annual conference of the Fishermen and Scientists Research Society in Truro, Nova Scotia, and heard a presentation by scientist Dounia Daoud of Homarus, a non-profit organization whose mandate it is to "find a solution to the decline of lobster catches" in the southern Gulf of St. Lawrence. Daoud's presentation was about the effects of the insecticide endosulfan on lobster and whether it could be behind the decline in catches. Endosulfan has been used extensively in Prince Edward Island, particularly on potato fields. It is highly toxic to lobsters and fish: scientists believe it to be responsible for numerous fish kills around the world and it is thought to affect crustacean molt cycles. It also has the potential to bio-accumulate. In humans it is known to cause reproductive and developmental damage. As a result, Canada is phasing it out, but, as Daoud pointed out in her presentation, it will continue to persist and affect ocean life long after it is no longer in use. Daoud's presentation indicated that, based on her studies, endosulfan affected the long-term behaviour and survival of lobsters in the southern Gulf.

I wanted to ask Fairchild about the effects of these chemicals on fish and whether the bio-accumulation of toxic contaminants in adult cod could be contributing to killing them. While I wasn't able to interview Fairchild, I did discover in the ATIP file that in February 2012, shortly after my request, he did send DFO communications advisors two studies regarding pesticides and cod, which were never forwarded to me. It was only after I filed the ATIP request that I learned of them.

In the attempt to bring "closure" to my file, Carkner sent me two other outstanding documents. One was a document with "pre-approved" answers to my questions for Steve Campana about shark finning and shark bycatch. The other was Doug Swain's responses to a list of questions I had sent him seven months earlier. But what I discovered was that the answers I received from Doug, via DFO Communications, were not exactly the same as the answers he supplied to them. I noticed that in the ATIP file some sections had been redacted — censored — and I have no idea why. Swain would know, but my sense was he wouldn't be allowed to tell me.

The control of information on the part of DFO is certainly not new. Back in 1997, the year the late Ransom Myers, a distinguished marine biologist and conservationist, left the DFO to become the Killam Chair of Ocean Studies at Dalhousie University, he testified before a House of Commons Committee on Fisheries and Oceans that was looking at the role of science in fisheries management.[140] Myers had been a DFO scientist based in Newfoundland for thirteen years, beginning in 1983, during the years leading up to and immediately following the cod collapse. He described and documented for the Committee how certain data relevant to cod stocks were "kept secret" or withheld, how researchers were intimidated by senior bureaucrats and how reports were censored. He said that if the research "did not show what was desired by Ottawa bureaucrats," then it was sytematically suppressed.

As an example, Myers described one of his own reports, co-authored in 1995 with Alan Sinclair and Jeff Hutchings, examining whether there was any change in the mortality of cod as a result of the increase in the harp seal population. "We found out we could not detect the effect of seals with the data we had. Because we did not show what was desired by Ottawa bureaucrats, that research was suppressed." In other words, the scientists' conclusions were not in line with official DFO statements about seals and cod at the time — statements that implicated the seals in the collapse and downplayed the role of overfishing. Not only were Myers and his colleagues not allowed to present their paper at an international symposium on the subject, though an oral presentation was finally permitted, the DFO also withheld the manuscript from being published in leading journals. "They censored the paper and then denied the paper existed," he told the Committee.

Myers also revealed why, after the moratorium on cod fishing was declared on northern cod in 1992, there was a one-year delay in examining the other cod stocks in eastern Canada and announcing a moratorium in the Gulf and on the eastern Scotian Shelf. He said "direct suppression of information from scientists to the [Atlantic Groundfish Advisory Committee]," was to blame. He also described the delay as "a crime beyond imagination," because during this time "seventy percent of the remaining cod were removed and this caused a much greater collapse in the rest of eastern Canada than was needed."

Myers told the Committee that when he was quoted in the *Globe and Mail* saying the collapse had "nothing to do with the environment, nothing to do with the seals. It is simply overfishing," he was officially reprimanded.[141] He told the Committee that "the bureaucratic and authoritarian control" over science resulted in "pseudoscience, not science," and the system would "inevitably fail and lead to scientific blunders."

In 1997 Jeff Hutchings, Carl Walters and Richard Haedrich brought the issue out of the shadows and onto the international stage in a paper titled "Is Scientific Inquiry Incompatible with Government Information Control?" which was published in the *Canadian Journal of Fisheries and Aquatic Sciences*. In it they concluded that, within the DFO, nonscience influences were interfering with the dissemination of scientific information as well as the conduct of science. They said a system in which fisheries science is linked to fisheries management — as it is within the DFO — resulted in the "suppression of scientific uncertainty and a failure to document comprehensively legitimate differences in scientific opinion." They called for the replacement of the existing framework of government-sponsored fisheries science with the creation of a "politically independent" research body of fisheries scientists — whose advice would have to be followed by the minister — or at a minimum, a reorganization of the link between science and management. Neither of these ideas have since been implemented.

In his 1998 book, *Lament for an Ocean*, Michael Harris painstakingly documents the events of those years and the controversy that ensued. Senior bureaucrats within DFO went on the defensive, attacking the journal for publishing Hutchings' paper. Hutchings made it clear that the paper was not attacking DFO science; rather it was critical of the way the science was filtered to the minister. According to Harris, the scientific community, both inside and outside DFO were supportive of Hutchings and his co-authors.

The two senior bureaucrats whose names had appeared in an article in the *Ottawa Citizen* — Scott Parsons, the Assistant Deputy Minister for Science, and William Doubleday, the Director General of Fisheries and Oceans Science — threatened to file a lawsuit against the paper; they also named Myers in the suit, who had gone public with his views on the suppression of science and ironically, the intimidation of scientists at DFO. It had become clear that the atmosphere within DFO did not encourage the free debate and exchange of scientific ideas or the sharing of scientific findings and uncertainty with the public.

For a period of time since then, according to some scientists, there has been some improvement. One DFO scientist told me that information was provided more freely once a number of senior bureaucrats retired. To offset any embarrassment, the government would simply state that the views of the scientist did not necessarily represent the views of the department. A DFO communications advisor told me that, just a few years ago, scientists were encouraged to help non-specialists — journalists like me — with interpreting published papers. He said it was much easier then for a journalist to interview a scientist: usually it involved the journalist making the request and one communications person making the arrangement. Today, as my experience illustrates, the communication of science has been centralized. Requests are frequently handled in Ottawa where they can be more easily controlled.

A recent *Globe and Mail* article reported that in five years of government under Stephen Harper the number of information officers in the federal government increased by 16 percent. At the same time, much less information has actually been communicated. The article attributed this growth in communications to a preoccupation with controlling and disseminating information — information that should be provided without constraint since it has been funded by the public purse and collected for the public's benefit.[142]

According to Hutchings — and this says a lot coming from him — information control today is much worse than he has ever personally witnessed in the past. He says that while there is more scientific information available to the public (such as electronic documents of published reports) "there is no question that there is far greater government control over the communication of scientific information by government scientists in the past five years than existed previously."

A recent case that was widely reported in the media was the "muzzling" of DFO molecular geneticist Kristi Miller. In 2011 Miller was the lead scientist in a study published in the journal *Science* that suggested a virus referred to as salmon leukemia may have been a major factor in the 2009 collapse of the Fraser River sockeye salmon — when only one million of an anticipated ten million returned to the river to spawn.[143] After her study was published Miller was not allowed to speak to the media about her findings. She was, however, called to testify before the Cohen Commission, a public inquiry into the cause of the collapse: while on the stand, flanked by a security guard, she revealed that the directives that kept her off-limits to the media were not from within DFO but, she discovered, from the Privy Council Office, which serves the prime minister.

But why was there worry about her speaking to the media? "If we bring out that there could be a disease issue in sockeye salmon without really understanding how far and widespread it might be … the worry would be that it would automatically be assumed to be associated with aquaculture, and we really didn't even have any data at that time," she said.[144]

Critics of the growing salmon farming industry in B.C. argue that only those sockeye that swam past the salmon farms — which had been known to harbour the virus identified by Miller — collapsed. Was the gag order an attempt by government to protect the aquaculture industry? Chances are good that this is the case since it is within the mandate of the DFO to actively promote salmon farming and farmed salmon. Justice Cohen made two important recommendations in this case: that the mandate to promote salmon farming be removed, and that the DFO instead act in accordance with its "paramount regulatory objective to conserve wild fish." With respect to the siting of fish farms, among his seventy-five recommendations, the result of months of testimony and access to databases that were previously not made public, Justice Cohen urged the DFO to "explicitly consider the proximity to migrating Fraser River sockeye salmon when siting salmon farms." Cohen also had something to say about DFO's role in ensuring the transparency and accessibility of fish health data, when he called on the DFO to require fish farms to provide fish samples not just for monitoring purposes, but also for research purposes. He also recommended the DFO provide timely access to these fish health data to non-government researchers.[145]

According to Hutchings, the communication and the execution of science are connected: "Anything that inhibits the communication of science inhibits the science. Current government policy on the granting of interviews to the media is clearly not something that best serves society. Rather the policy is meant to exert government control of information and the communication of that information to society."

While I was very grateful to have been granted interviews with Bowen and Bundy, I am still unclear as to why the interviews were shadowed by communications manager Carl Myers. When I asked Myers if he usually sits in on interviews he said he tries "to sit in on interviews where possible." He said he makes a point of doing so "if the scientist rarely does interviews, for their support and to keep current on their research." In those cases, he says the scientist often requests his presence. I certainly want to believe Myers. I want to have confidence that the workings of government are transparent, that there's a free flow of scientific information between federal scientists and the public, and that I still live in a democracy. But according to news reports, there is good reason to believe that occupational free speech among scientists is being eroded. The International Polar Year conference in Montreal in 2012 is a case in point.[146] Federal scientists with Environment Canada were set to present their latest findings on a number of issues related to climate change but according to an internal memo that was leaked to the media, when it came to answering any questions from media, they were to follow strict measures issued from Ottawa. Communications staffers within Environment Canada would double as "media minders" and would attend, monitor, and record interviews with federal scientists, a move which some say was a form of intimidation.

After hearing about this and other stories like it, I couldn't help but wonder if Myers, who sat in on my interviews with two DFO scientists, was really just being helpful and trying to stay current with the science, as he said, or if he was instructed to keep tabs on what the scientists told me, making sure they stuck to their "media lines."

Dean Bavington of Memorial University argues that part of the reason why more control is being exerted is because the science itself is becoming more uncertain. He says scientists today are discovering how complex the marine ecosystem really is and this "new science of complexity" is not very welcome by governments wanting to attract investment. "It seems the more we learn about these systems the less we're able to control them. It leads to more uncertainty. So the leap between the state and science was developed to answer questions that were on the minds of investors and now we're in a situation where that's breaking down." Bavington says this is why government scientists are being muzzled and why scientific uncertainty has to be kept out of the media.

For Hutchings it's the silence from the public that is most deafening. "The extremely sad element to this, in my view, is not that the government is exerting that control, but that the Canadian public, through its silence, is implicitly accepting this control over it," he says. "Even the Soviet Union had its dissidents."

Some Recent Developments

As this book was going to print the fate of the grey seals was still up in the air. Chair of the Senate Committee Fabian Manning recommended the cull begin in the southern Gulf as early as the winter of 2013, during the whelping season. But that winter has come and gone. In order for a cull to take place it would have to receive the green light from the Minister of Fisheries and Oceans and a decision in this matter has yet to be made public.

As for Sable Island, it is now Canada's forty-third national park. In June 2013 *Bill S-15*, the bill designating Sable Island, was passed through the House of Commons, but not without dissent. Green Party leader and Member of Parliament for Saanich-Gulf Islands, Elizabeth May, voted against the bill, arguing that it would allow oil and gas exploration, including drilling and fracking underneath the island. According to a media release issued by her office, ExxonMobil agreed to give up its decades-old rights to drill on the island but still maintained rights to do seismic testing on the island as well as horizontal drilling for natural gas below the island, starting one nautical mile away. According to the release, the bill also set a dangerous precedent, further weakening Canada's national park system, by giving the Canada-Nova Scotia Offshore Petroleum Board — whose mandate is to promote oil and gas development — power to make regulations inside a national park.

As for the grey seals, in February 2013, when the legislation that would formally protect the island as a national park was tabled in the Senate, Peter Kent, Minister of the Environment, told a press conference in Halifax that the park would extend beyond the land itself to a distance of one nautical mile offshore. Martin Willison, a biology professor at Dalhousie University, then posed the question: "In that respect, can I assume talk about a seal cull is therefore off the table?" to which Kent replied, "It is off the table." Sheryl Fink, IFAW's seal program director, commented that while there isn't anything in the national park legislation to prevent culling, and while the matter still ultimately falls within the jurisdiction of the DFO, she hopes that positive feedback on Kent's remarks will "entice the Conservative [government] to stick to his word on this one."

Not long after this I learned of some startling new research initiatives, one with respect to grey seals and the other involving cod. In regard to the seals, research is currently underway out of the University of Saskatchewan that shows that the grey seal population on Sable Island may be doing much more to benefit the island than was previously imagined. Through a process called stable isotope analysis, graduate student Kenton Lysak and his team found that grey seals transport marine-derived nutrients — identified by the greater presence of nitrogen 15 (^{15}N), a heavier and rarer isotope of nitrogen — onto the island, which in turn fertilizes the plants, increases the total vegetation cover and potentially promotes further productivity and enhances the stability of the island's fragile ecosystem. Lysak explains:

> Wherever there are seals we have more nutrients being input into the system, more enrichment. That might seem like a basic thought but why that's important is that the seals are supplementing the ecosystem by providing nutrients to relatively isolated parts of the island. That means plants in these areas can uptake them in a highly concentrated form and this means greater plant growth wherever seal permeability is highest.

The increase in plant growth, particularly in the areas where the seals congregate, may also be helping to stabilize the island's shifting dunes. "These seals may be providing a pretty important support by imputing more nutrients into the nutrient-deficient system which promotes plant growth that in turn may limit eroding processes," he says. New information coming out of Lysak's research involves the island's most famous inhabitants, the wild horses. "The funny thing about this project is that it all seems very simple. It's the great circle of life: seals are enriching soils and the nutrients are being taken into the plants and we would think that this is going into the higher trophic levels — the horses — and it is true, it is." Using samples of horse hair to analyze what the horses have been eating, Lysak and his team found that, wherever there was a greater abundance of seals, the horses possessed the corresponding ^{15}N signature. "What we're just starting to see is that the animals that possess a greater fitness, that may be better at reproducing and more apt to survive also tend to exhibit this higher nutrient enrichment," he says.

While further work is required, Lysak says his preliminary findings indicate that the growth of the grey seal population since the 1960s and the resultant nutrient subsidy could have contributed to the increasing vegetation cover on the island over time. In turn, this would be contributing to the survivorship of the horses, whose population has increased from a hundred and fifty to two hundred in the 1950s to roughly five hundred today. Lysak says that, if there were a cull of grey seals on the island, it could result in community instability, for the plants and for the horses. "It's a fragile ecosystem and a change in nutrients from extrinsic sources could drastically change the stability and productivity of the island," he says.

As for the research involving cod, it's not positive. A study published in 2013 in the journal *Science* looked at depleted fish stocks around the globe and found that, if decisive action in reducing fishing is taken in a timely manner, stocks can rebound. However, the evidence seems to suggest that if this doesn't happen — as in the case of the cod — recovery is unlikely. "Prolonged intense overexploitation, especially for collapsed stocks, not only delays rebuilding but also substantially increases the uncertainty in recovery times, despite predictable influences of fishing and life history." The study goes on to say that "current harvest and low biomass levels render recovery improbable for the majority of the world's depleted stocks."[147] In other words, no matter what happens now, it may be too late for this species to recover.

Notes

Chapter 1

1. DFO, 2011, *Impacts of Grey Seals on Fish Populations in Eastern Canada*, p. 3.
2. At the time, the motion about controlling the seal population was said to have been put forward by Diana Whalen, the representative for Halifax-Clayton Park, but when asked about her motivation for putting forward the resolution, she said she didn't know anything about it. She said that, as a representative of an urban area, seals have not really been one of her concerns. So she looked into it and found out from the Chief Clerk at the Legislature that there are rules about putting forward motions for debate and that in theory each Member can submit a motion of their own on any matter that is of personal interest to them. But in practice each opposition caucus picks one motion and faxes over separate notices for the motion under the name of each Member of caucus to increase the odds of their motion getting picked for debate. A draw is held and whichever one is drawn is then read by the Speaker. According to the Chief Clerk: "The two caucuses could agree to submit only one notice each under the name of the real mover. This would slightly reduce the statistical advantage currently enjoyed by the larger caucus." Whalen says this is why her name was attached to the motion, but it was Harold Theriault who actually spoke to it.
3. *Hansard Debates and Proceedings* March 29, 2007.
4. Harris, 1990, p. 43.
5. Nova Scotia Department of Fisheries and Aquaculture, 2008, *Winter 2008 Hay Island Grey Seal Harvest: Follow-up Report. Final Copy*, p. 10.
6. Quote taken from Wark, B, 2009, "NDP Deliver Protected Wilderness to Seal Hunters." *The Coast*, November 12.
7. Worm's comments are taken from the unpublished transcript of the Committee on Law Amendments, November 4, 2009.
8. Unpublished transcript of the Committee of Law Amendments, November 3, 2009.
9. Quotes from Denny Morrow and Ernest Fage are from *Hansard*, April 18, 2006.
10. Dwyer, 1998, pp. 72–73.

Chapter 2

11. Kovacs et al., 2012, *Global Threats to Pinnipeds*, Table 1.
12. Mowat, 1984, pp. 355–61.
13. The phrase "quickly and humanely" taken from DFO, 2009, *Amendments to the Marine Mammal Regulations — Seal Harvest*.
14. Furlong, 2012, *CBC News Online*.
15. Curran and Morrow quotes are taken from interviews conducted for an article I co-wrote with Bruce Wark for *The Coast* in 2010.
16. DFO, 2009, *Proceedings of the National Workshop on the Impacts of Seals on Fish Populations in Eastern Canada*, p. 5.

Chapter 3

17. Robert O'Boyle and Mike Sinclair question a high historical abundance of grey seals. See their 2012 paper, p. 11.

18. Mike Hammill leads the federal government's population surveys for the Gulf herd. He takes a sample of the population to figure out the proportion of female seals that are pregnant. From this information he generates what he calls an "age specific reproductive rate," which in turn, gives him the adult female population estimate. "We assume that for every female there is a male, so essentially we multiply the number of females by two and this gives the number of animals one year and older." Then, he adds in the number of pups born to get the total population size.

19. To get a sense of the fluctuation, the Gulf herd pup estimate jumped from 5,436 in 1984 to 10,700 in 1996, then back down to 5,300 in 2000, up to 14,200 in 2004, down to 11,400 in 2007 and then 11,228 in 2010. Gulf herd pup counts from Hammill and Stenson, 2011, *Pup production of Northwest Atlantic grey seals in the Gulf of St. Lawrence*, Table 6, p. 18.

20. All Pauly quotes in this and in the previous paragraph are from Pauly, 1995, p. 430.

21. All Pauly quotes in this paragraph are from *The Green Interview* with Silver Donald Cameron. Recorded in October 2011.

22. Jackson et al., 2001, Table 1.

23. Bowen says the reasons why there are so few examples of this kind of growth among pinnipeds is because "the oceanic life style, long lives, and history of heavy exploitation by man have made it difficult to collect adequate time series of population trends for many species until relatively recently." Bowen et al., 2003, p. 1265.

24. Study by MacIntyre, Estep and Noji was cited in Pauly, 1995, p. 430.

25. Myers and Worm, 2003, pp. 280–283.

26. Brodie and Beck, 1983, p. 268.

27. A scathing critique of Marine Stewardship Certification can be found in Jacquet, Pauly, Ainley, Holt, Dayton and Jackson, 2010, pp. 28–29.

28. Hurley, 1998, p. 110.

29. Cambi et al. 2009.

30. Aging a Greenland shark is not possible because, unlike other shark species, they do not have annual growth rings on their vertebrae. Aging one would require capturing a newborn and then periodically recapturing and measuring it for the duration of its natural life, a task that could require several generations of researchers and would be logistically very difficult. Shark experts estimate they can live to two hundred years of age based on one scientific study that showed that the shark grows by 0.5 to 1.0 cm per year. This is based on one shark that was captured and tagged in 1936 and then recaptured in 1952 and in that sixteen-year period had grown only six centimetres. Assuming constant growth, it would take more than two hundred years to reach seven metres, the size of a mature Greenland shark.

31. From personal communication with Susanna Fuller, Marine Conservation Coordinator at the EAC, as well as from the transcript of the Standing Senate

Committee Hearing, March 29, 2012, Halifax.

32. Mowat, 1985, p. 325.
33. Denys, 1908, p. 130.
34. Denys, 1908: cod, p. 257; noise of salmon, p. 199; quantity of birds, p. 266; size of salmon, p. 166; size of mackerel, p. 184.
35. Myers and Cadigan, 1995, p. 1274.
36. Jackson et al., 2001, p. 629.

Chapter 4

37. Carson, 1941, p. 138.
38. Ibid., pp. 169–70.
39. McQuinn, 2009, p. 2256.
40. DFO, 2011, *Impacts of Grey Seals on Fish Populations in Eastern Canada*, p. 16.
41. Based on personal communication with DFO marine mammal specialist, Mike Hammill, July 23 and 24, 2012.
42. Savenkoff et al., 2004, p. 2194.
43. Bavington quote from David Caley's book, *Ideas on the Nature of Science*, based on a radio program that aired on CBC radio's *Ideas* program, also by David Cayley, p. 248. Unless referenced in an endnote, all Bavington quotes are from personal communication.
44. While the media characterized the study as being "independent," it wasn't entirely so: O'Boyle and Sinclair did do the study independently from the seal-cod team at the DFOs BIO, but some of the initial modelling and literature search was done with the financial support of DFO. Some of their findings were first reported at the DFO seal-cod workshop in fall 2010. After retiring from BIO, O'Boyle founded and is president of a private consulting firm Beta Scientific Consulting. See O'Boyle and Sinclair, 2012.
45. Trzcinski et al., 2006, p. 2286.
46. O'Boyle and Sinclair, 2012, p. 11.
47. Grahl-Nielsen et al., 2011, p. 263.
48. If you're interested in the controversy around fatty acid analysis and prey consumption estimates please refer to Grahl-Nielsen et al., 2003, 2004 and 2011; and G.W. Thiemann et al., 2004.
49. This recommendation appeared in a letter from the FRCC to the fisheries minister at the time, David Anderson, and was dated March 24, 1999. Fisheries Resource Conservation Council, 1999, p. 43.
50. DFO scientists rely heavily on fisheries data to come up with estimates on fish populations. Information about landings — the fish that are taken out of the sea — and the age of the fish caught (based on their size) is used along with a wide range of data that come from the DFO's annual summer survey, which includes information on the relative abundance and age structure of fish as well as the reproductive power of a population. Fish populations are often characterized by years in which there are very large numbers of juveniles produced. These are called year classes. The presence of especially large year classes can be tracked through time in the population surveys and the fishery landings. Fisheries often rely on these large year classes and will exploit them over successive years until

they have been exhausted. The data from the fishery and the data from the fish surveys are brought together using what resembles an accounting method called "virtual population analysis." According to Ian Boyd, it's extraordinarily difficult to measure how many fish are in the sea. An additional problem is that all the information is historical: telling us roughly what things were like but not necessarily what they will be like in the future.

51. Pauly quote taken from *The Green Interview* with Silver Donald Cameron, Recorded October 2011.
52. Bundy and Fanning, 2005, p. 1474.

Chapter 5

53. Swain and Chouinard, 2008, p. 2318.
54. Rose, 2007, p. 507.
55. Swain and Chouinard, 2008, p. 2318.
56. DFO, 2009, *Minister Shea announces 2009 fisheries management decisions for the Gulf of St. Lawrence.* Media Release, June 16.
57. Based on personal communication with George Rose, Director of the Centre for Fisheries Ecosystem Research at Memorial University, September 13, 2012.
58. See Ransom Myers testimony to the House of Commons Standing Committee, December 9, 1997. See Proceedings of the Standing Commettee on Fisheries and Oceans, 1997.
59. Hutchings, 2000, pp. 882–83.
60. Income assistance was first provided through the $484 million Northern Cod Adjustment and Recovery Program; this was followed in 1994 by The Atlantic Groundfish Strategy (TAGS), which cost in the order of $1.9 billion. When this program ended in 1998, an additional $730 million package was announced for retraining and other support.
61. Lavigne et al, 2011.
62. Dufour and Ouellet, 2007, p. 49; Benoit et al., 2012, p. 4. Each one of these major impact areas could easily be the subject of a book. However, due to time and space limitations, only four are addressed briefly here: bycatch, seismic testing, hypoxia and ocean acidification.
63. Monosson and Lincoln, 2006, p. 595.
64. 1985 report cited in the Royal Society of Canada, 2012, pp. 127–28. See Hutchings et al., 2012.
65. DFO, 2011, *Recovery Potential Assessment for the Laurentian South Designatable Unit of Atlantic Cod,* p. 24.
66. For a summary on DFO and its progress in the area of protecting habitat from trawling and dredging see Hutchings et al., 2012.
67. DFO, 2011, *Impacts of Grey Seals on Fish Populations in Eastern Canada,* p. 31.
68. Harold Theriault, quote from *Hansard,* January 23, 2007, p. 20. See Nova Scotia Legislature 2007.
69. Gavaris et al., 2010, p. iv, 51.
70. Harris, 1998, p. 223.
71. References for a number of studies about the effects of siesmic operations on the hearing of marine organisms including Atlantic cod can be found in Landon

and Pannozzo, 2001, pp. 39–52.

72. Galloway, 2013, *Globe and Mail*.

73. Lethal and sub-lethal effects of hypoxia are based on DFO laboratory experiments using northern Gulf cod. See Chabot and Couturier, 2002, p. 35.

74. Chabot and Couturier, 2002, p. 45.

75. All Alanna Mitchell quotes in this section taken from *The Green Interview*, by Silver Donald Cameron. Recorded October 2011.

Chapter 6

76. Lidgard et al., 2012, p. 7. Some of the benefits that seals might derive from being part of a group include reduction of predation risk, being able to efficiently locate prey, greater foraging efficiency and access to mates.

77. Lucas and Natanson, 2010, pp. 64–88.

78. Bexton et al., 2012, pp. 229–40.

79. More than a year after the shipwreck, the hulking mass still looms strangely close to Scatarie's coastline, awaiting removal, which was expected to take several months. After numerous delays, it was finally scheduled to be completed by early December, 2012, but the start date was once again pushed back. At the time of writing, the shipwreck salvager — U.S-based Bennington Group — had backed out of the deal. According to news reports at the time, the province's premier, Darrell Dexter, said the whole problem was "created by the federal government because of lax regulations governing the towing of ships through Canadian waters." MacIntyre, 2012, *Chronicle Herald*.

80. Gulland and Hall, 2007, p. 136.

81. The other major threat facing belugas is that their habitat also happens to be the St. Lawrence Seaway, a major navigation corridor where in one six-month period in 2007 it was estimated that 52,000 boat trips, from cruise ships and freighters to pleasure craft, were taken. It is well known that the noise and disturbance from ship traffic affects the behaviour of the small cetacean and interrupts its normal activities affecting its ability to successfully feed, socialize and reproduce.

82. Hobbs, Lebeuf and Hammill, 2001, pp. 1–18.

83. For more on infectious diseases found in marine mammals and potential harmful effect on consumers of seal meat products see MacKenzie's web site: <fishery-crisis.com/seals/seal%20products.htm>.

84. One 2008 study that appeared in *Diseases of Aquatic Organisms* reported the results of a survey of 483 people who work in close contact with marine mammals in a variety of occupations, but mostly in the fields of research and rehabilitation. The study noted that while prolonged malaise or respiratory illnesses — suspected to be caused by brucellosis or tuberculosis — were infrequently reported, the diseases could be debilitating and potentially life-threatening and therefore workers and volunteers should be educated about them. Hunt et al., 2008, p. 87.

85. Hammill and Stenson, 2011, *Modellling Grey Seal Abundance in Canadian Waters*, pp. 7–10.

86. CBC News online, February 2, 2006.

87. Johnston, Bowers, Friedlaender and Lavigne, 2012.

88. NOAA, 2012. Because it was previously thought that the ribbon seal was less

dependent on sea ice than the other ice seals, it was not proposed for listing until 2011, when new information had become available, including data on ribbon seal movements and diving behaviour. As a result, the NOAA Fisheries is conducting a new staus review for this species. At the time of writing, a decision had not yet been made with regard to listing this species.

89. Kovacs, 2008.
90. This view was expressed by the DFO marine mammal scientist based in Newfoundland, Garry Stenson, and reported by the *Canadian Press*, and appeared in the *Cape Breton Post* on January 4, 2102.
91. DFO, 2011, *A Review of Ice Conditions and the Harp Seal Total Allowable Catch (TAC) for 2010*, p. 2.
92. Galloway, 2012, *Globe and Mail*.

Chapter 7

93. The phytoplankton study did generate some debate among scientists. For more detail on this please see <wormlab.biology.dal.ca/ramweb/papers-total/Boyce_etal_2011.pdf>.
94. For more information on the externalization of costs, the value of ecosystem services, and the delusionary approach of measuring progress using the Gross Domestic Product (GDP), please refer to the work of Genuine Progress Index Atlantic.
95. The Gardner Pinfold report was finally released in March 2013 under an Access to Information request by IFAW, roughly a year after it was submitted to DFO. The consulting firm recommended, "based on interviews with key stakeholders and an analysis of vessel operating costs" that the "reasonable price per confirmed kill under a strategic targeted removal involving observers" would be $100. Using this method — where sealers would target seals where they pup or haul out — the firm estimated that as many as two hundred seals could be killed per trip. Under an "incentive-based reward system," where seals would be killed during the course of other fisheries, the firm estimated the price per jaw should be set at $150. This "hunt" would take place during fishing trips in areas where seals are known to congregate and, because of the difficulty in recovering wounded or dead seals at sea, it was estimated that only three to six jawbones could be reasonably retrieved per day, from as many as ten to twenty seals killed.
96. For more information on how the "aggregated diet" was derived please refer to Benoit et al., 2011.
97. DFO, 2011, *Impacts of Grey Seals on Fish Populations in Eastern Canada*, p. 5; and Swain, Benoit and Hammill, 2011, p. 2.
98. DFO, 2011, *Impacts of Grey Seals on Fish Populations in Eastern Canada*, p. 47.
99. Reasons given not to list cod taken from the Government of Canada, *Canada Gazette, Part II*, April 19, 2006, p. 291, and DFO, 2005, *Socioeconomic Considerations to Inform a Decision Whether or Not to List Three Populations of Atlantic Cod under SARA*.
100. Hutchings quote taken from the *Canadian Press*. 2012.
101. Laylin, 2012.
102. Bowen and Lidgard, 2011, p. 18.

103. From ICES advice regarding Icelandic cod, June 2012.
104. Morissette, Hammill and Savenkoff, 2006, p. 98.
105. Morissette and Hammill, 2011, p. 1.
106. Morissette, Christensen and Pauly, 2012.
107. Holt, 2004, pp. 25–26.
108. Ibid., p. 26.
109. For more information on the E.U. seal policy, see Curry, 2012, *Globe and Mail.*

Chapter 8

110. In addition to John Lien, Jeff Hutchings and Ian Boyd were also interviewed on the same program focusing on seal-fishery politics. *Open Air: Natural History Radio from Newfoundland and Labrador*, April 13, 2000.
111. Rose, 2007, pp. 412–15.
112. Rose, 2007, pp. 413.
113. Bavington quote taken from David Caley's book *Ideas on the Nature of Science*, based on a radio program that aired on CBC radio's *Ideas* program. Cayley, 2009, p. 248. Unless specified, all other Bavington quotes are from personal communication.
114. Myers and Cadigan, 1995, p. 1274.
115. Myers, Hutchings and Barrowman, 1996, p. 304.
116. Myers quote taken from Myers and Worm, 2003, media release.
117. Summary of Peter Larkin's critique of MSY found in Mace, 2001, pp. 2–5.
118. Larkin, 1977, p. 3.
119. George Rose wrote: "With politics dictating that harvests from the sea be as large as possible, the need to count fish and determine how many fish could be caught became pressing." He refers to MSY, the mathematical approach that would be used to achieve this end, as the "holy grail" of fisheries science in the 1950s. See Rose, 2007, p. 450.
120. Bolster et al., 2011, pp. 96–97. Bolster and his colleagues note the conventional wisdom that technological progress was sequential is not reflective of their analysis of early logbooks from the age of sail, which show that these technologies actually overlapped and that during the transition from hand-lining to long-lining (tub trawling), for instance, "fishermen on individual vessels employed some or all of these methods during the same season, and often during the same day."
121. Quote from DFO scientist Nancy Shackell. DFO, 2012, *Historical Data Sheds Light on Ecosystem Impacts in the Gulf of Maine Area.*
122. Bavington quote from Cayley, 2009, p. 240.
123. Lavigne, 2003, pp. 31–32.
124. FAO, 2012, p. 11.
125. Pauly, 2010, "The State of Fisheries," pp. 118–19.
126. Pauly, 2011, *The Green Interview*, with Silver Donald Cameron, October.
127. Ibid.
128. Pauly, 2010, "The State of Fisheries," p. 119.
129. Here is a further breakdown of these figures: In 2010, the commercial value of lobsters, shrimp and crab (including queen and other crab) landed in the Atlantic region was $576 million, $254 million and $287 million, respectively. Shrimp

and crab were really important for Newfoundland — comprising 66 percent of the total value of commercial fisheries in that province while lobsters were the mainstay for Nova Scotia (at 53 percent), New Brunswick (at 63 percent) and Prince Edward Island (78 percent). DFO, *Commercial Fisheries: 2010 Value of Atlantic Coast Commercial Landings, by Region.*

130. Charles et al., 2009, p. 25.
131. Koeller et al., 2009, pp. 791–93.
132. Allain, 2012, p. 23.
133. This observation is based on research conducted by Patricia Marchak on the forest industry and forestry-based communities in her 1995 book *Logging the Globe.*
134. Worm et al., 2006, pp. 789–90.
135. White, 2007.
136. Davis, 2009, p. 121.
137. Thurston, 2004, p. 17.
138. Pauly, 2010, "The State of Fisheries," p. 119.
139. Girard, 2001, p. 155.

Epilogue

140. Proceedings of the Standing Committee on Fisheries and Oceans. House of Commons, 1997, 36th Parliament, 1st Sesson, December 9.
141. Ibid.
142. J. Simpson, 2012, *Globe and Mail.* Also see *Canadian Press*, 2013.
143. Miller et al., 2011.
144. *Canadian Press*, 2011.
145. Cohen, 2012, Cohen Commission of Inquiry into the Decline of Sockeye Salmon in the Fraser River, Vol. 3, p. 10.
146. *CBC News Online*, 2012, "Federal Scientists Closely Monitored during Polar Conference," April 24.
147. Neubauer et al., 2013, p. 347.

Select Bibliography

Allain, M. 2012. "Good for Nothing." International Collective in Support of Fishworkers. *Samudra Report* 61: 23–25.

Armstrong, B. 1981. *Sable Island*. Halifax: Formac Publishing.

Aurioles, D., and F. Trillmich. 2008. *Antarctic Fur Seal: Arctocephalus Gazella*. At <iucnredlist.org/details/2058/0> IUCN Red List of Threatened Species.

Baum, J.K., and B. Worm. 2009. "Cascading Top-Down Effects of Changing Oceanic Predator Abundances." *Journal of Animal Ecology* 78, 4: 699–714.

Bavington, D. 2009. "Science Manages the Sea." In D. Caley (ed.), *Ideas on the Nature of Science*. Fredericton: Goose Lane Editions.

___. 2010. *Managed Annihilation: An Unnatural History of the Newfoundland Cod Collapse*. Vancouver: U.B.C. Press.

Benoit, H.P., J.A. Gagne, C. Savenkoff, P. Ouellet and M-N Bourassa (eds.). 2012. *State-of-the-Ocean Report for the Gulf of St. Lawrence Integrated Management (GOSLIM) Area*. Canadian Manuscript Report of Fisheries and Aquatic Sciences 2986.

Benoit, H.P., M.O. Hammill and D.P. Swain. 2011. *Estimated Consumption of Southern Gulf of St. Lawrence Cod by Grey Seals: Bias, Uncertainty and Two Proposed Approaches*. DFO Canadian Science Advisory Secretariat Res. Doc. 2011/041.

Beverton, R.J.H., and S.J. Holt. 1957. *On the Dynamics of Exploited Fish Populations*. Dordrecht: Springer Science and Business Media.

Bexton, S., D. Thompson, A. Brownlow, J. Barley, R. Milne and C. Bidewell. 2012. "Unusual Mortality of Pinnipeds in the United Kingdom Associated with Helical (Corkscrew) Injuries of Anthropogenic Origin." *Aquatic Mammals* 38, 3: 229–40.

BirdLife International 2008. *Pinguinus impennis (Great Auk)*. At <iucnredlist.org/details/106003305/0> IUCN Red List of Threatened Species.

Bolster, W.J., K.E. Alexander and W.B. Leavenworth. 2011. "The Historical Abundance of Cod on the Nova Scotian Shelf." In J.B.C Jackson, K.E. Alexander, and E. Sala (eds.), *Shifting Baselines: The Past and the Future of Ocean Fisheries*. Washington: Island Press.

Bowen, W.D. 1997. "Role of Marine Mammals in Aquatic Ecosystems." *Marine Ecology Progress Series* 158: 267–74.

___. 2011. *Sources of Bias and Uncertainty in Seal Diet Composition: Hard Part and Fatty Acid Analysis*. DFO Can. Sci. Advis. Sec. Res. Doc. 2011/025.

___. 2011. *Historical Grey Seal Abundance and Changes in the Abundance of Grey Seal Predators in the Northwest Atlantic*. DFO Canadian Science Advisory Secretariat Res. Doc. 2011/026.

Bowen, W.D., C.A. Beck, S.J. Iverson, D. Austin and J.I. McMillan. 2006. "Linking Predator Foraging Behaviour and Diet with Variability in Continental Shelf Ecosystems: Grey Seals in Eastern Canada." In I.L. Boyd, S. Wanless and C.J. Camphuysen (eds.), *Top Predators in Marine Ecosystems*. Cambridge: Cambridge University Press.

Bowen, W.D., C. den Heyer, J.I. McMillan and M.O. Hammill. 2011. *Pup Production at Scotian Shelf Grey Seal (Halichoerus grypus) Colonies in 2010*. DFO Can. Sci. Advis. Sec. Res. Doc. 2011/066.

Bowen, W.D., and D.C. Lidgard. 2011. *Vertebrate Predator Control: Effects on Prey*

Populations in Terrestrial and Aquatic Ecosystems. DFO Can. Sci. Advis. Sec. Res. Doc. 2011/028.

Bowen, W.D., J. McMillan and R. Mohn. 2003. "Sustained Exponential Population Growth of Grey Seals at Sable Island, Nova Scotia." *ICES Journal of Marine Sciences* 60: 1265–74.

Boyce D.G., M.R. Lewis and B. Worm. 2010. "Global Phytoplankton Decline over the Past Century." *Nature* 466: 591–96.

Boyd, I., S. Wanless and C.J. Camphuysen (eds.). 2006. *Top Predators in Marine Ecosystems: Their Role in Monitoring and Management.* Cambridge: Cambridge University Press.

Brodie, P., and B. Beck. 1983. "Predation by Sharks on the Grey Seal (*Halichoerus Grypus)* in Eastern Canada." *Canadian Journal of Fisheries and Aquatic Sciences* 50: 1768–78.

Brown, D.H., H. Ferris, S. Fu and R. Plant. 2004. "Modeling Direct Positive Feedback between Predators and Prey." *Theoretical Population Biology* 65: 143–52.

Bundy, A. 2005. "Structure and Functioning of the Eastern Scotian Shelf Ecosystem Before and After the Collapse of Groundfish Stocks in the Early 1990s." *Canadian Journal of Fisheries and Aquatic Sciences* 62: 1453–73.

Bundy, A., and L.P. Fanning. 2005. "Can Atlantic Cod (Gadus Morhua) Recover? Exploring Trophic Explanations for the Non-Recovery of the Cod Stock on the Eastern Scotian Shelf, Canada." *Canadian Journal of Fisheries and Aquatic Sciences* 62: 1474–89.

Bundy, A., J.J. Heymans, L. Morissette and C. Savenkoff. 2009. "Seals, Cod and Forage Fish: A Comparative Exploration of Variations in the Theme of Stock Collapse and Ecosystem Change in Four Northwest Atlantic Ecosystems. *Progress in Oceanography* 81: 188–206.

Camhi, M.D., S.V. Valenti, S.V. Fordham, S.L. Fowler and C. Gibson. 2009. *The Conservation Status of Pelagic Sharks and Rays: Report of the IUCN Shark Specialist Group — Pelagic Shark Red List Workshop.* Newbury, U.K.: IUCN Species Survival Commission's Shark Specialist Group. At <cmsdata.iucn.org/downloads/ssg_pelagic_report_final.pdf>.

Campagna, C. 2008. *Northern Elephant Seal: Mirounga Angustirostris.* IUCN Red List of Threatened Species. At <iucnredlist.org/details/13581/0>.

Campana, S.E., J. Branding and W. Joyce. 2011. *Estimation of Pelagic Shark Bycatch and Associated Mortality in Canadian Atlantic Fisheries.* Canadian Science Advisory Secretariat Research Document 2011/067.

Canada Ice Service online. n.d. "Same Week: Historical Ice Coverage by Stage of Development for the Week of 0129, Seasons: 1968/69–2011/12. Gulf of St. Lawrence." Environment Canada.

___. n.d. "Sea Ice Climatic Atlas for the East Coast 1981–2010: The Ice Regime." Environment Canada. At <ec.gc.ca/glaces-ice/default.asp?lang=En&n=AE4A459A-1>.

Canadian Environmental Assessment Agency. n.d. "Corridor Resources Inc. Exploration Well on the Old Harry Prospect — EL 1105." At <ceaa.gc.ca/050/details-eng.cfm?evaluation=60633>.

Canadian Press. 2011. "Kristi Miller, Fisheries Scientist, Tells Inquiry Her Work Was Muzzled by Feds." At <huffingtonpost.ca/2011/08/25/kristi-miller-fisheries-

scientist_n_937247.html> August 25.

___. 2012. "Senate Wants to Kill 70,000 Seals." At <oncampus.macleans.ca/educa-tion/2012/10/24/senate-wants-to-kill-70000-seals/> October 24.

Candow, J.E. 1989. *Of Men and Seals: A History of the Newfoundland Seal Hunt.* Ottawa: Ministry of the Environment.

Carson, R. 1941. *Under the Sea-Wind: A Naturalist's Picture of Ocea Life.* New York: Oxford University Press.

___. 1962. Silent Spring. Boston: Houghton Mifflin.

CBC *News online [digital archive].* 1977. "The Atlantic Seal Hunt: Seal Hunt Protest Is 'the New Paganism.' Richard Cashin on the Newfoundland Fishermen Food and Allied Workers' Union Defends the Seal Hunt." At <cbc.ca/player/Digital+Archives/CBC+Programs/Television/Take+30/ID/1614430458/?page=3>.

___. 2006. "Seal Pups Washed Away in Storm Surge." At <cbc.ca/news/canada/nova-scotia/story/2006/02/02/ns-storm-seals20060201.html> February 2.

___. 2009. "Canada to Fight E.U. Seal Product Ban." At <cbc.ca/news/world/story/2009/07/27/seal-hunt-ban-eu476.html> July 27.

___. 2012. "*MV Miner* Salvage Delayed Yet Again." At <cbc.ca/news/canada/nova-scotia/story/2012/11/06/ns-mv-miner-salvage-delays.html> November 6.

___. 2012. "Federal Scientists Closely Monitored During Polar Conference." At <cbc.ca/news/canada/montreal/story/2012/04/24/scientists-muzzling-canada.html> April 24.

CBC Radio. 2010. "Interview with Paul Brodie." *Mainstreet,* May 31.

CBCL Ltd. 2009. *Logistical Evaluation of Options to Manage the Grey Seal Population on Sable Island.* Prepared for Fisheries and Oceans Canada. Halifax: CBCL Land Use and Environment Division. At <thecoast.ca/pdfs/Sable_Island_seal_re-port_high_res_searchable.pdf>.

Chabot D., and C. Couturier. 2002. "Estimating the Impact of Naturally Occurring Hypoxia on Growth Production of Atlantic Cod (*Gadus Morhua*) from the Northern Gulf of St. Lawrence (Canada)." In D. Randall and D. MacKinlay (eds.), *Responses of Fish to AquaticHhypoxia, 5th International Congress on the Biology of Fish, Physiology Section.* American Fisheries Society 35–53.

Chantraine, P. 1980. *The Living Ice: The Story of the Seals and the Men Who Hunt Them in the Gulf of St. Lawrence.* Toronto: McClelland and Stewart.

Charles, A. 1999. "The Atlantic Canadian Groundfishery: Roots of a Collapse." *Dalhousie Law Journal* 18, 1: 65–83.

Charles, A., C. Burbidge, H. Boyd and A. Lavers. 2009. *Fisheries and the Marine Environment in Nova Scotia: Searching for Sustainability and Resilience.* Halifax: Genuine Progress Index Atlantic.

Choi, J.S., K.T. Frank, W.C. Leggett, and K. Drinkwater. 2004. "Transition to an Alternate State in a Continental Shelf Ecosystem." *Canadian Journal of Fisheries and Aquatic Sciences* 61: 505–10.

Choi, J.S., K.T. Frank, B.D. Petrie and W.C. Leggett. 2005. "Integrated Assessment of a Large Marine Ecosystem: A Case Study of the Devolution of the Eastern Scotian Shelf, Canada." *Oceanography and Marine Biology: An Annual Review* 43: 47–67.

Cohen, B.I. 2012. *The Uncertain Future of Fraser River Sockeye.* Commission of Inquiry into the Decline of Sockeye Salmon in the Fraser River (Canada). Final Report. At <cohencommission.ca/en/FinalReport/> October.

CTV News online. 2011. "Thousands of Seals in Grave Danger from Storm." At <ctvnews.ca/thousands-of-seals-in-grave-danger-from-storm-1.596094> January 15.

Curry, B. 2012. "E.U.'s Seal Policy Raises Eyebrows." *Globe and Mail*, October 9.

Davies, B. 1970. *Savage Luxury.* New York: Ballantine Books.

Davis, W. 2009. *The Wayfinders: Why Ancient Wisdom Matters in the Modern World.* Toronto: Anansi Press.

Davison, J. 2012. "Are Canada's Federal Scientists Being Muzzled?" *CBC News online.* At <cbc.ca/news/canada/story/2012/03/23/f-federal-scientists.html> March 27.

De La Mare, W. 1970. *The Massacre.* In The Complete Poems of Walter De La Mare. New York: Alfred A. Knopf.

De Villiers, M., and S. Hirtle. 2004. *Sable Island: The Strange Origins and Curious History of a Dune Adrift in the Atlantic.* New York: Walker and Company.

Denys, N. 1908 [1672]. *Description and Natural History of the Coasts of North America (Acadia).* Translated and edited by William F. Ganong. Toronto: The Champlain Society.

DFO (Department of Fisheries and Oceans). 1993. *Report on the Status of Groundfish Stocks in the Canadian Northwest Atlantic.* At <dfo-mpo.gc.ca/CSAS/Csas/Publications/SSR-RES/1993/1993_001_e.pdf>.

____. 2001. *Fisheries Management Policies on Canada's Atlantic Coast.* At <dfo-mpo.gc.ca/afpr-rppa/Doc_Doc/FM_Policies_e.htm>.

____. 2005. *Socioeconomic Considerations to Inform a Decision Whether or Not to List Three Populations of Atlantic Cod under SARA. Discussion Document.* Economic Analysis and Statistics Policy Sector. Ottawa: Fisheries and Oceans Canada.

____. 2005. "Will 'Dead Zones' Spread in the St. Lawrence River?" At <dfo-mpo.gc.ca/science/Publications/article/2005/01-12-2005-eng.htm>.

____. 2007. *National Plan of Action for Reducing Incidental Catch of Seabirds in Longline Fisheries.* At <dfo-mpo.gc.ca/npoa-pan/npoa-pan/npoa-seabirds-eng.htm>.

____. 2007. *Science Annual Report, 2006–2007.* At <dfo-mpo.gc.ca/science/Publications/annualreport-rapportannuel/ar-ra0607/ScienceAR_English.pdf>.

____. 2007. *Science Annual Report, 2007–2008.* At <dfo-mpo.gc.ca/science/Publications/annualreport-rapportannuel/ar-ra0708/ar-ra0708-eng.pdf>.

____. 2009. *Minister Shea Announces 2009 Fisheries Management Decisions for the Gulf of St. Lawrence.* Media Release. At <dfo-mpo.gc.ca/media/npress-communique/2009/hq-ac31-eng.htm> June 16.

____. 2009. *Proceedings of the National Workshop on the Impacts of Seals on Fish Populations in Eastern Canada (Part 2)*, 24–28 November 2008. DFO Can. Sci. Advis. Sec. Proceed. Ser. 2009/020.

____. 2009. *Amendments to the Marine Mammal Regulations — Seal Harvest.* At <dfo-mpo.gc.ca/media/back-fiche/2009/seal_hunt-chasse_au_phoque-eng.htm>.

____. 2010. *A Review of Ice Conditions and the Harp Seal Total Allowable Catch (TAC) for 2010.* Canadian Science Advisory Secretariat. Science Response 2010/004.

____. 2010. *Science Annual Report, 2008–2009.* At <dfo-mpo.gc.ca/science/publications/annualreport-rapportannuel/ar-ra0809/ar-ra0809-eng.pdf>.

____. 2010. *Science Advice on Harvesting of Northwest Atlantic Grey Seals (Halichoerus Grypus) on Hay Island.* Canadian Science Advisory Secretariat. Science Advisory Report 2009/067.

___. 2011. *Impacts of Grey Seals on Fish Populations in Eastern Canada.* Canadian Science Advisory Secretariat, Science Advisory Report. 2010/071.

___. 2011. *Stock Assessment of Northwest Atlantic Grey Seals (Halichoerus Grypus).* DFO Canadian Science Advisory Secretariat. Science Advisory Report 2010/091.

___. 2011. *Recovery Potential Assessment for the Laurentian South Designatable Unit of Atlantic Cod (Gadus Morhua).* Canadian Science Advisory Secretariat. Science Advisory Report 2011/028.

___. 2011. *Recovery Potential Assessment for the Laurentian North Designatable Unit (3Pn, 4RS and 3Ps) of Atlantic Cod (Gadus Morhua).* Canadian Science Advisory Secretariat. Science Advisory Report 2011/026.

___. 2011. *Annual Report on the Science Activities of Fisheries and Oceans Canada, 2009–2010.* At <dfo-mpo.gc.ca/science/Publications/annualreport-rapportannuel/ar-ra0910/DFO-MPO_AR-RA_0910-eng.pdf>.

___. 2012. *Recovery Strategy for the Beluga Whale (Delphinapterus Leucas) St. Lawrence Estuary Population in Canada.* Species at Risk Act Recovery Strategy Series. Ottawa: Fisheries and Oceans Canada.

___. 2012. *Historical Data Sheds Light on Ecosystem Impacts in the Gulf of Maine.* At <dfo-mpo.gc.ca/science/publications/article/2012/03-09-12-eng.html> March 9.

___. n.d. *The Canadian Seal Harvest — A Timeline.* At <dfo-mpo.gc.ca/fm-gp/seal-phoque/reports-rapports/facts-faits/facts-faits_tl-eng.htm>.

___. n.d. *Atlantic Coast Commercial Landings by Region and by Year.* At <dfo-mpo.gc.ca/stats/commercial/sea-maritimes-eng.htm>.

___. n.d. *Commercial Fisheries: 2010 Value of Atlantic Coast Commercial Landings, by Region.* At <dfo-mpo.gc.ca/stats/commercial/land-debarq/sea-maritimes/s2010av-eng.htm>.

___. n.d. *Commercial Fisheries. License Holders: Number of Commercial Fish Harvesters Registered by Category, by Province, by Region, by Year.* At <dfo-mpo.gc.ca/stats/commercial/licences-permis/licences-permis-atl-eng.htm>.

___. n.d. *Commercial Fisheries: Vessel Information: Number of Vessels by Length (in Feet) by Province and Region, by Year.* At <dfo-mpo.gc.ca/stats/commercial/licences-permis/licences-permis-atl-eng.htm>.

Downie, D.L., and T. Fenge (eds.). 2003. *Northern Lights Against POPs. Combatting Toxic Threats in the Arctic.* Inuit Circumpolar Conference of Canada. Montreal: McGill-Queens University Press.

Dufour, R., and P. Ouellet. 2007. "Estuary and Gulf of St. Lawrence Marine Ecosystem Overview and Assessment Report." *Can. Tech. Rep. Fish. Aquat. Sci.* 2744E.

Dwyer, M.J. 1998. *Over the Side, Mickey: A Sealer's First Hand Account of the Newfoundland Seal Hunt.* Halifax: Nimbus Publishing.

EAC (Ecology Action Centre). 2012. "Canadian Swordfish Eco-Certified Despite Deaths of Endangered Sea Turtles and Sharks." At <ecologyaction.ca/content/canadian-swordfish-eco-certified-despite-deaths-endangered-sea-turtles-and-sharks> April 20.

Ecotrust Canada. 2004. "Catch-22: Conservation, Communities and the Privatization of B.C. Fisheries. An Economic, Social, and Ecological Impact Study."

Vancouver.

Fisheries Resource Conservation Council. 1999. "1999 Conservation Requirements for the Gulf of St. Lawrence Groundfish Stocks and Cod Stocks in Divisions 2GH and 3Ps." At <frcc.ca/1999/frccr199.pdf> April.

___. 2011. "Towards Recovered and Sustainable Groundfish Fisheries in Eastern Canada. A Report to the Minister of Fisheries and Oceans." At <frcc.ca/2011/FRCC2011.pdf>.

Food and Agriculture Organization of the United Nations. n.d. *Fishing Gear Types: Hooks and Lines.* Fisheries and Aquaculture Department. At <fao.org/fishery/geartype/109/en>.

___. 2012. *State of the World Fisheries and Aquaculture, 2012.* Rome: Fisheries and Aquaculture Department. At <fao.org/docrep/016/i2727e/i2727e.pdf>.

Forbes, A., and S. Forbes. 2004. *One More Dead Fish.* Documentary film. United States: Interpositive Media.

Frank, K.T., B. Petrie, J.S. Choi and W.C. Leggett. 2005. "Trophic Cascades in a Formerly Cod-Dominated Ecosystem." *Science* 308, 5728: 1621–23.

Frank, K.T., B. Petrie, J.A.D. Fisher and W.C. Leggett. 2011. "Transient Dynamics of an Altered Large Marine Ecosystem." *Nature* 477: 86–89.

Frouin, H., M. Lebeuf, M.O. Hammill, B. Sjare and M. Fournier. 2011. "PBDEs in Serum and Blubber of Harbor, Grey and Harp Seal Pups from Eastern Canada." *Chemosphere* 82: 663–69.

Furlong, J. 2012. "Death on the Ice: Time to Pull the Plug on the Seal Hunt?" At <cbc.ca/news/canada/newfoundland-labrador/story/2012/01/20/nl-john-furlong-seal-hunt-121.html> January 21.

Galloway, G. 2012. "Record Harp-Seal Quota May not Save an Industry without a Market." *Globe and Mail,* March 21.

___. 2013. "Review of Oil Well for Gulf of St. Lawrence Terminated." *Globe and Mail,* February 28.

Gardner Pinfold Consultants Inc. 2012. *Grey Seals in Atlantic Canada.* Submitted to Fisheries and Oceans Canada.

Gavaris S., K.J. Clark, A.R. Hanke, C.F. Purchase and J. Gale. 2010. *Overview of Discards from Canadian Commercial Fisheries in NAFO Divisions 4V, 4W, 4X, 5Y and 5Z for 2002–2006.* Can. Tech. Rep. Fish. Aquat. Sci. 2873.

Genuine Progress Index Atlantic. 2009. "Written Submission to the Law Amendments Committee Re: Proposed Amendments to the Wilderness Area Protection Act." (Unpublished.) Halifax, November 3.

Gibson, G. 2009. *A Bedside Book of Beasts: A Wildlife Miscellany.* New York: Random House.

Girard, R. 2001. *I See Satan Fall Like Lightning.* Maryknoll, NY: Orbis.

Government of Canada. 2006. "Order Giving Notice of Decisions Not to Add Certain Species to the List of Endangered Species." Canada Gazette, Part II 140(8). At <gazette.gc.ca/archives/p2/2006/2006-04-19/html/si-tr61-eng.html>.

___. 2012. *Marine Mammal Regulations.* Department of Justice. At <laws-lois.justice.gc.ca/PDF/SOR-93-56.pdf>.

Government of Iceland. n.d. *Icelandic Fisheries in Figures, 2008.* Ministry of Fisheries and Agriculture. At <sjavarutvegsraduneyti.is/media/sjavarutvegur_i_tolum/

Sjavarutvegur_i_tolum_2008_allur.pdf>.

Grahl-Nielsen, O., M. Anderson, A.E. Derocher, C. Lydersen, O. Wiig and K. Kovacs. 2003. "Fatty Acid Composition of the Adipose Tissue of Polar Bears and of their Prey: Ringed Seals, Bearded Seals and Harp Seals. *Marine Ecology Progress Series* 265: 275–82.

___. 2004. "Reply to Comment on Grahl-Nielsen et al. (2003): Sampling, Data Treatment and Predictions in Investigations on Fatty Acids in Marine Mammals." *Marine Ecology Progress Series* 281: 303–306.

Grahl-Nielsen, O., T. Haug, U. Lindstrom and K.T. Nilssen. 2011. "Fatty Acids in Harp Seal Blubber Do Not Necessarily Refect Their Diet." *Marine Ecology Progress Series* 426: 263–76.

Green Interview. 2011. Alanna Mitchell with Silver Donald Cameron. October. At <TheGreenInterview.com>.

___. 2011. Daniel Pauly with Silver Donald Cameron. October. At <TheGreenInterview.com>.

Green Party of Canada. 2013. "Bill S-15 Would Allow Oil and Gas Activities Inside Sable Island National Park Reserve." Media release, June 7.

Greenland Shark and Elasmobranch Education and Research Group. n.d. "The Greenland Shark." At <geerg.ca/gshark_1.html>.

Gulland, F.M.D., and A.J. Hall. 2007. "Is Marine Mammal Health Deteriorating? Trends in Global Reporting of Marine Mammal Disease." *EcoHealth* 4: 135–50.

Haedrich, R.L., and L.C. Hamilton. 2000. "The Fall and Future of Newfoundland's Cod Fishery." *Society and Natural Resources* 13: 359–72.

Hamilton, L.C., and M.J. Butler. 2001. "Outport Adaptations: Social Indicators through Newfoundland's Cod Crisis." *Human Ecology Review* 8, 2: 1–11.

Hammill, M.O., J.F. Gosselin and G.B. Stenson. 2007. "Changes in Abundance of Grey Seals in the NW Atlantic." In T. Haug, M. Hammill and D. Olafsdottir (eds.), "Grey Seals in the North Atlantic and the Baltic." *NAMMCO Scientific Publications* 6: 99–115.

Hammill, M.O., and G.B. Stenson. 2011. *Pup Production of Northwest Atlantic Grey Seals in the Gulf of St. Lawrence.* DFO Can. Sci. Advis. Sec. Res Doc. 2010/122.

___. 2011. *Modelling Grey Seal Abundance in Canadian Waters.* DFO Can. Sci. Advis. Sec. Res. Doc. 2011/014.

Hammill, M.O., G.B. Stenson, T. Donoil-Valcroze and A. Mosnier. 2011. *Northwest Atlantic Harp Seals Population Trends, 1952–2012.* DFO Can. Sci. Advis. Sec. Res Doc. 2011/099.

Hammill, M.O., G.B. Stenson and M.C.S. Kingsley. 2011. *Historical Abundance of Northwest Atlantic Harp Seals (Pagophilus Groenlandicus): Influence of Harvesting and Climate.* DFO Can. Sci. Advis. Sec. Res. Doc. 2011/100.

Hammill, M.O., G.B. Stenson, F. Proust, P. Carter and D. McKinnon. 2007. "Feeding by Grey Seals in the Gulf of St. Lawrence and Around Newfoundland." *NAMMCO Scientific Publications* 6: 135–52.

Harkonen, T, et al. 2006. "The 1988 and 2002 Phocine Distemper Virus Epidemics in European Harbour Seals." *Diseases of Aquatic Organisms* 68, 2: 115–30.

Harris, L. 1990. *Independent Review of the State of the Northern Cod Stock (Harris Report).* Department of Fisheries and Oceans.

Harris, M. 1998. *Lament for an Ocean: The Collapse of the Atlantic Cod Fishery: A True Crime*

Story. Toronto: McClelland and Stewart.

Hartwell, S.I. 2011. "Chesapeake Bay Watershed Pesticide Use Declines but Toxicity Increases." *Environmental Toxicology and Chemistry* 30, 5: 1223–31.

Harwood, J. 2001. "Marine Mammals and Their Environment in the Twenty-First Century." *Journal of Mammalogy* 82, 3: 630–40.

Hobbs, K.E., M. Lebeuf and M.O. Hammill. 2001. "PCBs and OCPs in Male Harbour, Grey, Harp and Hooded Seals from the Estuary and Gulf of St. Lawrence, Canada." *The Science of the Total Environment* 296: 1–18.

Holt, S. 2004. "Preliminary Thoughts." In *Investigating the Roles of Cetaceans in Marine Ecosystems*. Monaco: CIESM Workshop Mongraph. At <ciesm.org/online/monographs/Venise.pdf> January 28–31.

Hunt, T.D., M.H. Ziccardi, F.M.D. Gulland, P.K. Yochem, D.W. Hird, T. Rowles and J.A.K. Mazet. 2008. "Health Risks for Marine Mammal Workers." *Diseases of Aquatic Organisms* 81: 81–92.

Hurley, P.C.F. 1998. "A Review of the Fishery for Pelagic Sharks in Atlantic Canada." *Fisheries Research* 39: 107–13.

Hutchings, J.A. 2000. "Collapse and Recovery of Marine Fishes." *Nature* 406: 882–85.

Hutchings, J.A., I.M. Cote, J.J. Dodson, I.A. Fleming, S. Jennings, N.J. Mantua, R.M. Peterman, B.E. Riddell, A.J. Weaver and D.L. VanderZwaag. 2012. *Sustaining Canadian Marine Biodiversity: Responding to the Challenges Posed by Climate Change, Fisheries, and Aquaculture*. Ottawa: Royal Society of Canada.

Hutchings, J.A., C. Walters and R.L. Haedrich. 1997. "Is Scientific Inquiry Incompatible with Government Information Control?" *Canadian Journal of Fisheries and Aquatic Sciences* 54: 1198–210.

ICES (International Council for the Exploration of the Sea). 2012. *Advice June 2012: Cod in Division Va (Iceland Cod)*. At <ices.dk/committe/acom/comwork/report/2012/2012/cod-iceg.pdf>.

Jackson, J.B.C., K.E. Alexander and E. Sala (eds.). 2011. *Shifting Baselines: The Past and the Future of Ocean Fisheries*. Washington: Island Press.

Jackson, J.B.C., M.X. Kirby, W.H. Berger, K.A. Bjorndal, et al. 2001. "Historical Overfishing and the Recent Collapse of Coastal Ecosystems." *Science* 293: 629–38.

Jacquet, J., D. Pauly, D. Ainley, S. Holt, P. Dayton and J. Jackson. 2010. "Seafood Stewardship in Crisis." *Nature* 467, 2: 28–29.

Jenson, L.B. 1980. *Fishermen of Nova Scotia*. Halifax: Petheric Press.

Johnston, D.W., M.T. Bowers, A.S. Friedlaender and D.M. Lavigne. 2012. "The Effects of Climate Change on Harp Seals (*Pagophilus Groenlandicus*)." *PLoS ONE* 7, 1: e29158.

Kirkman S.P., and D.M. Lavigne. 2010. "Assessing the Hunting Practices of Namibia's Commercial Seal Hunt." *South African Journal of Science* 106, 3/4: 1–3.

Koeller, P., C. Fuentes-Yaco, T. Platt, S. Sathyendranath et al. 2009. "Basin-Scale Coherence on Phenology of Shrimps and Phytoplankton in the North Atlantic Ocean." *Science* 329, 5928: 791–93.

Kovacs, K.M. 2008. *Pagophilus Groenlandicus (Harp Seal)*. In IUCN 2012. IUCN Red List of Threatened Species. At <iucnredlist.org/details/41671/0>.

___. 2008. *Cystophora Cristata (Hooded Seal)*. In IUCN 2012. IUCN Red List of Threatened Species. At <iucnredlist.org/details/6204/0>.

Kovacs, K.M., A. Aguilar, D. Aurioles, V. Burkanov et al. 2012. "Global Threats to Pinnipeds." *Marine Mammal Science* 28, 2: 414–36.

Kurlansky, M. 1997. *Cod: A Biography of the Fish that Changed the World.* New York: Penguin Books.

Landon, L., and L. Pannozzo. 2001. *Crude Costs: A Framework for a Full-Cost Accounting Analysis of Oil and Gas Exploration off Cape Breton, Nova Scotia.* Halifax: Save our Seas and Shores Coalition (SOSS).

Lapp, C. 1997. *Fishing on the Brink.* Documentary film. Halifax: Envision Productions.

____. 2002. *Clearing the Waters.* Documentary film. Halifax: Envision Productions.

Larkin, P.A. 1977. "An Epitaph for the Concept of Maximum Sustainable Yield." *Transactions of the American Fisheries Society* 106, 1: 1–11.

Lavigne, D.M. 2003. "Marine Mammals and Fisheries: The Role of Science in the Culling Debate." In N. Gales, M. Hindell and R, Kirkwood (eds.), *Marine Mammals: Fisheries, Tourism and Management Issues.* Collingwood, Australia: CSIRO Publishing.

____. 2011. *IFAWs Response to Proposals to Cull Grey Seals in Atlantic Canada, with Specific Reference to DFOs Science Advisory Report (SAR) on the Impacts of Grey Seals on Fish Populations in Eastern Canada.* (Unpublished.)

____. 2012. *Grey Seals, Cod, and Culling: Notes for a Presentation to the Standing Senate Committee on Fisheries and Oceans, Ottawa.* International Fund for Animal Welfare. (Unpublished.) Februrary 14.

Lavigne, D.M., and S. Fink. 2009. *Comments on "Regulations Amending the Marine Mammal Regulations" (Canada Gazette Part 1: 3268-3276, December 27, 2008).* (Unpublished.) January.

Lavigne, D.M., S. Iverson, H. Whitehead, S. Holt, L. Weilgart and B. Worm. 2011. "Open Letter to the Honorable Keith Ashfield, Minister of Fisheries and Oceans Canada. Re: FRCC Recommendation to Kill Some 140,000 Grey Seals." (Unpublished.) September 26.

Lavigne, D.M., and K.M. Kovacs. 1988. *Harps and Hoods: Ice-Breeding Seals of the Northwest Atlantic.* Waterloo: University of Waterloo Press.

Laylin, T. 2012. "Namibia's 'Cruel' Seal Hunt Sparks Calls for Tourism Boycott." *The Ecologist.* At <theecologist.org/News/news_analysis/1304083/namib-ias_cruel_seal_hunt_sparks_calls_for_tourism_boycott.html> April 12.

Lidgard, D.C., D.W. Bowen, I.D. Jonsen and S.J. Iverson. 2012. "Animal-Borne Acoustic Transceivers Reveal Patterns of at-Sea Associations in an Upper-Trophic Level Predator." *PLoS ONE* 7, 11: e48962. doi:10.1371/journal.pone.0048962.

Lilly, G.R., K. Wieland, B.J. Rothschild, S. Sundby, et al. 2008. *Decline and Recovery of Atlantic Cod (Gadus Morhua) Stocks throughout the North Atlantic.* Resiliency of Gadid Stocks to Fishing and Climate Change. Alaska Sea Grant College Program, 39–66.

Lister-Kay, J. 1979. *Seal Cull: The Grey Seal Controversy.* Harmondsworth, England: Penguin Books.

Lotze, H.K. 2007. "Rise and Fall of Fishing and Marine Resource use in the Wadden Sea, Southern North Sea." *Fisheries Research* 87: 208–18.

Lotze, H.K., and I. Milewski. 2004. "Two Centuries of Multiple Human Impacts and Successive Changes in a North Atlantic Food Web." *Ecological Applications*

14, 5: 1428–47.

Lotze, H.K., and B. Worm. 2009. "Historical Baselines for Large Marine Animals." *Trends in Ecology and Evolution* 24, 5: 254–62.

Lowry, L., K. Kovacs and V. Burkanov. 2008. *Odobenus Rosmarus (Atlantic Walrus)*. IUCN Red List of Threatened Species At <iucnredlist.org/details/15106/0>.

Lucas, Z., and L.J. Natanson. 2010. "Two Shark Species Involved in Predation on Seals at Sable Island, Nova Scotia, Canada." *Proceedings of the Nova Scotian Institute of Science* 45: 64–88.

Lyndersen, C., and K.M. Kovacs. 1999. "Behaviour and Energetics of Ice-Breeding, North Atlantic Phocid Seals during the Lactation Period." *Marine Ecology Progress Series* 187: 265–81.

MacDonald, M. 2011. "*MV Miner*: Nova Scotia Premier Darrell Dexter Aims Broadside at Ottawa over Federal Response to Stuck Ship." *Macleans*, October 11. At <macleans.ca/article.jsp?content=n10874672>.

Mace, P.M. 2001. "A New Role for MSY in Single-Species and Ecosystem Approaches to Fisheries Stock Assessment and Management." *Fish and Fisheries* 2: 2–32.

MacIntyre, M.E. 2012. "Sealers, Foes Brace for Encounter." *Chronicle Herald*, February 29.

___. 2012. "Shipwreck Salvager Backs Out." *Chronicle Herald*, November 15.

MacKenzie, D. 2008. "Hay Island Grey Seal Hunt, 2008." Letter to The Honorable Mark Parent. At <fisherycrisis.com/seals/Hay%20Island%20grey%20seal%20 hunt%202008.htm> February 17.

Malik, S., P.J. Wilson, R.J. Smith, D.M. Lavigne and B.N. White. 1997. "Pinniped Penises in Trade: A Molecular-Genetic Investigation." *Conservation Biology* 11, 6: 1365–94.

Marchak, P. 1995. *Logging the Globe*. Montreal: McGill-Queens University Press.

McQuinn, I.H. 2009. "Pelagic Fish Outburst or Suprabenthic Habitat Occupation: Legacy of the Atlantic Cod (*Gadus Morhua*) Collapse in Eastern Canada." *Canadian Journal of Fisheries and Aquatic Science* 66: 2256–62.

Miller, K.M., S. Li, K.H. Kaukinen, N. Ginther, et al. 2011. "Genomic Signatures Predict Migration and Spawning Failure in Wild Canadian Salmon." *Science* 331, 6014: 214–17.

Ministry of Fisheries and Marine Resources, Namibia. n.d. "Table 7. Seal Harvest, 2006–2010." At <mfmr.gov.na/>.

___. 2009. *Annual Report*. At <209.88.21.36/opencms/export/sites/default/grnnet/ MFMR/downloads/docs/MIN_OF_FISHERIES_2009_Annual_report.pdf>.

Mitchell, A. 2009. *Sea Sick: The Global Ocean in Crisis*. Toronto: McLelland and Stewart.

Monosson, E., and D. Lincoln. 2006. "Comparison of PCBs, Organochlorine Pesticides, and Trace Metals in Cod Liver from Georges Bank and Stellwagen Bank, U.S.A and Canada." *Marine Pollution Bulletin* 52: 572–97.

Morissette L., V. Christensen and D. Pauly. 2012. "Marine Mammal Impacts in Exploited Ecosystems: Would Large Scale Culling Benefit Fisheries?" *PLoS ONE* 7, 9: e43966. doi: 10.1371/journal.pone.0043966.

Morissette, L., and M.O. Hammill. 2011. *A Preliminary Evaluation of the Impacts of Grey Seal (Halichoerus Grypus) Predation on the 4T Ecosystem and Possible Effects of their Removal on Cod Recovery*. DFO Canadian Science Advisory Secretariat Res. Doc. 2011/016.

Morissette, L., M.O. Hammill and C. Savenkoff. 2006. "The Trophic Role of Marine Mammals in the Northern Gulf of St. Lawrence." *Marine Mammal Science* 22, 1: 74–103.

Mowat, F. 1984. *Sea of Slaughter.* Toronto: McClelland and Stewart-Bantam, Ltd.

Myers, R.A., and N.G. Cadigan. 1995. "Was an Increase in Natural Mortality Responsible for the Collapse of Northern Cod?" *Canadian Journal of Fish and Aquatic Sciences* 52: 1274–85.

Myers, R.A., J.A. Hutchings and N.J. Barrowman. 1996. "Hypothesis for the Decline of Cod in the North Atlantic." *Marine Ecology Progress Series* 138: 293–308.

___. 1997. "Why Do Fish Stocks Collapse? The Example of Cod in Atlantic Canada." *Ecological Applications* 7, 1: 91–106.

Myers, R.A., and B. Worm. 2003. "Rapid Worldwide Depletion of Predatory Fish Communities." *Nature* 423: 280–83.

___. 2003. "Cover Study of *Nature* Provides Startling New Evidence that Only 10% of All Large Fish Are Left in Global Ocean." Media Release. At <ram.biology.dal.ca/~myers/depletion/docs/MyersWormFinalPR.pdf> May 14.

National Oceanic and Atmospheric Association. 2012. "NOAA Lists Ringed and Bearded Ice Seal Populations under the Endangered Species Act." Media release. At <alaskafisheries.noaa.gov/newsreleases/2012/icesealsesa1212.pdf> December 21.

Neubauer, P., O.P. Jensen, J.A. Hutchings and J.K. Baum. 2013. "Resilience and Recovery of Overexploited Marine Populations." *Science* 340: 347–49.

North Atlantic Marine Mammal Commission. 2005. "Status of Marine Mammals in the North Atlantic: The Atlantic Walrus." At <nammco.no/webcronize/images/Nammco/654.pdf>.

Nova Scotia Department of Environment. 2010. *Protecting Wilderness: A Summary of Nova Scotia's Wilderness Areas Protection Act.* At <gov.ns.ca/nse/protectedareas/docs/Wilderness_Act_Sum.pdf>.

Nova Scotia Department of Fisheries and Aquaculture. 2008. *Winter 2008 Hay Island Grey Seal Harvest: Follow-up Report. Final Copy.* Prepared for the Nova Scotia Department of Environment. Halifax.

___. 2008. *Limited Grey Seal Harvest on Hay Island.* At <novascotia.ca/news/release/?id=20080208006> February 8.

Nova Scotia Legislature. 2006. "Proceedings of the Nova Scotia House of Assembly Committee on Resources: Grey Seal Research and Development Society." *Nova Scotia Hansard Reporting Services.* At <gov.ns.ca/legislature/hansard/comm/r/re_2006apr18.htm> April 18.

___. 2006. "Proceedings of the Nova Scotia House of Assembly Committee on Resources: Grey Seal Conservation Society." *Nova Scotia Hansard Reporting Services.* At <gov.ns.ca/legislature/hansard/comm/r/re_2006oct03.htm> October 3.

___. 2007. "Proceedings of the Nova Scotia House of Assembly Committee on Resources: The State of the Ocean with Boris Worm." *Nova Scotia Hansard Reporting Services.* At <nslegislature.ca/index.php/committees/committee_hansard/C10/re_2007jan23> January 23.

___. 2007. "Hansard Debates and Proceedings, Assembly 60, Session 1." At <nslegislature.ca/index.php/proceedings/hansard/C48/60_1_house_07mar29/> March 29.

___. 2009. "Transcript of the Committee on Law Amendments." Unpublished. Provided by Bob Kinsman, *Hansard Reporting Service*, Halifax. November 3 and 4.

O'Boyle, R., and M. Sinclair. 2012. "Seal-Cod Interactions on the Eastern Scotian Shelf: Reconsideration of Modeling Assumptions." *Fisheries Research* 115–116: 1–13.

Ocean Tracking Network. n.d. *Ocean Tracking Network Annual Report 2011–2012*. Halifax: Dalhousie University.

___. n.d. "Ocean Monitoring." *Online* At <oceantrackingnetwork.org/about/ocean>.

Open Air: Natural History Radio from Newfoundland and Labrador. 2000. "Seal-Fishery Politics." At <myweb.dal.ca/jhutch/media.html> April 13.

Pannozzo, L. 1999. "Fish Full of Dollars." *The Coast*, p. 9-12. Halifax: November 18.

___. 2010. "How to Kill 220,000 Seals on Sable Island: The DFO plan." *The Coast*. At <thecoast.ca/RealityBites/archives/2010/05/26/how-to-kill-220000-seals-on-sable-island-the-dfo-plan> May 27.

___. 2012. "Sealfall, Licence to Cull." *The Coast*. At <http://www.thecoast.ca/halifax/seafall-license-to-cull/Content?oid=3482101> November 15.

Pannozzo, L., and R. Colman. 2009. *New Policy Directions for Nova Scotia: Using the Genuine Progress Index to Count What Matters*. Halifax: Genuine Progress Index Atlantic.

Pannozzo, L., and B. Wark. 2010. "Sable Island's Cod Killer?" *The Coast*. At <thecoast.ca/halifax/sable-islands-cod-killer/Content?oid=1708783> July 1.

Pauly, D. 1995. "Anecdotes and the Shifting Baseline Syndrome of Fisheries." *Trends in Ecology and Evolution* 10, 10: 430.

___. 2010. "The State of Fisheries." In S.N.S. Sodhi and P.R. Ehrlich (eds.), *Conservation Biology for All*. Oxford: Oxford University Press.

___. 2010. *Five Easy Pieces: The Impact of Fisheries on Marine Ecosystems*. Washington, DC: Island Press.

Pauly, D., V. Christensen, S. Guenette, T.J. Pitcher, U.R. Sumaila, C.J. Walters, R. Watson and D. Zeller. 2002. "Towards Sustainability in World Fisheries." *Nature* 418: 689–95.

Pauly, D., and J. Maclean. 2003. *In a Perfect Ocean: The State of Fisheries and Ecosystems in the North Atlantic Ocean*. Washington, DC: Island Press.

Pitcher, T.J., J.J. Heymans, and M. Vasconcellos (eds.). 2002. *Ecosystem Models of Newfoundland for the Time Periods 1995, 1985, 1900, and 1450*. Fisheries Centre, University of British Columbia.

Proceedings of the Standing Senate Committee on Fisheries and Oceans on the Management of the Grey Seal Population, 41st Parliament, 1st Session. 2011. October 25.

___. 2012. March 13.

___. 2012. March 29.

Proceedings of the Standing Committee on Fisheries and Oceans. House of Commons, 36th Parliament, 1st Session. 1997. December 9.

Roman, J., and J.J. McCarthy. 2010. "The Whale Pump: Marine Mammals Enhance Primary Productivity in a Coastal Basin." *PLoS ONE* 5, 10: e13255.

Rooney, N., K. McCann, G. Gellner and J.C. Moore. 2006. "Structural Asymmetry and the Stability of Diverse Food Webs." *Nature* 442: 265–69.

Rose, G. 2007. *Cod: The Ecological History of the North Atlantic Fisheries*. St. John's: Breakwater Books.

Sandler, M.W. 2008. *Atlantic Ocean: The Illustrated History of the Ocean that Changed the World.* New York: Sterling Publishing.

Savenkoff, C., M. Castonguay, A.F. Vezina, S.P. Despatie, D. Chabot, L. Morissette and M. Hammill. 2004. "Inverse Modeling of Trophic Flows through an Entire Ecosystem: The Northern Gulf of St. Lawrence in the mid-1980s." *Canadian Journal of Fisheries and Aquatic Sciences* 61: 2194–214.

Savenkoff, C., D.P. Swain, J.M. Hanson, M. Castonguay, M.O Hammill, H. Bourdages, L. Morissette and D. Chabot. 2007. "Effects of Fishing and Predation in a Heavily Exploited Ecosystem: Comparing Periods Before and After the Collapse of Groundfish in the Southern Gulf of St. Lawrence (Canada)." *Ecological Modelling* 204: 115–28.

Scheffer, M., S. Carpenter, J.A. Foley, C. Folke and B. Walker. 2001. "Catastrophic Shifts in Ecosystems." *Nature* 413: 591–96.

Shelton, P., and J. Morgan. 2005. "Is By-Catch Mortality Preventing the Rebuilding of Cod (*Gadus Morhua)* and American Plaice (*Hippoglossoides Platessoides)* Stocks on the Grand Bank?" *Journal of the Northwest Atlantic Fisheries Science* 36: 1–17.

Shiva, V. 2011. "Real Science Is Spiritual." Clear Compass Media. At <youtube. com/watch?feature=player_embedded&v=RzrRIOsWnNo>.

Simpson, J. 2012. "More Information Offices, Less Information." *Globe and Mail,* January 27.

Sinclair, A., R.A. Myers and J.A. Hutchings. 1995. "Seal Predation: Is There Evidence of Increased Mortality on Cod?" NAFO/ICES Symposium on the Role of Marine Mammals in the Ecosystem, September 1995, Dartmouth, Nova Scotia.

Standing Senate Committee on Fisheries and Oceans. 2012. *The Sustainable Management of Grey Seal Populations: A Path Toward the Recovery of Cod and other Groundfish Stocks,* 1st Session, 41st Parliament, October.

Stanford, J. 2008. *Economics for Everyone: A Short Guide to the Economics of Capitalism.* Halifax: Fernwood Publishing.

Steele, D.H., R. Anderson and J.M. Green. 1992. "The Managed Commercial Annihilation of Northern Cod." *Newfoundland Studies* 8, 1: 34–68.

Stenson, G.B., and M.O. Hammill. 2012. *Living on the Edge: Observations of Northwest Atlantic Harp Seals in 2010 and 2011.* DFO Can. Sci. Advis. Sec. Res. Doc. 2011/ 108.

Swain, D.P. 2011. "Life-History Evolution and Elevated Natural Mortality in a Population of Atlantic Cod (*Gadus Morhua)." Evolutionary Applications* 4: 18–29.

Swain, D.P., H.P. Benoit and M.O. Hammill. 2011. *Grey Seal Reduction Scenarios to Restore the Southern Gulf of St. Lawrence Cod Population.* DFO Can. Sci. Advis. Sec. Res. Doc. 2011/035.

Swain, D.P., and G.A. Chouinard. 2008. "Predicted Extirpation of the Dominant Demersal Fish in a Large Marine Ecosystem: Atlantic Cod (*Gadus Morhua)* in the Southern Gulf of St. Lawrence." *Canadian Journal of Fisheries and Aquatic Sciences* 65: 2315–19.

Swain, D.P., and R.K. Mohn. 2012. "Forage Fish and the Factors Governing Recovery of Atlantic cod (*Gadus Morhua)* on the Eastern Scotian Shelf." *Canadian Journal of Fisheries and Aquatic Sciences* 69: 997–1001.

Swain, D.P., L. Savoie, T. Hurlbut, T. Surette and D. Daigle. 2009. *Assessment of the Southern Gulf of St. Lawrence Cod Stock.* DFO Can. Sci. Advis. Sec. Res. Doc.

2009/037.

Thiemann, G.W., S.M. Budge, W.D. Bowen and S.J. Iverson. 2004. "Comment on Grahl-Nielsen et al. (2003): Fatty Acid Composition of the Adipose Tissue of Polar Bears and of their Prey: Ringed Seals, Bearded Seals and Harp Seals." *Marine Ecology Progress Series* 281: 297–301.

Thomas, L., M.O. Hammill and W.D. Bowen. 2011. "Estimated Size of the Northwest Atlantic Grey Seal Population 1977–2010." DFO Can. Sci. Advis. Sec. Res. Doc. 2011/017.

Thurston, H. 2001. "Marram." In H. MacDonald and B. MacLain (eds.), *Landmarks: An Anthology of New Atlantic Canadian Poetry of the Land*. Charlottetown: The Acorn Press.

___. 2004. *A Place Between the Tides: A Naturalist's Reflections on the Salt Marsh*. Vancouver: Greystone Books.

___. 2012. *The Atlantic Coast: A Natural History*. Vancouver: Greystone Books.

Toropova, C., I. Meliane, D. Laffoley, E. Matthews and M. Spalding (eds.). 2010. *Global Ocean Protection: Present Status and Future Possibilities*. Gland, Switzerland: International Union for the Conservation of Nature's World Commission on Protected Areas.

Trzcinski, M.K., R. Mohn and W.D. Bowen. 2006. "Continued Decline of an Atlantic Cod Population: How Important Is Gray Seal Predation?" *Ecological Applications* 16, 6: 2276–92.

Walters, C., and J.F. Kitchell. 2001. "Cultivation/Depensation Effects on Juvenile Survival and Recruitment: Implications for the Theory of Fishing." *Canadian Journal of Fisheries and Aquatic Sciences* 58, 1: 39–50.

Wark, B. 2009. "NDP Deliver Protected Wilderness to Seal Hunters." *The Coast*. At <thecoast.ca/halifax/ndp-deliver-protected-wilderness-to-seal> November 12.

Watson, P. 2002. *Seal Wars. Twenty-five Years on the Front Lines with the Harp Seals*. Toronto: Key Porter Books.

White, C. 2007. "The Idols of Environmentalism." *Orion Magazine*. At <orionmagazine.org/index.php/articles/article/233> March/April.

Worm, B., E.B. Barbier, N. Beaumont, J.E. Duffy, C. Folke, et al. 2006. "Impacts of Biodiverstiy Loss on Ocean Ecosystem Services." *Science* 314: 787-790.

Worm, B., R. Hilborn, J.K. Baum, T.A. Branch, J.S. Collie, et al. 2009. "Rebuilding Global Fisheries." *Science* 325: 578-585.

Legislation

Endangered Species Act. 1973. 16 U.S.C., 1531.
Fish Inspection Act. R.S.C., 1985, c. F-12.
Marine Mammal Protection Act of 1972 as Amended. 2007. 16 U.S.C., Chapter 31.
Species at Risk Act. S.C. 2002, c. 29.
Wilderness Areas Protection Act. 1998, c. 27, s. 1.

Index